Skeul an

LYVER ON/
BOOK ONE

STEUS DHIEN A'N YETH KERNEWEK
A COMPLETE COURSE IN THE CORNISH LANGUAGE

Wella Brown

Kesva an Taves Kernewek
The Cornish Language Board

Delinyansow gans
Drawings by
Julian Kitt

First published in 1996 by
THE CORNISH LANGUAGE BOARD
KESVA AN TAVES KERNEWEK
Reprinted with corrections and additions June 2003

ISBN 0 907064 21 3

Printed by Four Way Print Limited,
Saltash, Cornwall.

CONTENTS

GENERAL INTRODUCTION

This course, in three books, has been devised primarily for the use of those who are studying Cornish as members of a group where conversational practice can take place and where a teacher is at hand to direct the students' progress. I have also had in mind the needs of those who are studying on their own and for that reason there are very full sets of examples given at every stage.

Book 1 covers the syllabus for the First Grade, including all recommended vocabulary, and part of the Second Grade of the examinations of **Kesva an Taves Kernewek**, *The Cornish Language Board*. Book 2 continues with material for the Second Grade and part of the Third Grade, and Book 3 covers the remainder of the syllabus for Grade Three and all of Grade Four.

As to the design of the course, it has as its basic idea that of a series of themes such as 'existence and non-existence', 'looking for things' and so on.

The various parts bring in units of grammar as appropriate. The use of grammatical terms is, in my view, a positive aid to acquiring a language and not an aim in itself and further, far from being an obstacle to beginners, a working knowledge of grammar makes the process of learning easier and quicker.

A glossary of the commonest and most useful grammatical terms and ideas is provided for reference on pages vi-viii of this first book since these terms will be used throughout the course in describing the way Cornish works.

Each part of the course is made up of, firstly an explanation of its theme with examples, then a word list followed by more examples relevant to the theme and finally a section of general examples in order to keep previously learnt matter under constant review.

A series of exercises has been incorporated as an extension to the main text. There are also cassettes to accompany the exercises to provide practice in listening and in speaking so that the all-important matter of good pronunciation can be given due attention.

I must here acknowledge the help given by members of the Cornish language class at Saltash who used the course as it was being constructed and who offered valuable suggestions as it proceeded and in particular the corrections and amendments proffered by Julian Davey. David Balhatchet painstakingly scrutinised the provisional edition and I am grateful to him for the care with which he examined every line of the book. The excellent illustrations are the work of Julian Kitt of Saltash and I am indebted to him for the many hours he spent in devising suitable sketches. Gary Angove supplied one of the voices for the cassette recordings which are part of the course. Finally, without the encouragement of Graham Sandercock and his willingness to re-record the whole manuscript and prepare it for publication, this course would have been very much longer in the preparation. The cover design is by Chris Bowden.

THE PHONEMIC SYSTEM AND **KERNEWEK KEMMYN**

This course is in **Kernewek Kemmyn**, *Common Cornish*. Modern Cornish is ultimately based on the language used in the period centring on the year 1500, the 'golden period' of Cornish literature. The modern spelling is phonemic, that is to say, the pronunciation of each word is accurately reproduced in the spelling so that once the system is grasped, reading Cornish is quite straightforward. A full description of the system will be found in *The Pronunciation and Spelling of Revived Cornish* by Dr Ken George or in the first chapter of my *A Grammar of Modern Cornish* 3rd edition.

Consonants are pronounced as in English but the following should be noted:
dh the E. 'th' in 'with'
gh when final is like the Scottish 'ch' in *'loch'*. When between two vowels or in the groups 'lgh' and 'rgh' it is a strongly stressed 'h' as in the E. word 'aha!'. When this sound is doubled it is written **ggh**
hw is so written to preserve the influence of the 'h' as in E. 'when' emphatically spoken
th the E. 'th' in 'thin'. When doubled it is written **tth**

Vowels should be pronounced pure as follows:
a the vowel of E. 'ah' when long; when short, the 'a' of E. 'bat'
e the 'e' of E. 'bet'
eu the 'eu' as in French *'peur'*
i the 'ee' in E. 'beet'
o when long the 'ou' in E. 'sought' and when short is as the 'o' in E. 'got'
oe long, the 'oa' of E. 'boat'; short, the 'u' of E. 'cut'
ou the 'oo' of E. 'boot'
u the 'u' of French *'tu'*
y the 'i' of E. 'bit'. Note that this is also a semi-vowel, the E. 'y' in 'yet'

Diphthongs
aw the 'ow' of E. 'how'
ay the 'y' of E. 'by'
ew the 'ew' of Welsh *'tew'* 'fat'
ey the 'ei' of E. 'veil'
iw the 'ew' of E. 'dew' but narrower
ow a sound between the 'ow' of E. 'owe' and the 'aw' of E. 'awe'
oy the 'oy' of E. 'boy'
yw the 'ew' of E. 'flew'

MUTATIONS

In Cornish, as in other Celtic languages, the initial consonant of a word may change in a regular manner in certain circumstances. These changes are known as mutations. They will be described as they occur but the table below is provided for reference purposes.

Original letter	2 soft	3 breathed	4 hard	5 mixed	5 after 'th
B	V		P	F	V
CH	J				
D	DH		T	T	T
GA	} the G = A		KA	HA	HA
GE	} is dropped = E		KE	HE	HE
GI	} and the = I		KI	HI	HI
GY	} next = Y		KY	HY	HY
GL	} letter = L		KL		
GR	} becomes = R		KR		
GW	} the initial = W		KW	HW	W
GO	WO		KO	HWO	WO
GU	WU		KU	HWU	WU
GRO	WRO		KRO	HWRO	WRO
GRU	WRU		KRU	HWRU	WRU
K	G	H			
M	V			F	V
P	B	F			
T	D	TH			

There is a special form of the fifth mutation used after the word **'th** 'you', 'your' and this will be described in the text.

To help the learner, a small numeral after a word and corresponding to the numbered columns above indicates the mutation change it causes, e.g. **war**[2] 'on' causes second state mutation and **kyn**[5] 'although' is followed by fifth state mutation. These numbers are not used in ordinary texts, of course.

GLOSSARY

◆ *adjective:*
a word that is linked to a noun to describe it. It answers the question 'What kind of...?': 'What kind of car?' 'A powerful car'; 'What kind of person is Sheila?' 'Sheila is kind' Note that words like 'my' and 'that' accompanying a noun are also adjectives.

◆ *adverb:*
a word that gives information about when, where or how an action takes place: 'He came yesterday'; 'She lived there'; 'I slept soundly'.

◆ *affirmative:*
any statement other than a question or a denial: 'The sky is blue'.

◆ *article:*
the word 'the' (definite article) and the words 'a', 'an' (indefinite article) in English.

◆ *auxiliary:*
a verb which when used with a verbal noun (see below) makes a verbal phrase. The verbal noun names the action or state while the auxiliary verb provides the other verbal information such as the tense, person, etc. In the statements 'I can go', 'Rita will drive', 'He does say so', the verbs 'can', 'will' and 'does' are the auxiliary verbs while 'go', 'drive' and 'say so' name the action.

◆ *clause:*
part of a complex sentence which has its own verb and subject and which is equivalent to a noun, adjective or adverb: 'He came when I called him' contains an adverbial clause denoting time. We might say that it is a sentence embedded in another sentence.

◆ *collective:*
a noun is called a collective noun if it denotes a class or group: **gwydh** is 'trees' in general; **kommol** is 'clouds'. We might say 'Clouds cause rain'; **Kommol a wra glaw.**

◆ *complement:*
that part of the sentence which completes the meaning of the verb 'to be' and its tenses: 'I am the *secretary*'; 'All the dishes had been *washed*'; 'The train will be *late*'.

◆ *conditional:*
describes a state or action about which there is some doubt, it being dependent upon some other state or action occurring: 'I would like to go'. There is usually an 'if' clause, expressed or understood, to go with it, e.g. 'if no-one else wants to'.

◆ *conjunction:*
a word which joins other words as units of a statement: 'and', 'when', 'but', 'or', for example.

◆ *dual:*
is the term used when two things are habitually pairs, for example the limbs or other parts of the body. So in Cornish 'your eyes' becomes **agas dewlagas**, **dew** '2' + **lagas** 'eye' = 'two eyes'.

◆ *future:*
any state not yet achieved. In English 'will', 'shall', 'going to' are used to indicate the future. In Cornish there are also special ways of doing this by the use of a number of phrases or by a form of the verb in a few cases.

◆ *indicative:*
when a verb is used to state a fact as contrasted with a supposition or an oder, it is said to be in the indicative mood: 'Tamsyn **works** in the garden'

◆ *imperfect:*
the tense of the verb which indicates an action or state in the past which continued or was repeated or was intermittent. In English it is expressed by phrases like 'used to', 'would': 'We used to live there'; 'The old men would sit on the bench and talk'. It contrasts with the preterite (see below) which indicates an action completed at a definite time.

◆ **inflected:**
any verb form which changes (usually by adding syllables) to indicate tense, person, etc. **kavsens** 'they had got' is an inflected form because to the basic part **kav** is added -s- to indicate past completed time and -ens to indicate the meaning 'they'

◆ **interrogative:**
any sentence which asks a question as contrasted with affirmative (above) and negative (below).

◆ **intransitive:** (see 'transitive'.)

◆ **mutation:**
a change in the original initial letter of a word in certain defined circumstances. The word **penn** 'head' can appear as **benn** or **fenn**. See page v for a full description.

◆ **negative:**
any sentence which denies a state or action: 'This dog is not well trained', as contrasted with affirmative and interrogative.

◆ **noun:**
a word which names something or someone: 'road', 'George'. For the various sorts of nouns, see the text.

◆ **object:**
of a sentence is that thing or person which, the subject having been named, receives the action: 'Mary kissed *her husband'*. See also 'subject', 'transitive' and 'intransitive'.

◆ **passive:**
is a sentence in which the subject (see below) is described as having had something done to it or him/her. The passive form of the sentence 'Everyone praised James' is 'James was praised by everyone'. It can be seen that the former object, 'James', has become the subject of the second sentence.

◆ **past:**
when referring to a verb denotes the form which has the appropriate verb endings. See 'inflected'. **kempennas** has the verbal part **kempenn** giving the idea of 'tidying' with ending -as which signifies action completed in the past.

◆ **periphrastic:**
is the term used to describe a verb phrase which is made up of an auxiliary verb and a verbal noun. The phrase **Hi a vynn mos** is periphrastic because it is made up of an auxiliary verb **vynn** 'will' and a verbal noun **mos** 'the action of going'.

◆ **person:**
relates the action to the person performing it. The speaker - first person: 'I', 'we'. The person who is addressed - second person: 'thou', 'you'. The person or thing spoken about - third person: 'he', 'she', 'it', 'they'.

◆ **pluperfect:**
is a tense which shows that the action took place before another action already completed in the past. In English the word 'had' forms part of this tense: 'George had written the letter when I arrived'. See 'tense', 'preterite', 'imperfect', 'future'.

◆ **plural:**
the form of a word which shows that it refers to more than one person or thing: 'heads' is the plural of 'head'. In Cornish **pennow** is the plural of **penn**. It is contrasted with dual and singular.

◆ **preposition:**
a word that denotes a relationship in the world of actual things, persons and ideas as distinct from a conjunction which links words in a sentence. Usually a preposition refers to place: 'The meal is *on* the table', sometimes to time: 'Don't read *during* the meal'. Often the reference is to abstract ideas: *'Through* your interference'.

♦ *present perfect:*
the tense which says that some action has been completed at the time of speaking. In English it is expressed by using 'have', 'has': 'I have seen her'; 'She has not seen me'. See also 'preterite', 'imperfect', 'pluperfect', 'future'.

♦ *preterite:*
is the form of the verb which denotes completed action in past time. It is the usual form in narrative: 'Molly *came* to the door, *opened* it, *saw* who was there and *shut* it again'. Compare this with the imperfect.

♦ *pronoun:*
is a word used to refer to some thing or person already known, mentioned or named: 'The cup fell off the table and *it* broke'; '*I* rang John and gave *him* the message'; '*That* (some action or state) was a pity'.

♦ *singular:*
that form of a word which denotes one person or thing: **my** 'I' is singular, **ni** 'we' is plural; **hanaf** 'cup' is singular, **hanafow** 'cups' is plural. See also dual and plural.

♦ *singulative:*
a word which indicates one member of a class. It usually has the ending -*enn* added to a collective noun in Cornish: **Kommolenn** 'a single cloud'

♦ *stem:*
is that part of a word, usually a noun or a verb, which contains the basic idea and to which syllables may be added to modify that idea: **moes** 'table' **moesow** 'tables'; **skrif-** 'write' **skrifav** 'I write'.

♦ *subject:*
is that part of the sentence which names the doer of the action, the person or thing which performs it or about whom the statement is made. It may consist of one word, a phrase or a whole sentence (see clause, above): '*I* came home'; '*All the children* played'; 'It is true that *everyone paid more*'. It is contrasted with the object which is the person or thing receiving the action.

♦ *subjunctive:*
this is the form of the verb in which the speaker can imply doubt of uncertainty. In English the subjunctive is heard in expressions such as, '**If it be** your wish, it will be done'. It is more common in Cornish than in English where its use is rather formal.

♦ *syntax*:
the structure of the sentence and the way the various parts relate to each other. So in identifying the subject and object in a sentence we are talking about the syntax of the sentence.

♦ *tense:*
is shown by the form of the verb and gives an indication of the time, duration and completeness of the action. See 'perfect', 'preterite', 'imperfect', 'future', 'pluperfect'.

♦ *transitive:*
is a term applied to verbs in which the action passes on to or is done to another person or thing: 'He helps *the children*'. By contrast an intransitive verb confines its action to the doer of the action: '*The stone* fell'. See also 'subject' and 'object'.

♦ *verb:*
the word or words which indicates the action or state: 'ate', 'will eat', 'falls'. The verb 'is' in its various forms can mean 'existence' or can link two ideas: 'There is a cat in the garden'; 'She is lucky'. This is the case also in Cornish.

♦ *verbal noun:*
the word which in Cornish names the action or state. It is called the verbal noun because although related to the verb it is grammatically a noun and is so treated. It is the form under which, for convenience, the verb is found in dictionaries: **tewlel** 'the act of throwing'; **bos** 'the state of being'. The English equivalent is expressed by what is called the infinitive, 'to throw', 'to be' or by a form ending in '-ing': 'throwing', 'being', in these two cases.

ix

xi

1 KORTESI - *COURTESY*

A greeting of some sort is usually exchanged when people meet, as a preliminary to more specific conversation. Here are some commonly used greetings.

Meeting in the evening

Greeting	Response
Gorthugher da! *Good evening!* **Fatla genes?** *How are you?*	**Gorthugher da!** *Good evening!* **Yn poynt da, meur ras - ha ty?** *Well, thanks - and you?* **Yn poynt da, meur ras.** *Well, thanks.* **Da lowr, meur ras.** *Well enough, thanks.*

Parting in the evening

Greeting	Response
Nos dha! *Good night!*	**Nos dha!** *Good night!*

Meeting at other times

Greeting	Response
Dydh da! *Good day!* **Myttin da!** *Good morning!* **Dohajydh da!** *Good afternoon!*	**Dydh da!** *Good day!* **Myttin da!** *Good morning!* **Dohajydh da!** *Good afternoon!*

Another person can be introduced by saying:

Ottomma Jori!
Here's George! (This is George!)

Saying 'goodbye'

Dyw genes! (to one person)
Dyw genowgh! (to more than one person)

GERVA - *Vocabulary*

dohajydh	*afternoon*	**myttin**	*morning*	**genes**	*with you*
dydh	*day*	**nos**	*night*		(singular)
Dyw	*God*	**oll**	*all*	**genowgh**	*with you*
gorthugher	*evening*	**lowr**	*enough*		(plural)

DASWELES - *Review*

Kernewek	Sowsnek
Dydh da, Ken. Fatla genes?	*Hullo, Ken. How are you?*
Dydh da, Charles.	*Hullo, Charles.*
Yn poynt da, meur ras, ha ty?	*Fine, thanks, and you?*
Myttin da, Maria. Fatla genes?	*Good morning, Mary. How are you?*
Da lowr, Maureen - ha ty, - fatla genes?	*Fairly well, Maureen - and you, how are you?*
Yn poynt da, meur ras.	*Very well, thanks.*
Gorthugher da, Loveday.	*Good evening, Loveday.*
Gorthugher da, Jane.	*Good evening, Jane.*
Ottomma Jori.	*Here's George.*
Gorthugher da, Jori - fatla genes?	*Good evening, George - how are you?*
Yn poynt da, meur ras.	*Fine, thanks.*
Nos dha, oll!	*Good night, all.*
Nos dha, Wella!	*Good night, Wella.*
Dohajydh da, Ann.	*Good afternoon, Ann.*
Dohajydh da, Malcolm - fatla genes?	*Good afternoon, Malcolm - how are you?*
Da lowr, meur ras - ha ty?	*Well enough, thanks - and you?*
Da lowr, meur ras.	*Quite well, thanks.*
Dydh da, Maria.	*Hullo, Mary.*
Dydh da, Wella - ottomma Stefan.	*Hullo, Wella - here's Stephen.*
Dydh da, Stefan.	*Hullo, Stephen.*

2 BOSVA - *EXISTENCE*

There is frequently a need to find out whether or not something exists or to say that it does exist: 'Is there a post-office here?'; 'Are there people in the room?'.

In English the sense of existing is expressed by a tense of the verb 'is' together with the word 'there': 'There is a bird on the roof'; 'There had been more rain in the night'.

In Cornish the corresponding verb **bos** 'to be' has special forms to carry the meaning of existence:

The question:	**eus ..?**	*Is there..? Are there..?*
The answer:	**eus!**	*There is! There are!*
or	**nag eus!**	*There is not! There are not!*
The statements:		
positive	**yma...**	*There is. There are.*
negative	**nyns eus...**	*There is not. There are not.*

Question	Response
Eus chi ena? 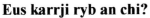	**Eus!**
Is there a house there?	*There is!*
Eus karrji ryb an chi?	**Eus! Yma karrji ena.**
Is there a garage by the house?	*There is. There is a garage there.*
Eus karr a-rag an karrji?	**Nag eus! Nyns eus karr ena.**
Is there a car in front of the garage?	*There isn't! There isn't a car there.*
Ottomma an karr a-ji dhe'n karrji!	
Look here's the car inside the garage!	

Notice the absence of words for 'yes' and 'no' in the above. It is usual to answer a question by repeating the verb of the question.

The same singular verb forms (**yma, eus**) are used to translate both 'there is' and 'there are':

ottomma	*look! see here!*	Use these two words for
ottena	*look! see there!*	pointing things out.

GERVA - *Vocabulary*

Kernewek	English	Kernewek	English	Kernewek	English
a-ji dhe	*inside*	**ha** *conj.*	*and*	**mes** *conj.*	*but*
a-rag	*in front of*	(**hag** before a	vowel)	**moes** *f.*	*table*
aval *m.*	*apple*	**jynn-skrifa** *m.*	*typewriter*	**omma** *adv.*	*here*
avalow *pl.*	*apples*	**kador** *f.*	*chair*	**pluvek** *f.*	*cushion,*
chi *m.*	*house*	**karr** *m.*	*car*		*pillow*
eglos *f.*	*church*	**karrji** *m.*	*garage*	**pluvenn** *f.*	*pen*
ena *adv.*	*there*	**le** *m.*	*place*	**pluvennow** *pl.*	*pens*
gesys *adj.*	*remaining,*	**leow** *pl.*	*places*	**ryb** *prep.*	*beside*
	left,	**lyver** *m.*	*book*	**sur** *adv.*	*surely*

DASWELES - *Review*

Kernewek	Sowsnek
Ottena eglos!	*Look, a church there!*
Yma chi ryb an eglos.	*There's a house beside the church.*
Eus karrji ena ryb an chi?	*Is there a garage there beside the house?*
Nag eus! Nyns eus karrji ena.	*No! There isn't a garage there.*
Mes yma karr a-rag an chi.	*But there is a car in front of the house.*
Ottomma lyver!	*Look, here's a book!*
Yma pluvenn a-ji dhe'n lyver.	*There's a pen inside the book.*
Eus pluvennow genes? Nag eus!	*Are there pens with you? No!*
Gorthugher da! Eus le gesys, mar pleg?	*Good evening! Is there a place left, please?*
Eus! Yma leow gesys.	*Yes! There are places left.*
Eus kador ena?	*Is there a chair there?*
Eus, sur!	*There is, certainly!*
Eus kador ha pluvek ena?	*Is there a chair and a cushion there?*
Nag eus!	*There isn't!*
Eus jynn-skrifa war an desk?	*Is there a typewriter on the desk?*
Eus avalow gesys?	*Are there any apples left?*
Eus! Ottena! Yma avalow ena.	*There are! Look! There are apples there!*

3 DIBLANSNETH - *DEFINITENESS*

In English when definite things are referred to, words like 'the', 'this', 'that', and so on are used.

In Cornish the corresponding word is **an** 'the'. This is the 'definite article'.

an lyver	*the book*
an karr	*the car*
an chi	*the house*

If the short word **ma** is added to these phrases, the meaning becomes 'this', 'these'.

If the short word **na** is added, the meaning becomes 'that', those'.

an lyver ma	*this book*
an lyvrow ma	*these books*
an karr na	*that car*
an kerri na	*those cars*

ma and **na** never stand alone. They always follow the word they apply to and **an** 'the' always precedes.

Now let us look at the word **moes** 'table'. We say **moes** 'table' but **an voes** 'the table', **an voes ma** 'this table' and **an voes na** 'that table'. The initial **m-** of the word has changed to **v-** after the word **an**.

This change is called 'mutation' and is explained at the beginning of this book where there is a reference table. Don't worry about it. Your attention will be drawn to it when it occurs.

This particular type of mutation is the commonest and it occurs with certain types of noun. These nouns are called 'feminine' nouns. All other nouns are 'masculine' but this topic will be dealt with in detail in Part 8.

Ensamplow *(Examples)*	davas	*sheep*	**an dhavas**	*the sheep*	**D** to **DH**
	garr	*leg*	**an arr**	*the leg*	**G** dropped
	goen	*down*	**an woen**	*the down*	**GO** to **WO**
	kador	*chair*	**an gador**	*the chair*	**K** to **G**
	mowes	*girl*	**an vowes**	*the girl*	**M** to **V**
	pluvenn	*pen*	**an bluvenn**	*the pen*	**P** to **B**
	tesenn	*cake*	**an desenn**	*the cake*	**T** to **D**

4 ANDHIBLANSNETH - *INDEFINITENESS*

What happens when there is no word **an** before the noun? The meaning in that case is the English 'a' or 'an'.

chi	*house* or *a house*
pluvenn	*pen* or *a pen*
aval	*apple* or *an apple*

Notice that English has to use the word 'a' or the word 'an', whereas Cornish does not.

We can however say **unn chi**, **unn karr**, **unn eglos** and so on with the meaning 'a certain house', 'a certain car', 'a certain church'. In this way there is a limit to the indefiniteness.

Ensamplow (Examples)	*I would like to climb a mountain.* (any one)	Use **menydh** *a mountain*
	*I would like to climb a certain mountain* (but not naming it)	Use **unn menydh** *a certain mountain*
	I would like to climb the mountain (Cader Idris)	Use **an menydh** *the mountain*

This word, **unn** 'one', 'a certain' has the same effect as **an** 'the' in that it changes - mutates - certain initial letters of feminine words: **moes** *f.* 'table'; **unn voes** 'a certain table'.

There are several other useful words:

nebonan *someone*

Yma nebonan a-ji dhe'n eglos na
There is someone inside that church

neppyth *something*

Yma neppyth a-rag an chi ma
There is something in front of this house

7

GERVA - *Vocabulary*

brithel *m.*	*mackerel*	**lestrier** *m.*	*kitchen dresser*
bryntin! *excl.*	*fine! grand!*	**leurlenn** *f.*	*carpet*
dell hevel	*so it seems*	**mebyl** *coll.*	*furniture*
gweder *m.*	*glass, mirror*	**pras** *m.*	*meadow*
hel an dre *m.*	*town hall*	**sinema** *m.*	*cinema*
kador-vregh *f.*	*armchair*	**stamp** *m.*	*postage stamp*
kenter *f.*	*nail*	**war²** *prep.*	*on*

DASWELES - *Review*

Kernewek	Sowsnek
An brithel ma yw bryntin.	*This mackerel is excellent.*
Yma an gador-vregh ena.	*The armchair is there.*
Eus sinema ryb hel an dre?	*Is there a cinema by the town hall?*
Nyns eus kenter omma, dell hevel.	*There is no nail here, it seems.*
Ottena - yma an genter war an leurlenn.	*Look there - there's the nail on the carpet.*
Eus stamp gesys? Nag eus!	*Is there a stamp left? No!*
Yma mebyl gesys ena y'n chi: kador-vregh, kador, gweder ha lestrier mes nyns eus moes ena.	*There is furniture left in the house: an arm-chair, chair, mirror and dresser but there isn't a table there.*
Eus nebonan ena a-ji dhe'n pras?	*Is there anyone there in the field?*
Eus stamp genes?	*Have you a stamp?*
Yma pras war an woen hag yma chi ryb an pras na.	*There's a field on the down and there's a house by that field.*
Sur, yma lyver war an voes.	*Certainly there is a book on the table.*
Eus neppyth gesys ena? Eus!	*Is there anything left? Yes!*
Yma avalow gesys, dell hevel.	*There are apples left, it seems.*
Yma an dhavas ena y'n pras na.	*The sheep is in that field.*

5 HEVELEPTER - *IDENTITY*

When we say, for example,

	An diwes ma yw gwin frynkek	*This drink is French wine*
or	**An chi na yw ostel**	*That house is an hotel*

it is easy to see that we are saying that one thing is identical with another.

The link between them is the word **yw** which does the same work as the English word *is*. It joins the subject of the sentence to the complement (see the Glossary). The person or the thing about which the information is given or sought is made the subject of the sentence and may be represented by a noun or pronoun.

Some more examples:

Hemm yw an gegin	*This is the kitchen*
Henn yw Frank	*That is Frank*
Frank yw henna	*Frank is that one/man*

The first mentioned thing can refer to a number of things, and then the word is plural. We still use **yw** as the link word although in English is changes to 'are'.

An losow yw eythin	*The plants are gorse*
An traow ma yw prenn	*These things are wood*

We may want to say that two things are not the same, the statement is negative.

To say that two things are not the same, are not identical, we use the following form of words:

nyns 'not' + **yw** 'is' = **nyns yw** *is not*. This is said first.

Then the two things are mentioned, one after the other:

an chi na - ostel

9

Nyns yw an chi na ostel	*That house is not an hotel*
Nyns yw an diwes ma gwin	*This drink is not French wine*
frynkek	

In the same way we say:

Nyns yw henna Frank	*That is not Frank*
Nyns yw hemma an gegin	*This is not the kitchen*
Nyns yw an losow eythin	*The plants are not gorse*
Nyns yw an traow ma prenn	*These things are not wood*
Nyns yw Frank henna	*Frank is not that one/man*

If we want to ask if two things are the same, we use the words we already know.

The order of the words and the way in which they are said will show that it is a question we are asking.

Yw an chi na ostel?	*Is that house an hotel?*
Yw an diwes ma gwin frynkek?	*Is this drink French wine?*

The linking word **yw** is comes first.

Then the two things we are enquiring about are named:

Yw henna Frank?	*Is that Frank?*
Yw hemma an gegin?	*Is this the kitchen?*
Yw an losow eythin?	*Are the plants gorse?*
Yw an traow ma prenn?	*Are these things wood?*

Cornish speakers do not say *yes* or *no*. They say **yw** 'it is' or **nag yw** 'it is not'.

Yw an diwes ma gwin frynkek?	*Is this drink French wine?*
Yw	*It is (= yes)*
Yw henna Frank?	*Is that Frank?*
Nag yw	*It is not (= no)*

Jori

10

Ensamplow

Yw an dre ma Essa?	*Is this town Saltash?*
Yw	*It is (= yes)*
Yw an drehevyans na hel an dre?	*Is that building the town hall?*
Nag yw	*It is not (= no)*

When the question is about a number or things, for example,

Yw an losow eythin?	*Are the plants gorse?*

then the answer word must show this, since the things are not named in the reply, so instead of **yw**, we say **yns** which by itself means 'they are'.

Yw an gwydh ma derow?	*Are these trees oaks?*
Yns	*They are (= yes)*
Yw an chiow na ostelyow?	*Are those houses hotels?*
Nag yns	*They are not (= no)*

'THIS', 'THAT', 'THESE', 'THOSE'

hemma	*this thing* or *male person*
henna	*that thing* or *male person*
homma	*this thing* or *female person*
honna	*that thing* or *female person*
re	*some, ones*
an re ma	*these things* or *persons*
an re na	*those things* or *persons*

The masculine forms **hemma**, **henna**, are used as a kind of neutral reference when the identity of an object has not been identified or is irrelevant. This can be explained by assuming that the two pronouns stand for **tra** 'thing'. See further the notes on page 64. If the object is identified, then the appropriate gender of pronoun is employed.

Pyth yw hemma?	*What is this?*
Pluvek yw	*It's a cushion*
Homm yw da	*This (= the cushion) is good*

11

WHAT IS THAT?

Pyth yw henna? *What is that?*
Maylyer gwag yw *It's an empty envelope*

Pyth yw an re na? *What are those?*
Skeusennow koth yns *They are old photographs*

If there is no noun accompanying the word 'what' in questions, the Cornish word is **pyth** at the head of the sentence. It can stand for either one thing or many. No mutation follows **pyth**.

GERVA - Vocabulary

chi *m.*	house	**losow** *coll.*	plants
chiow *pl.*	houses	**ostel** *f.*	hotel
derow *coll.*	oak	**prenn** *m.*	wood (material)
diwes *m.*	drink	**tra** *m./f.*	thing, object
drehevyans *m.*	building	**traow** *pl.*	things, objects
eythin *coll.*	gorse	**tre** *f.*	town, farm, home
gwin *m.*	wine	**an dre**	the town, etc.
kegin *f.*	kitchen	**yn** *prep.*	in
an gegin	the kitchen	**y'n** (= yn an)	in the

DASWELES - Review

Kernewek	Sowsnek
Hemm yw pluvenn.	*This is a pen.*
An re ma yw pluvennow.	*These are pens.*
Henn yw chi.	*That is a house.*
An re na yw chiow.	*Those are houses.*
An drehevyans na yw eglos.	*That building is a church.*
An eglos yw an drehevyans na.	*The church is that building.*
An dre ma yw Logh.	*This town is Looe.*
Homm yw Myrna ha honn yw Pat.	*This is Myrna and that is Pat.*
An diwes ma yw gwin.	*This drink is wine.*
Pyth yw an dra ma?	*What is this object?*
Henn yw kenter.	*That is a nail.*

Kernewek	Sowsnek
Nyns yw an dra ma prenn.	This object is not wood.
Nyns yw hemma an gegin.	This is not the kitchen.
Nyns yw an drehevyans ma ostel.	This building is not an hotel.
Pyth yw an mebyl omma?	What is the furniture here?
An re ma yw an mebyl, an voes ma, an gador-vregh ma ha'n lestrier na.	These (things) are the furniture, this table, this armchair and that dresser.
Yw henna brithel? Yw!	Is that a mackerel? It is!
Yw an re ma losow? Yns!	Are these plants? They are!

DASWELES KEMMYSKYS - *Miscellaneous Review*

Kernewek	Sowsnek
Eus eglos y'n dre ma?	Is there a church in this town?
Eus! Yma an eglos ryb hel an dre	There is! The church is beside the town hall.
Yw an gwin ma bretonek?	Is this wine Breton?
Hemma. Hemm yw bretonek.	This. This is Breton.
Eus pluvek war an gador-vregh na?	Is there a cushion on that arm-chair?
Eus, dell hevel.	There is, it seems.
Eus diwes gesys?	Is there (any) drink left?
Nag eus! Nyns eus tra omma.	There isn't. There's nothing here.

6 STUDH - *STATE*

In saying

An chi yw koth *The house is old*

we are telling someone what state the house is in and the same linking word **yw** is used as before to join the subject to the complement. The word following **yw** is an adjective, **koth** 'old'.

Again, there is no need to change the linking word if the speaker is talking about a number of things, that is to say, if the noun is plural.

An chiow yw nowydh *The houses are new*
The English version has *are* of course. .

Other examples

Hemm yw brav! *This is fine*
An pluvennow ma yw rudh *These pens are red*

When it is necessary to deny or to question that a thing has a certain quality, the same patterns as before are used.

Denying something

Nyns yw an maw lowen *The boy is not happy*
Nyns yw an fordhow salow *The roads are not safe*

Asking and answering:

Yw an vowes yowynk? *Is the girl young?*
Yw! *She is! (= yes)*
Yw an boes parys? *Is the food ready?*
Nag yw! *It is not! (= no)*
Yw an fleghes parow? *Are the children equals?*
Yns! *They are! (= yes)*
Yw an lyvrow gwerthys? *Are the books sold?*
Nag yns! *They are not! (= no)*

In these last two replies, the words **fleghes** and **lyvrow** are not repeated so the verb has to be plural in each case, **yns** 'they are', **nag yns** 'they are not'.

We can also ask a negative question, 'is not?', 'are not?' by beginning the question with the phrase **a nyns**:

A nyns yw an boes parys?   *Isn't the food ready?*
A nyns yw an fleghes parow?   *Aren't the children equals?*

GERVA - *Vocabulary*

brav *adj.*	*fine, excellent*	**kul** *adj.*	*narrow*
byw *adj.*	*alive*	**lemmyn** *adv.*	*now*
dell dybav	*so I think*	**les** *m.*	*use, advantage*
den *m.*	*person*	**dhe les**	*of use, useful*
tus *pl.*	*people*	**lowen** *adj.*	*happy*
feusik *adj.*	*lucky*	**maw** *m.*	*boy*
flogh *m.*	*child*	**mes** *conj.*	*but*
fleghes *pl.*	*children*	**nowydh** *adj.*	*new*
fol *adj.*	*foolish*	**par** *m.*	*equal*
fordh *f.*	*road*	**parow** *pl.*	*equals*
gwann *adj.*	*weak*	**parys** *adj.*	*ready*
gwerthys *adj.*	*sold*	**salow** *adj.*	*safe*
hweg *adj.*	*sweet*	**skav** *adj.*	*light, nimble*
koth *adj.*	*old*		

DASWELES - *Review*

An den na yw feusik, dell hevel.	*That man is lucky, it seems.*
An fordh ma yw kul.	*This road is narrow.*
James ha Lowena yw parow.	*James and Lowena are equals.*
Yw an mebyl parys? Nag yns.	*Is the furniture ready? No.*
An lyver ma yw dhe les, dell dybav.	*This book is useful, I think.*
Ottomma kenter war an gador ma.	*Look, here's a nail on this chair.*
Homm yw fol, sur.	*This is silly, surely.*
Hel an dre yw nowydh mes an eglos yw koth.	*The town hall is new but the church is old.*

15

An gwin ma yw hweg. Bryntin!	*This wine is sweet. Fine!*
An chi yw gwerthys lemmyn.	*The house is sold now.*
An voes ma yw derow.	*This table is oak.*
An gweder ma yw dhe les.	*This mirror is useful.*
Yw an maw salow ena?	*Is the boy safe there?*
Hemm yw brav!	*This is grand!*
Nyns yw an losow byw.	*The plants are not alive.*
A nyns yw an maw ma skav?	*Isn't this boy quick?*
Yw, sur.	*He is, certainly.*
A nyns yw an re ma parow?	*Aren't these equal?*
Yns, dell hevel.	*They are, it seems.*

DASWELES KEMMYSKYS - *Miscellaneous Review*

Dydh da, Maureen. Brav yw lemmyn.	*Hello, Maureen. It's grand now.*
Eus gwin gesys? Eus! Yma gwin y'n gegin.	*Is there (any) wine left? There is! There's wine in the kitchen.*
Fatla genowgh hwi oll?	*How are you all?*
Eus fordh ryb an pras na?	*Is there a road beside that field?*
Ottena pluvek war an gador na.	*Look there's a cushion on that chair.*
Yma nebonan y'n gegin lemmyn.	*There is someone in the kitchen now.*
An ostel na yw bryntin.	*That hotel is fine.*
Dyw genes, Peder!	*Goodbye, Peter!*
An drehevyans a-rag an chi yw karrji.	*The building in front of the house is a garage.*
Eus traow gesys war an lestrier?	*Are there things left on the dresser?*
Eus! Yma traow gesys ena	*There are. There are things left there.*
Eus leow gesys y'n sinema lemmyn?	*Are there places left in the cinema now?*
An re ma yw nowydh, dell dybav.	*These are new, I think.*
Pyth yw hemma?	*What's this?*
An dra na yw pluvenn.	*That object is a pen.*
Pyth yw hweg?	*What is sweet?*
An aval ma yw hweg, sur.	*This apple is sweet, for sure.*
A nyns eus davas y'n pras na?	*Isn't there a sheep in that field?*
Py tus yw kernewek omma?	*Which people are Cornish here?*
Oll an re na, dell dybav.	*All of those, I think.*

16

7 DASWRIANS - *REPETITION*

Often in ordinary conversation it is necessary to ask people to repeat something they have said. To do this in Cornish, say:

Arta, mar pleg!   *Again please!*

You may also want to find out if you yourself have been understood.

A wodhesta konvedhes?   *Do you understand?*

The answer will be either:

Gonn!   *I understand (= yes!)*

or

Na wonn!   *I do not understand (= no!)*

In a class or group situation the question might be put to a number of people and so the verb would be plural:

A wodhowgh hwi konvedhes?   *Do you understand?*

Each person would then probably answer as before with **Gonn!** or **Na wonn!**

PY LYVER? - *Which book?*

Py lyver yw henna?	*What book is that?*
Gerlyver yw.	*It's a dictionary.*
Py gwin yw gwin bretonek?	*What wine is a Breton wine?*
Muscadet yw gwin bretonek.	*Muscadet is a Breton wine.*
Py mebyon yw drog?	*Which boys are naughty?*
Py re yns?	*Which ones are they?*
An re na yw drog, sur.	*Those ones are naughty, certainly.*

The word **py** comes before a noun, singular or plural, and translates the English 'what', 'which' in questions. It does not cause mutation.

GERVA

Powyow - Countries

Alban *f.*	Scotland	**Kembra** *f.*	Wales
Albanek *adj.*	Scottish	**Kembrek** *adj.*	Welsh
Almayn *f.*	Germany	**Kernow** *f.*	Cornwall
Almaynek *adj.*	German	**Kernow** *m.*	Cornishman
Breten *f.*	Britain	**Kernewek** *adj.*	Cornish
Breten Veur *f.*	Great Britain	**Kernowes** *f.*	Cornishwoman
Breten Vyghan *f.*	Brittany	**Manow** *f.*	Isle of Man
Breton *m.*	Breton (person)	**Pow Frynk** *m.*	France
Iwerdhon *f.*	Ireland	**Pow Sows** *m.*	England
Iwerdhonek *adj.*	Irish	**Sowsnek** *adj.*	English

The name of a language, **Kernewek** for instance, will be written with an upper case initial. If the same form is an adjective, it can be written with either an upper case or a lower case initial, usually the latter: **Almaynek** 'the German language'; **karr almaynek/Almaynek** 'a German car'.

GERYOW AN GEWER - *Weather terms*

awel *f.*	wind, gale	**kommolek** *adj.*	cloudy
awelek *adj.*	very windy	**niwl** *m.*	mist
ergh *m*	snow	**niwlek** *adj.*	misty
ergh a wra hi	it's snowing	**oer** *adj.*	very cold
glaw *m.*	rain	**poeth** *adj.*	very hot
glaw a wra hi	it's raining	**splann** *adj.*	bright
glyb *adj.*	wet	**sygh** *adj.*	dry
gwyns *m.*	wind	**teg** *adj.*	fine
gwynsek *adj.*	windy	**toemm** *adj.*	warm
kewer *f.*	weather	**yeyn** *adj.*	cold
fatell yw an gewer?	how is the weather?	**yma anwoes warnav**	I have a cold
kosel *adj.*	calm		

The weather is regarded as a feminine entity, thus:

Hi a wra glaw	It rains
Hi yw kosel	It is calm

DASWELES - *Review*

Pyth yw hemma, Pol?	*What's this, Paul?*
Arta, mar pleg!	*Again, please!*
An gwin ma yw almaynek.	*This wine is German.*
A wodhesta konvedhes Kernewek?	*Do you understand Cornish?*
Gonn, dell dybav.	*I do, I think.*
Py lyver yw kembrek?	*Which book is Welsh?*
Hemm yw kembrek.	*This (one) is Welsh.*
Py lyver yw dhe les?	*Which book is useful?*
Hemm yw dhe les, sur.	*This (one) is useful, certainly.*
An pow na yw Pow Sows.	*That country is England.*
An stamp ma yw iwerdhonek.	*This stamp is Irish.*
Fatell yw an gewer lemmyn?	*What is the weather like now?*
Yma awel.	*There's a wind.*
Poeth yw an gewer lemmyn.	*The weather is now very hot.*
An gewer yw splann ha kosel, dell hevel.	*The weather is calm and fine, it seems.*
Brav! Hi yw teg.	*Splendid! It's fine.*
Ergh a wra hi yn Alban lemmyn.	*It's snowing in Scotland now.*
Ott! An pras yw niwlek.	*Look! The field is misty.*

Poeth yw an gewer lemmyn.

DASWELES KEMMYSKYS - *Miscellaneous Review*

Fatla genes, Mighal?	*How are you, Michael?*
Yn poynt da, Les, meur ras. Ha ty?	*Well, Les, thanks. And you?*
Ogh! Da lowr. Mes yma anwoes warnav.	*Oh! Well enough. But I have a cold.*
Gwynsek yw hi an dohajydh ma.	*It's windy this afternoon.*
Yw, sur.	*It is, certainly.*
Eus glaw?	*Is there rain?*
Eus. Hi a wra glaw lemmyn.	*There is. It's raining now.*
An karr ma yw gwerthys.	*This car is sold.*
An voes ma yw nowydh.	*This table is new.*
A nyns yw an maw ma lowen?	*Isn't this boy happy?*
Yw, dell dybav.	*He is, I think.*
Homm yw feusik. Yma aval gesys.	*This is lucky. There's an apple left.*
Yma ostel yn unn dre yn Breten Vyghan. Ostel dha yw.	*There's an hotel in a certain town in Brittany. It's a good hotel.*
Pyth yw an drehevyans ma?	*What is this building?*
Henn yw hel an dre.	*That's the town hall.*
An brithel ma yw brav!	*This mackerel is fine!*
Dyw genes lemmyn - ha meur ras!	*Goodbye now - and thanks!*
Py re yw parys lemmyn?	*Which ones are ready now?*
Honn yw Kernewes.	*That woman is a Cornishwoman.*
Ottomma Karl! Almaynek yw.	*This is Karl! He's German.*
Kernow ha Breten Vyghan yw parow. Sur, parow yns.	*Cornwall and Brittany are equals. Certainly, equals they are.*
An gwyns yw skav lemmyn, dell hevel.	*The wind is light now, it seems.*
An gador ma yw kembrek, dell dybav.	*This chair is Welsh, I think.*
A wodhowgh hwi oll konvedhes Kernewek?	*Do you all understand Cornish?*
Gonn! Gonn!	*I do! I do!*
Sur, an eglos ma yw oer.	*Certainly this church is very cold.*

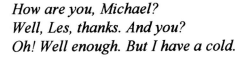

8 GOROW ha BENOW - *MASCULINE and FEMININE*

It is obvious that boys and men are masculine by nature or sex and that girls and women are feminine by nature or sex.

In addition to this natural difference in living beings, Cornish also marks words themselves as being masculine or feminine and in this it is like many other languages. This grammatical characteristic is usually called 'gender'.

In Cornish, for example, **chi** *house* is masculine and **moes** *table* is feminine in gender although there is nothing about these objects themselves to mark such a distinction.

In some cases the meaning or appearance of a word will show whether it is masculine or feminine and these characteristics will be mentioned from time to time. One obvious way is to see whether the word means a male or a female being. If it does then the likelihood is that the gender will follow the sex.

Gorow *Masculine*
maw *boy*, **ewnter** *uncle*, **gour** *husband*, **kulyek** *cock*, **margh** *stallion*

Benow *Feminine*
mowes *girl*, **modrep** *aunt*, **gwreg** *wife*, **yar** *hen*, **kasek** *mare*

The form of a word as it is heard in speech or seen in writing may show the gender of a word. It was explained in the chapter on Definiteness (Part 3) that the initial letter of some words changes in a regular way after the word **an** '*the*', and examples were given there of this 'mutation' process. Feminine singular nouns are the most common of such words and repeating the feminine words given in the list above we have:

an vowes *the girl*, **an vodrep** *the aunt*, **an wreg** *the wife*, **an yar** *the hen* (no change), **an gasek** *the mare*.

This change also happens after the word **UNN** *one, a certain*, as we have seen, so that we have again:

unn vowes *one/a certain girl*, **unn vodrep** *one/a certain aunt*, **unn wreg** *one/a certain wife*, **unn yar** *one/a certain hen* (no change), **unn gasek** *one/a certain mare*.

By way of contrast, masculine nouns only have this change (mutation) when they are plural and refer to people:

pyskador *fisherman,* **an pyskador** *the fisherman,* **unn pyskador** *one fisherman,* where, as can be seen, there is no mutation but:

pyskadoryon *fishermen,* **an byskadoryon** *the fishermen.*

GERVA

AN TEYLU - *The Family*

broder *m.*	*brother*	**benow** *f./adj.*	*female*
ewnter *m.*	*uncle*	**gwreg** *f.*	*wife*
gorow *m./adj.*	*male*	**hweger** *f.*	*mother-in-law*
gour *m.*	*man, husband*	**hwoer** *f.*	*sister*
hwegron *m.*	*father-in-law*	**kares** *f.*	*relative*
kar *m.*	*relative*	**keniterow** *f.*	*cousin*
kenderow *m.*	*cousin*	**mamm** *f.*	*mother*
mab *m.*	*son*	**mammik** *f.*	*mummy*
noy *m.*	*nephew*	**mamm-wynn** *f.*	*grandmother*
tas *m.*	*father*	**modrep** *f.*	*aunt*
tas-gwynn *m.*	*grandfather*	**myrgh** *f.*	*daughter*
tasik *m.*	*daddy*	**nith** *f.*	*niece*

In referring to *father*, *mother*, etc. when particular persons in a family are being spoken of, Cornish usually puts the definite article in front: **an vamm-wynn** *grandmother.*

GERVA

anwoes *m.*	*cold* (ailment)	**le'ti** *m.*	*dairy*
yma anwoes war Beder	*Peter has a cold*	**ke** *m.*	*hedge*
		koes *m.*	*wood(land)*
tiek *m.*	*farmer*	**tioges** *f.*	*farmwife*
namoy *adj., adv.*	*any more* (with neg. *no more*)		

DASWELES - *Review*

An broder ha'n hwoer yw parow.	*The brother and sister are equals.*
Nyns yw an vamm ha'n vyrgh parow.	*The mother and daughter are not equals.*
An vodrep yw koth.	*The aunt is old.*
Yma anwoes war an vamm-wynn.	*The grandmother has a cold.*
An tas, an ewnter ha'n mab oll yw gorow.	*Father, uncle and son are all male.*
An vamm, an vyrgh ha'n vodrep oll yw benow.	*Mother, daughter and aunt are all female.*
A nyns yw an hweger lowen namoy?	*Isn't mother-in-law happy any more?*
An vowes yw yowynk.	*The girl is young.*
An byskadoryon yw parys lemmyn.	*The fishermen are ready now.*
An diogyon na yw feusik, dell dybav.	*Those farmers are lucky, I think.*
Yma an dioges yn le'ti lemmyn.	*The farmwife is in the dairy now.*
A nyns eus ke ryb an koes? Nag eus!	*Isn't there a hedge by the wood? No!*

DASWELES KEMMYSKYS - *Miscellaneous Review*

An jynn-skrifa na yw koth mes da.	*That typewriter is old but good.*
Yma neppyth nowydh y'n dre lemmyn. Henn yw bryntin!	*There's something new in the town now. That's splendid!*
Nyns eus pluvennow gesys namoy.	*There are no pens left any more.*
A wodhesta konvedhes hemma?	*Do you understand this?*
Na wonn.	*I do not understand.*
Fatell yw an gewer lemmyn?	*What's the weather like now?*
Glyb ha kommolek, dell hevel.	*Wet and cloudy, it seems.*
Py mowes yw Karol?	*Which girl is Carol?*
Honna y'n gador-vregh.	*That (one) in the armchair.*
Py lyver yw gesys?	*What book is left?*
Pyth yw hemma, an dra ma, yn Kernewek?	*What is this, this object, in Cornish?*
'Gweder' yw. A wodhesta konvedhes?	*It's 'gweder'. Do you understand?*
Gonn, meur ras.	*Yes, thank you.*
Ottomma diwes. Gwin yw, dell dybav, ha yeyn. Bryntin!	*Here's (some) drink. It's wine I think, and cold. Splendid!*
Eus pluvenn genes, mar pleg? Eus!	*Have you a pen, please? Yes!*
An gegin yw kul.	*The kitchen is narrow.*

23

9 DESKRIFA TRAOW - *DESCRIBING THINGS*

An gwin ma yw frynkek, sur　　*This wine is French, surely*

Gwin frynkek yw ytho　　*It's French wine then*

A noun can have an adjective attached to it to describe it as in the second example. This adjective follows its noun in Cornish whereas in English the adjective comes first. There are a few exceptions to this as will be seen at a later stage.

Hemm yw lyver berr　　*This is a short book*
Homm yw notenn verr　　*This is a short note*

Although the same adjective, **berr**, is used in both these statements, in the second example the noun, **notenn**, is feminine in gender and singular in number. The adjective is mutated by softening in such cases. Other examples:

padell goth (koth)　　*an old saucepan*
avon dhown (down)　　*a deep river*
fordh arow (garow)　　*a rough road*

No mutation takes place if the noun ends in -**s** or in -**th** and the adjective begins with **k-**, **p-** or **t-**: **eglos teg** not *eglos deg, **an yeth kernewek** not *an yeth gernewek.

The same mutation of an adjective is used when the noun is masculine in gender, plural and denotes persons:

pyskadoryon vrav (brav)　　*fine fishermen*
tus wann (gwann)　　*weak people*
Again there is no mutation of **k-**, **p-** or **t-** after -**s** or -**th**:
tus keltek　　*Celtic people*

If another word intervenes between the noun and the adjective, then then there is no mutation. This is a general rule in Cornish; the word causing the mutation and the word mutated must come together: **padell goth (koth)** *an old saucepan*; **padell blos (plos)** *a dirty saucepan*, but **padell blos, koth** *a dirty old saucepan*.

You learnt earlier how to say, *What is the weather like?*, **Fatell yw an gewer?**. This word **fatell** meaning *how* can be used in a general way to find out what something is like: **Fatell yw an chi?** *What's the house like?*. The answer might be, **Nowydh yw** *It's new*. Notice that **fatell** is always followed by a verb, in this case **yw** *is*.

A similar question might be, *What kind of car is that?*. For this sort of query we use **Py par?** You have met **par** as a noun meaning *equal* in the sense of *equivalent*. So the answer to this question might be **Rolls Roys** or **Myni**. Here the next word is the name of the thing you are enquiring about.

PIW YW HENNA? - *WHO IS THAT?*

Gav dhymm mes piw yw henna, mar pleg?	*Excuse me but who is that, please?*	
Mr Grace yw henna	*That's Mr Grace*	

Piw yw Mr Lock ytho?	*Who is Mr Lock then?*	
Ottena! An gour ena yw Mr Lock, an gour hir na	*Look! that man there is Mr. Lock, that tall man.*	

Piw is the Cornish for *who* in questions. It is not the same as the English word *who* in statements like '*That's the man who bought our house*', a construction which will be dealt with later.

GERVA

avon *f.*	river		**keltek** *adj.*	Celtic
benyn *f.*	woman		**kewsys** *adj.*	spoken
benynes *pl.*	women		**notenn** *f.*	note
berr *adj.*	short		**padell** *f.*	saucepan
bras *adj.*	big		**tus (an dus)**	people
byghan *adj.*	small		**yeth** *f.*	language
down *adj.*	deep		**ytho** *conj.*	so, then
Kelt *m.*	Celt			

25

DASWELES - *Review*

Hemm yw aval hweg.

An avon Tamer yw
avon vras, down.

Hemm yw koes bras.

Pow teg yw Breten Vyghan.

Ottomma kador-vregh vyghan.

Yma le gesys omma.

Yma kador gesys ryb an voes vras.

Hel an Dre yw drehevyans teg.

An gour yw den da, dell dybav.

A nyns yw hemma gwin almaynek?

Ny wonn!

Yeth dha yw Kernewek.

Tus dha yns, sur.

Kewer deg yw brav mes nyns yw an
gewer teg lemmyn.

Gwydhelek yw yeth keltek.

An voes ma ha'n lestrier na yw
mebyl koth, dell hevel.

Lyver berr yw lyver da, dell dybav.

Eus kenter vyghan berr ena genes,
mar pleg?

Tus keltek yns.

Henn yw flogh da.

An re na yw fleghes dha.

Fatell yw an karrji ytho?

Splann yw!

Py par pluvenn yw honna?

Pluvenn-fenten yw.

Piw yw honna? Honn yw Loveday.

Piw yw an re na ena?

Mr ha Mrs Harrison yns.

Piw yw an venyn voen ena?

Fiona yw. Tioges yw Fiona.

Piw yw an benynes koth na?

Ny wonn!

This is a sweet apple.

*The River Tamar is
a large, deep river.*

This is a big wood.

A beautiful country is Brittany.

Here's a small armchair.

There's a place left here.

There's a chair left beside the big table.

The town hall is a fine building.

The husband is a good person, I think.

Isn't this a German wine?

I don't know!

A good language is Cornish.

Good people they are, certainly.

*Fine weather is great but the weather
isn't fine now.*

Irish is a Celtic language.

*This table and that dresser are old
furniture, it seems.*

A short book is a good book, I think.

*Is there a small, short nail there with
you, please?*

They are Celtic people.

That's a good child.

Those are good children.

What's the garage like then?

It's fine.

What kind of pen is that?

It's a fountain pen.

Who is that? That's Loveday.

Who are those (people) there?

Mr and Mrs Harrison they are.

Who is that slim woman there?

Fiona it is. A farmwife is Fiona.

Who are those old women there?

I don't know!

DASWELES KEMMYSKYS - *Miscellaneous Review*

Yma anwoes war an flogh na, sur.	*That child certainly has a cold.*
Eus nebonan y'n le'ti ena?	*Is there anyone in the dairy there?*
Fatell yw an gewer an gorthugher ma?	*How is the weather this evening?*
Splann ha sygh yw hi.	*Fine and dry.*
A nyns eus yeth keltek yn Kembra?	*Isn't there a Celtic language in Wales?*
Yma avon vras ha hir yn Almayn.	*There is a large, long river in Germany.*
An avon na yw an Rayn.	*That river is the Rhine.*
Nyns yw an ostel ma da, dell hevel.	*This hotel is not good, it seems.*
Yw an maw parys lemmyn?	*Is the boy ready now?*
Yma bleujyow byw gesys war an fordh omma.	*There are live flowers left on the road here.*
An chi a-ji dhe'n koes yw chi nowydh.	*The house in the wood is a new house.*
A nyns eus notenn verr gesys y'n gegin?	*Isn't there a short note left in the kitchen?*
Eus gweder byghan genes, mar pleg?	*Have you got a small mirror with you, please?*
Py avon yw homma?	*What river is this?*
An avon Tavi yw hi.	*The river Tavy it is.*
Hi a wra glaw lemmyn mes toemm yw hi.	*It's raining now but it's warm.*
Dydh da, Charles. Fatla genes?	*Hullo, Charles. How are you?*
Yn poynt da, dell hevel.	*Well, it seems.*
Sur, nyns yw an vyrgh feusik.	*Certainly the daughter isn't lucky.*
Yw an dra ma 'kador' yn kernewek?	*Is this object 'kador' in Cornish?*
Yw, sur. Hemm yw 'kador' ha henn yw 'kador-vregh' yn kernewek.	*Certainly. This is 'kador' and that is 'kador-vregh' in Cornish.*
Tus fol yns.	*They are foolish people.*
Py yeth yw kewsys yn Kembra?	*What language is spoken in Wales?*
Kembrek yw kewsys ena ryb Sowsnek.	*Welsh is spoken there beside English.*

Sur, nyns yw an vyrgh feusik.

27

10 PERGHENNIETH - *BELONGING - POSSESSION*

In English we say *the end of the book*. In Cornish this same meaning is given by **penn an lyver**. Notice that:

1. The word **an** *the* is used only with the last word.
2. The English word *of* is not translated in the Cornish version.

Other examples:

Ottena tour an eglos	*See there the tower of the church* *(= the church tower)*;

Kemmer kres an lovan ma,
   mar pleg
	Take the middle of this rope,
	     please.

A whole string of ideas can be put togther in the same way. Remember that **an** '*the*' is only used with the last word of the string but not, of course, with the name of a person or other proper noun:

Toll alhwedh daras	*The keyhole of the town hall door*
hel an dre	*(Literally hole key door hall the town)*
Broder tas Kevyn	*Kevin's father's brother*
	(Literally brother father Kevin)

If an adjective goes with the first noun it keeps its normal place after that noun:

Dorn shyndys an flogh   *The child's injured hand*

In these expressions each successive word defines the one before it. If there is no **an** before the last word it remains indefinite:

Dorn an flogh	*The hand of the child*
but	*(= the child's hand)*
Dorn flogh	*The hand of a child*
and	
Lost an ki	*The tail of the dog*
but	
Lost ki	*The tail of a dog*

GERVA

daras *m.*	*door*		**lovan** *f.*	*rope*
dorn *m.*	*hand*		**penn** *m.*	*head, end*
hel *f.*	*hall*		**plos** *adj.*	*dirty*
kemmer! *vb.*	*take!*		**shyndys** *adj.*	*hurt, damaged*
ki *m.*	*dog*		**toll** *m.*	*hole*
kres *m.*	*centre*		**tour** *m.*	*tower*
lost *m.*	*tail, queue*			

DASWELES - *Review*

Mab Pol yw broder Simon.	*Paul's son is Simon's brother.*
Tour an eglos ma yw gwann.	*The tower of this church is weak.*
Toll an daras yw hir mes kul.	*The door opening is high but narrow.*
Gwreg an gour ma yw Kernewes dha.	*This man's wife is a good Cornishwoman.*
Ottena - daras an karr yw shyndys.	*Look there! The door of the car is damaged.*
Henn yw karr hwegron Jori.	*That's George's father-in-law's car.*
Honn yw kares hweger Myrna.	*That's a relation of Myrna's mother-in-law.*
Yma padell blos war voes an gegin.	*There's a dirty pan on the kitchen table.*
Hel an Dre yw bras.	*The town hall is large.*
Kemmer dorn an maw, mar pleg.	*Take the child's hand, please.*
A nyns yw bras an avon ha down?	*Isn't the river large and deep?*
Kres an koes yw le kosel.	*The middle of the wood is a quiet place.*
A nyns eus penn lovan omma?	*Isn't there a rope end here?*
Kemmer an penn ma ytho!	*Take this end then!*
Pluvek an gador-vregh yw plos, dell hevel.	*The armchair cushion is dirty, it seems.*
Lost an ki ma yw berr, sur.	*This dog's tail is short, certainly.*

**Toll an daras yw
hir mes kul**

**Kres an koes
yw le kosel**

DASWELES KEMMYSKYS - *Miscellaneous Review*

Eus moes dherow yn kres an hel?

Is there an oak table in the centre of the hall?

Gorthugher da, Jenefer. Kemmer an lyver ma, mar pleg!

Good evening, Jenefer. Take this book, please!

Eus anwoes war Jori? Eus!

Has George got a cold. Yes!

Noy Mr Toms ha mab Mr. Rickard yw parow, dell hevel.

Mr Tom's nephew and Mr. Rickard's son are equals, it seems.

Py hwedhel yw gwir?

Which story is true?

An notenn yw parys lemmyn.

The note is ready now.

Py drehevyans yw hel an dre.

Which building is the town hall?

Ottena! An drehevyans bras.

There look! The big building.

An maw yw shyndys mes salow yw.

The boy is hurt but he is safe.

Nos dha, Roy! Nos dha, Tom!

Good night, Roy! Good night, Tom!

Yma kenter vras y'n toll ma. Kenter goth yw homma sur.

There's a large nail in this hole. It's an old nail certainly.

Tour an eglos na yw nowydh.

That church tower is new.

Nyns eus le gesys yn kres an dre lemmyn.

There isn't a place left in the town centre now.

An ki ma yw gorow.

This dog is male.

Yma toll down yn kres an fordh.

There is a deep hole in the centre of the road.

Fatell yw an gewer genes?

How is the weather with you?

Hi yw kommolek omma.

It's cloudy here.

Yw an yeth kernewek dhe les? Yw, sur!

Is the Cornish language useful? It certainly is!

Pyth yw yeth Alban?

What is the language of Scotland?

Albanek yw kewsys ena ryb Sowsnek.

Gaelic is spoken there beside English.

Hi yw kommolek omma

30

11 SEYTH GER A VERN - *SEVEN IMPORTANT WORDS*

Once a thing or a person is identified, further reference can be made to the thing or to the person by the use of pronouns. In English these are words like *I, you, he, she, it,* and so on. Here are the Cornish equivalents:

MY	*I*	**NI**	*we*
TY	*you* (one person)	**HWI**	*you* (more than one person)
EV	*he* or *it*	**I**	*they*
HI	*she* or *it*		

As can be seen, there are two Cornish words for the English word *you*. English used to have two also, *thou* used when speaking to one person and *you* when speaking to more than one person. In French the similar use of *tu* 'thou' in speaking to close friends, relatives and children and *vous* 'you' for other occasions can give rise to some nice social questions as to which to use. There is no such problem in Cornish. Simply say **TY** to one person and **HWI** to a group.

EV is *he* and **HI** is *she* but remember that everything in Cornish is considered to be either masculine or feminine. So in referring to a house, **ev** in Cornish becomes *it* in English. Similarly in speaking of a table you will say **hi** which again becomes the English *it*.

An karr yw rudh.	**Ev yw nowydh.**	*The car is red. It's new.*
Ottomma tesenn.	**Hi yw da!**	*Here's a cake. It's good!*

Remember that the sound of the y in **my** and in **ty** is short, somewhere between the English *pen* and *pin*. Don't be tempted by the English *me* into saying *mee, tee*.

Notice that the verb used in this sort of statement remains **yw** *is* in every case: **my yw** *I am*, **i yw** *they are* even though these would be literally *I is, they is* in English.

Using these pronouns in place of nouns makes conversation and writing easier!

31

GERVA

dha weles!	*'see you!'*	**kloppek** *adj.*	*lame*
fur *adj.*	*wise*	**rudh** *adj.*	*red*
gwir *adj.*	*true*	**teg** *adj.*	*fine, pretty*
hwath *adv.*	*yet, still*	**warbarth** *adv.*	*together*
hwedhel *m.*	*story*		

DASWELES - *Review*

My yw lowen.	*I am happy.*
Ty yw fur.	*You are wise.*
Ev yw kloppek.	*He is lame.*
Ev yw gwir.	*It (a statement) is true.*
Hi yw teg.	*She is pretty.*
Hi yw gwag.	*It (a basket) is empty.*
Ni yw warbarth.	*We are together.*
Hwi yw parys.	*You are ready.*
I yw koth.	*They are old.*

Ev yw derow, derow kernewek.	*It is oak, Cornish oak.*
Ty yw Kelt.	*You are a Celt.*
I yw gesys warbarth y'n hel.	*They are left together in the hall.*
Ty yw tiek, dell dybav.	*You are a farmer, I think.*
Ev yw ki fol.	*He's a silly dog.*
Hi yw myrgh an teylu, mowes teg yw hi.	*She's the daughter of the family, she's a pretty girl.*
Ni yw lowen lemmyn.	*We are happy now.*
I yw dhe les.	*They are useful.*
Ha lemmyn hwi yw gour ha gwreg.	*And now you are man and wife.*

DASWELES KEMMYSKYS - *Miscellaneous Review*

Pyth yw penn an hwedhel? Ny wonn.	*What is the end of the story? I don't know.*
Fatell yw an tas lemmyn?	*How is father now?*
Gwann ha kloppek hwath yw ev.	*Weak and lame he is still.*
Nyns eus anwoes war Pam* namoy.	*Pam hasn't got a cold now.*
Yma kador gesys y'n hel.	*There is a chair left in the hall.*
Hemm yw fur, dell dybav.	*This is wise, I think.*
Ottena an ostel.	*There's the hotel.*
Kemmer an notenn, mar pleg!	*Take the note, please!*
Py par prenn yw hemma?	*What sort of wood is this?*
An prenn ma yw derow.	*This wood is oak.*
Noy Mr Turner yw maw bras.	*Mr Turner's nephew is a big boy.*
Nos dha, Maria, dha weles!	*Good night, Mary, see you!*
A nyns eus fordh dha a-rag an karrji?	*Isn't there a good road in front of the garage?*
Yw hi hweger Yowann?	*Is she John's mother-in-law?*
Fatell yw an dus ena lemmyn?	*How are the people there now?*
Brav yns hag yn poynt da, dell dybav.	*They are fine and in good health, I think.*
Awelek yw hi, sur.	*It is certainly very windy.*
Ni yw warbarth lemmyn.	*We are together now.*
An re ma, i yw parow, dell hevel.	*These, they are equal, it seems.*
Chi koth ha yeyn yw ev.	*An old, cold house it is.*

* *non-Celtic personal and place names are not usually mutated*

Gwann ha kloppek hwath yw ev.

33

12 DEGRE - *DEGREE*

An gegin yw byghan	*The kitchen is small*
An gegin yw pur vyghan	*The kitchen is very small*

Pur[2] *very* mutates all following words by softening where appropriate as in the table on page v at the beginning of the book:

pur vras (bras)	*very large*
pur dhu (du)	*very black*
pur arow (garow)	*very rough*
pur goth (koth)	*very old*
etc.	

An chambour yw re dewl	*The bedroom is too dark*
An fordh yw re arow	*The road is too rough*

Re[2] *too, excessively* mutates all following words by softening where appropriate just like **pur**.

re voen (moen)	*too thin*	
re boes (poes)	*too heavy*	
re der (ter)	*too eager*	

An hel yw bras lowr	*The hall is big enough*
An lovan ma yw hir lowr	*This rope is long enough*

Lowr *enough* follows its adjective so of course there is no mutation.

berr lowr	*short enough*
da lowr	*good enough*

The same word, **lowr**, can go with a noun to mean *enough of something*. It usually follows the noun:

bara lowr	*enough bread*
flows lowr	*enough silly talk*

34

GERVA

bara *m.*	*bread*	**hir** *adj.*	*long, tall*
chambour *m.*	*bedroom*	**moen** *adj.*	*thin*
da *adj.*	*good*	**poes** *adj.*	*heavy*
du *adj.*	*black*	**tew** *adj.*	*fat*
flows *m.*	*idle talk*	**tewl** *adj.*	*dark*

DASWELES - *Review*

Nyns yw hi pur lowen lemmyn.	*She is not very happy now.*
Ni yw pur doemm.	*We are very warm.*

Yma fordh pur gul
    ryb an pras.
	*There is a very narrow road
	    beside the field.*

A nyns yw an chambour ma pur deg?	*Isn't this bedroom very nice?*
An lovan ma yw re verr.	*This rope is too short.*
I yw re voen.	*They are too thin.*

Gour Morwenna yw re dew, a nyns
    yw ev?
	*Morwenna's husband is too fat, isn't
	    he?*

An gewer yw teg lowr.	*The weather is fine enough.*
Yw an gwin ma yeyn lowr?	*Is this wine cold enough?*
Hemm yw hweg lowr.	*This is sweet enough.*
Yw an karr salow lowr lemmyn?	*Is the car safe enough now?*
An re na yw lowr, meur ras.	*Those are enough, thanks.*
Eus avalow lowr genes?	*Have you got enough apples?*

Eus avalow lowr genes?

DASWELES KEMMYSKYS - *Miscellaneous Review*

Kemmer hemma mar pleg!	*Take this please!*
An bara ma yw sygh, pur sygh.	*This bread is dry, very dry.*
Ottomma Jori. Jori yw kenderow Mark, a nyns yw gwir, Jori?	*Here's George. George is Mark's cousin, isn't it true, George?*
Alban yw bras, pur vras.	*Scotland is large, very large.*
Eus bara gesys? Eus! Yma ev y'n gegin.	*Is there any bread left? Yes! It's in the kitchen.*
Shyndys yw penn an ki ma mes byw yw ev hwath.	*This dog's head is injured but it is alive still.*
Tewl yw hi yn kres an koes.	*It is dark in the centre of the wood.*
Nyns yw honna da.	*That is not good.*
Yma toll y'n bluvek ma.	*There's a hole in this cushion.*
Fatell yw an chambour? Pur dha, meur ras.	*How is the bedroom? Very good, thanks.*
An jynn-skrifa yw plos, dell hevel.	*The typewriter is dirty, it seems.*
Py lovan yw hir lowr?	*Which rope is long enough?*
Daras an eglos yw koth.	*The church door is old.*
Yma tus a-rag hel an dre. Lost hir yw.	*There are people in front of the town hall. It's a long queue.*
Dohajydh da, Lowena. Fatla genes lemmyn? Da lowr, meur ras.	*Good afternoon, Lowena. How are you now? Well enough, thanks.*
Glaw skav a wra hi.	*It's raining lightly.*
Yeth wir an den na yw Kernewek.	*That person's true language is Cornish.*
Hwi yw parys lemmyn, dell hevel.	*You are ready now, it seems.*
Pyth yw hemma? Lyver kembrek yw.	*What's this? It's a Welsh book.*

36

13 LIES TRA - *MANY THINGS*

The plural form of a noun is used to show that more than one thing is being spoken of. English usually adds an *s* to do this: *egg* and *eggs*, *girl* and *girls*.

Cornish commonly has the ending **-ow** or **-yow** to show the plural. Some examples have already been used and shown in the word lists:

chi	*house*	and	**chiow**	*houses*
an chi	*the house*	and	**an chiow**	*the houses*
leur	*floor*	and	**leuryow**	*floors*
an leur	*the floor*	and	**an leuryow**	*the floors*

Just as in English there are other ways of making the plural, e.g. *woman* and *women* with a change of *a* to *e*, so in Cornish there are other plural forms, for instance **flogh** *child* and **fleghes** *children*. These will be shown in the lists of words, the **Gervaow**, in the following way:

padell, -ow *f. saucepan*, where the letter *f.* means feminine and the letters **-ow** mean that adding these letters will make the plural, **padellow** *saucepans*. So the whole entry can be read as:

padell *saucepan*,   **an badell** *the saucepan*,
padellow *saucepans*,   **an padellow** *the saucepans*.

Another common way of making the plural, especially when persons are meant, is by adding **-yon** to the singular form:

tiek	*farmer*		and	**tiogyon**	*farmers*	
kaner	*singer*		and	**kanoryon**	*singers*	

Notice the change of **-ek** to **-og**, **-er** - to **-or** which is usual.

So the word list entry for **kaner** will be:

kaner, -oryon *m. singer*, from which we can say:

kaner *singer*,   **an kaner** *the singer*,
kanoryon *singers*,   **an ganoryon** *the singers*.

A noun may refer not to a particular thing but to a whole group as a class. **Del** in Cornish means *foliage, leaves*: **Yma an del ow treylya gell** *The leaves are turning brown.* They count as plural words and are called collectives. Most of them can, by adding the syllable **-enn**, make a word which refers to one individual of the group: **del + enn = delenn** *a leaf.* All the words so made are feminine: **an dhelenn** *the leaf.* Then by putting the plural ending on to this word we get **delennow** *individual leaves*: **Nebes delennow a goedhas a-dhiworth an skorrenn** *A few leaves fell from the branch.*

GERVA

del *coll.*	leaves, foliage	**kesten** *coll.*	chestnut trees
delenn, -ow *f.*	a leaf	**kestenenn, -ow** *f.*	chestnut tree
flogh, fleghes *m.*	child	**leur, -yow** *m.*	floor
gerva, -ow *f.*	word list	**skorr** *coll.*	branches
gwydh *coll.*	trees	**skorrenn, - ow**	a branch
gwydhenn *f.*	a tree	**tiek, -ogyon** *m.*	farmer
kaner,-oryon *m.*	singer		

DASWELES - *Review*

An chiow y'n dre ma yw pur goth.	The houses in this town are very old.
Kanoryon an eglos yw da. Gwir, kanoryon dha yns.	The church singers are good. True, good singers they are.
Nyns yw leuryow an chi salow lemmyn.	The floors of the house are not safe now.
An del y'n koes yw sygh.	The leaves of the wood are dry.
Yma delennow hir war an skorrenn verr na.	There are long leaves on that short branch.
Gwydh an koes ma yw koth.	The trees of this wood are old.
Yma skorrennow bras war an wydhenn na.	There are big branches on that tree.
Chambours an ostel ma yw byghan.	The bedrooms of this hotel are small.
Yma gervaow yn penn an lyver.	There are word lists at the end of the book.
Fleghes dha yns, sur.	They are good children certainly.
An lyvrow (lyver) yw gwerthys.	The books are sold.
Myrghes (myrgh) Tamsin yw teg, pur deg.	Tamsin's daughters are pretty, very pretty.

DASWELES KEMMYSKYS - *Miscellaneous Review*

Yw an losow byw hwath?
Are the plants alive still?

Hemm yw da lowr, meur ras.
This is good enough, thanks.

A nyns eus neppyth gesys?
Isn't there anything left?

Nyns yw hemma dhe les lemmyn.
This is no good now.

Yma padellow plos
    lowr y'n gegin!
There are enough dirty saucepans in the kitchen.

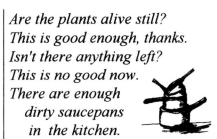

Eus stamp genes mar pleg? Eus!
Have you a stamp, please? Yes!

Py par stamp eus genes, ytho?
What sort of stamp have you got then?

Pow Frynk yw pow pur vras ha pur deg.
France is a very big country and very beautiful.

Py traow yw gwerthys lemmyn?
What things are sold now?

A wodhowgh hwi oll konvedhes hemma?
Do you all understand this?

Ni yw salow lemmyn, dell dybav.
We are safe now, I think.

Nyns eus nebonan gesys yn hel an dre.
There is no one left in the town hall.

Fatell yw an bara na?
What is that bread like?

    Brav yw, meur ras.
    It's fine, thanks.

Pyth yw an draow ma, an re byghan?
What are these objects, the small ones?

Kentrow (kenter) yns, dell hevel.
They are nails, it seems.

Avonyow Almayn yw hir.
The rivers of Germany are long.

Feusik yns, a nyns yns i?
They are lucky, aren't they?

Trevow (tre) Breten Vyghan yw teg, pur deg.
The towns of Brittany are beautiful, very beautiful.

Del an kesten yw bras.
The leaves of the chestnut are large.

An gestenenn goth na yw bras.
That old chestnut tree is large.

Dorn flogh yw byghan.
The hand of a child is small.

14 ONAN, DEW, TRI *ONE, TWO THREE*

One of the most frequently used parts of a language is its number system. In Cornish counting is in twenties. Here are the cardinal numbers up to twenty:

1 onan	**6 hwegh**	**11 unnek**	**16 hwetek**
2 dew	**7 seyth**	**12 dewdhek**	**17 seytek**
3 tri	**8 eth**	**13 trydhek**	**18 etek**
4 peswar	**9 naw**	**14 peswardhek**	**19 nownsek**
5 pymp	**10 deg**	**15 pymthek**	**20 ugens**

It will be seen that the '-teens' are made by adding **-ek** to forms of the simple number.

Onan is the word to use when 'one' stands by itself. When it accompanies a noun the word to use is **unn** which, as mentioned before, acts like **an** 'the' in mutating the first letter of a feminine noun by softening, the second state mutation:

Eus hwegynn gesys?	*Is there a sweet left?*
Eus! Yma onan hepken	*There is! There is one only*
Unn hwegynn yw lowr	*One sweet is enough*
Unn gador yw terrys	*One chair is broken*

For the numbers 'two', 'three' and 'four' there are special forms for use with feminine nouns. They are:

2 **diw**	3 **teyr**	4 **peder**

Dew and **diw** '2' mutate a following noun by softening and are themselves mutated after **an** 'the':

dew blat (plat)	*two plates*	**diw voes** (moes)	*two tables*
an dhew blat	*the two plates*	**an dhiw voes**	*the two tables*

40

Tri and **teyr** '3' mutate a following noun with the breathed mutation which is repeated here from the table on page v at the beginning of the book:

k- > h-   **p- > f-**   **t- > th-**

tri harr (karr)	*three cars*	**teyr hador** (kador)	*three chairs*
tri fysk (pysk)	*three fish*	**teyr fluvenn** (pluvenn)	*three pens*
tri foll (poll)	*three pits*	**teyr thigenn** (tigenn)	*three wallets*

In English, numbers are usually followed by a plural noun: 'six lights'. In Cornish the noun remains singular: **hwegh golow** and not *hwegh golowys.

GERVA

arghans *m.*	*silver, money*	**rag** *prep.*	*for*
boes *m.*	*food*	**redyans** *m.*	*reading*
golow, -ys *m.*	*light*	**seythun, -yow** *f.*	*week*
hepken *adv.*	*only*	**skon** *adv.*	*quickly*
hwegynn, -ow *m.*	*sweet*	**spas, -ow** *m.*	*space, opportunity*
karrek, kerrek *f.*	*rock*	**tanow** *adj.*	*thin, scarce*
lowarth, -yow *m.*	*garden*	**terrys** *adj.*	*broken*
plat, -ys *m.*	*plate*	**tigenn, -ow** *f.*	*wallet, handbag*
pysk, puskes *m.*	*fish*	**to, -how** *m.*	*roof*

DASWELES - *Review*

Yma tri fysk war an plat na.	*There are three fish on that plate.*
Onan yw brithel.	*One is a mackerel.*
Yma teyr gwydhenn y'n lowarth.	*There are three trees in the garden.*
Yma diw gestenenn ena.	*There are two chestnut trees there.*
An arghans yw tanow lemmyn.	*Money is scarce now.*
Nyns eus arghans lowr rag boes.	*There is not enough money for food.*
An dhew wour na yw parow, dell hevel.	*Those two men are equals, it seems.*
Mes sur, nyns yw an dhiw venyn parow.	*But certainly, the two women are not equals.*
Oll an mebyl yw diw voes koth ha peder kador.	*All the furniture is two old tables and four chairs.*
Yma unn karr a-rag an chi.	*There is one car in front of the house.*

Eus ostel yn kres an dre?	Is there an hotel in the town centre?
Eus! Yma pymp ostel ena.	Yes! There are five hotels there.
Kemmer teyr henter ytho!	Take three nails then!
Yma unnek mowes ha trydhek maw oll warbarth.	There are eleven girls and thirteen boys all together.
Yma deg hwegynn gesys, dell dybav.	There are ten sweets left, I think.
Yma unn garrek pur vras ena.	There is one very large rock there.
Ottena - teyr delenn rudh war an leur.	Look there are three red leaves on the ground.
Yma peswar stamp gesys y'n lyver.	There are four stamps left in the book.
Ugens lyver yw gwerthys lemmyn.	Twenty books are sold now.
Eus hwetek plat byghan war an lestrier?	Are there sixteen small plates on the dresser?
I yw tri flogh fol.	They are three foolish children.

DASWELES KEMMYSKYS - *Miscellaneous Review*

Del an gwydh ma yw tanow.	The leaves of these trees are thin.
Eus boes lowr gesys rag an ki?	Is there enough food left for the dog?
Eus! Yma boes war blat y'n gegin.	Yes! There is food on a plate in the kitchen.
An erva yw hir, re hir.	The word list is long, too long.
Pyth yw an re na, an tri thra dhu na ena? Ny wonn!	What are those, those three black things there? I don't know.
Dohajydh da, Maria. Fatla genes?	Good afternoon, Mary. How are you?
Brav, meur ras.	Fine, thanks.
Ni yw seyth kaner oll warbarth.	We are seven singers altogether.
Fatell yw an dhew garr?	What are the two cars like?
Onan yw rudh hag onan yw du.	One is red and one is black.
An lovan ma yw re verr. Eus onan hir genes?	This rope is too short. Have you a long one?
An dhiw gador ma yw an re poes.	These two chairs are the heavy ones.
Piw yw an re na - an dus koth?	Who are those - the old people?
An gour yw tas-gwynn Lowena mes ny wonn piw yw an venyn.	The man is Lowena's grandfather but I don't know who the woman is.

42

Py par del yw
   an re ma?
	What sort of leaves
	   are these?

Del derow yns, dell dybav.	*Oak leaves, I think.*
Yma anwoes war ewnter Tamsin.	*Tamsin's uncle has a cold.*
Nyns yw homma* da.	*This is not good.*

*The feminine pronoun **homma** is used to indicate that some condition is referred to rather than an action. In this latter case, **hemma** would be used. See also Part 15.

15 AN EUR - *THE TIME*

To ask about the time, say **Py eur yw hi, mar pleg?** 'What time is it, please?' Notice that the word **hi** 'it' is feminine. Time, weather and circumstances are regarded as feminine in Cornish.

If the time is on the hour, the answer will be: **Seyth eur** 'seven o'clock'; **Unnek eur** 'eleven o'clock' and so on. If the time is some minutes past the hour, the answer will be, for example, **ugens mynysenn wosa deg eur** 'twenty minutes (after) past ten'. The word **mynysenn** is feminine so remember to say **unn vynysenn** 'one minute', **diw vynysenn** 'two minutes', **teyr mynysenn** 'three minutes' and **peder mynysenn** 'four minutes'. If the time is some minutes to the hour there are several ways of putting it. The first is to say **deg eur marnas pymp mynysenn warn ugens** 'ten o'clock less twenty-five minutes'. The second way is to follow the English and say **pymp mynysenn warn ugens dhe dheg** 'twenty-five minutes to ten'.

Quarter hours are **kwarter** and half hours are **hanter**. So **kwarter wosa naw eur** 'a quarter after nine hours' = 'a quarter past nine'; **naw eur marnas kwarter** 'nine hours less a quarter' = 'a quarter to nine'; **Teyr eur hanter** 'half past three'. Midday is **hanter-dydh** and midnight is **hanter-nos**.

To specify the time precisely you can add **poran** 'exactly': **Py eur yw hi, mar pleg? Unn eur hanter poran** 'What time is it, please? Half past one exactly'.

If your reply is of the nature 'about six o'clock' then use the expression **a-dro dhe**[2]: **A-dro dhe bymp eur yw hi** 'It's about five o'clock'.'

To ask at what time something is to happen we use the phrase **Dhe by eur yth yw...?** 'At what time is...?'

Dhe by eur yth yw koen?   *At what time is dinner?*
Dhe seyth eur hanter yth yw   *It's at half past seven*

GERVA

dhe² *prep.*	*to*	**li, livyow** *f.*	*lunch*
hansel, -yow *m.*	*breakfast*	**mynys** *coll.*	*minutes*
kerdh, -ow *m.*	*walk*	**mynysenn, -ow** *f.*	*minute*
koen, -yow *f.*	*dinner, cooked supper*	**nessa** *adj.*	*next*
korev, -ow *m.*	*beer*	**niver,-ow** *m.*	*number*
kuntelles, -ow *m.*	*meeting*	**paper, -yow** *m.*	*paper*
kyns *adv.*	*before*	**prys, -yow** *m.*	*time, occasion*
kyttrin, -yow *m.*	*bus*	**tren, -ow** *m.*	*train*

Note that **dhe** 'to' followed by **an** 'the' makes **dhe'n** 'to the'.

DASWELES - *Review*

Py eur yw hi lemmyn?	*What time is it now?*
Eth eur marnas ugens mynysenn yw hi.*	*It's twenty to eight.*
Kwarter wosa deg eur yw hi.	*It's a quarter past ten.*
Unnek eur poran yw hi.	*It's exactly eleven o'clock.*
Teyr mynysenn warn ugens dhe hwegh eur yw hi.	*It's twenty-three minutes to six.*
Pymp eur hanter yw hi.	*It's half past five.*
Hanter dydh poran yw hi.	*It's exactly midday.*
A-dro dhe gwarter wosa naw eur yw hi.	*It's about a quarter past nine.*
Dhe by eur yth yw an kuntelles, mar pleg?	*At what time is the meeting, please?*
Dhe seyth eur hanter, dell dybav.	*At half past seven, I think.*
Dhe by eur yth yw an nessa kyttrin dhe Druru, mar pleg?	*At what time is the next bus to Truro, please?*
Nyns eus kyttrin dhe Druru kyns peder eur.	*There is no bus to Truro before four o'clock.*
Dhe by eur yth yw an nessa prys boes?	*At what time is the next meal?*
Ny wonn.	*I don't know.*

*This and similar phrases may in casual speech be shortened to **eth marnas ugens** = 'twenty to eight'

45

DASWELES KEMMYSKYS - *Miscellaneous Review*

Hemm yw kerdh hir mes brav yw.	*This is a long walk but it's grand.*
Yw an li parys?	*Is lunch ready?*
Yw. Yma hi war an voes y'n gegin.	*Yes. It's on the kitchen table.*
Py par diwes eus dhe brys koen?	*What kind of drink is there at dinner?*
Yma po korev po gwin gans an goen.	*There is beer or wine with the dinner.*
Dyw genes Tom - dha weles wosa prys te.	*Goodbye Tom - see you after tea.*
Fatell yw karr Mrs Trewartha?	*What is Mrs Trewartha's car like?*
Pur skav yw ev, dell hevel.	*It's very fast, it seems.*
Eus golow lowr rag an redyans?	*Is there enough light for the reading?*
Nag eus. Re dewl yw hi.	*No. It's too dark.*
Yma spas lowr y'n le na lemmyn.	*There is enough room in that place now.*

Gour kloppek yw ev.	*He is a lame man.*
An paper ma yw plos.	*This paper is dirty.*
Py par korev yw da?	*What kind of beer is good?*
Korev kernewek, sur.	*Cornish beer, of course.*
To an chi yw rudh.	*The roof of the house is red.*
Kerdh hir yw dhe'n eglos.	*It's a long walk to the church.*

46

16 HWILAS TRAOW - *LOOKING FOR THINGS*

In saying where things or people are, a very important word is needed.

It is **yma**, a word which we have met already. It means 'there is', 'it is' when speaking of a place or a position. It takes the place of **yw** which is the form of 'is' used in other cases, e.g. **An dra ma yw kenter** 'This object is a nail', **Hemm yw da** 'This is good'. Remember that unlike most Cornish words, **yma** has to be stressed on the last part, the syllable **-ma**, the first syllable being scarcely heard, **y`ma**. **Yma** usually comes first in a statement.

Examples:

Yma an amanenn war an voes   *The butter is on the table*
Yma an skath y'n porth   *The boat is in the harbour*

You will not be surprised to learn that **yma** can mean 'there are' when a plural noun is mentioned.

Examples:

Yma an fleghes y'n lowarth   *The children are in the garden*
Yma avalow y'n ganstell na   *There are apples in that basket*

If no plural noun is mentioned, then **yma** becomes **ymons** to show that the meaning must be 'they'. **Ymons** also is stressed on the last syllable, **y`mons**.

Examples:

Ymons omma   *They are here*
Ymons ryb an chi   *They are by the house*

You can add **i** 'they' for greater emphasis or clarity:

Ymons i omma   *They are here*
Ymons i ryb an chi   *They are by the house*

If we are asking where a thing or a person is and say, 'Where is?', 'Where are?', we use the phrase **ple'ma**.

The phrase **ple'ma** means both 'where is...?' and 'where are...?'. **Ple'ma** is short for **ple yma** 'what place is...?'.

So we say:

Ple'ma an ganstell?   *Where is the basket?*

In speech this will sound like, **pleman ganstell?** and in fact this would often be written, **plema'n ganstell?**.

Ple'ma an fleghes?   *Where are the children?*

To reply to these questions, one merely puts the required information in place of **ple**:

Ple'ma (= ple yma) an lyver?   *Where is the book?*

is answered by:

War an voes (yma an lyver   *On the table (is the book*
or **yma ev)**   or *it is)*

If the question is about a number of things, i.e. plural, and those things are named, then the question will be:

Ple'ma an fleghes?   *Where are the children?*

If no noun is used, then the question becomes:

Ple'mons? or **ple'mons i?**, and in that case the answer will be:

Y'n lowarth   *In the garden*
(yma an fleghes   *(are the children*
or **ymons** or **ymons i)**   or *they are)*

where the word **ymons** means 'they are', as we have seen.

GERVA

amanenn *m.*	*butter*	**kanstell, -ow** *f.*	*basket*
berrheans *m.*	*shortening,*	**kibell, -ow** *f.*	*bath, tub*
	abbreviation	**kresenn, -ow** *f.*	*centre*
dell vydh usys	*as is usual*	**podik, -igow** *m.*	*jug*
dre² *prep.*	*through*	**porth, -ow** *m.*	*port, harbour*
glan *adj.*	*clean*	**skath, -ow** *f.*	*small boat*
goen, -yow *f.*	*down moorland*	**spisti, -ow** *m.*	*grocery shop*
gow, -yow *m.*	*lie*	**tarow, terewi** *m.*	*bull*

DASWELES - *Review*

Ple'ma Yowann?	*Where is John?*
Y'n lowarth (yma ev).	*In the garden (he is).*
Ple'ma Tamsin?	*Where is Tamsin?*
Y'n gegin (yma hi).	*In the kitchen (she is).*
Ple'ma an karr?	*Where is the car?*
Y'n karrji (yma ev).	*In the garage (it is).*
Ple'ma gweder bras?	*Where is there a large mirror?*
Y'n hel (yma onan).	*In the hall (there is one).*
Ple'ma'n skathow?	*Where are the boats?*
Y'n porth (ymons i).	*In the harbour (they are).*
Ple'ma spisti Mr Pennros?	*Where is Mr Penrose's grocery shop?*
Yn kres an dre (yma ev).	*In the town centre (it is).*
Ple'ma an byskadoryon ytho?	*Where are the fishermen then?*
Y'n skath (ymons i).	*On board the boat (they are).*

Ottena ewnter Morwenna; gour da yw ev.

There's Morwenna's uncle; he's a good man.

Henn yw gow, sur.

That's a lie, certainly.

Yma fordh dre gres an dre.

There's a road through the town centre.

A nyns eus kanstell y'n gegin?

Isn't there a basket in the kitchen?

A ny wodhesta konvedhes hemma?

Don't you understand this?

Gonn, sur lowr.

I do, sure enough.

Re vyghan yw an spas ma, re gul.

This space is too small, too narrow.

Yma an re na omma dhe eth eur dell vydh usys.

Those (people) are here at eight o'clock usually.

An gibell yw pur vras, pur hir.

The bath is very large, very long.

An Gresenn Gernewek yw le da ha dhe les yw hi rag tus Kernow.

The Cornish Centre is a good place and is useful for the people of Cornwall.

Eus lyvrow genowgh hwi oll?

Have you all got books?

Yma niverow war an paper ma. Pyth yns i, a wodhesta?

There are numbers on this paper. What are they, do you know?

Na wonn. Ny wonn pyth yns.

No, I don't know what they are.

Py podigow yw glann? An re ma?

Which pots are clean? These?

A nyns yw henna tarow y'n pras na? Yw, dell hevel.

Isn't that a bull in that field? Yes, it seems.

Berrheans an lyver ma yw dhe les, dell dybav.

The abridgement of this book is useful, I think.

Eus amanenn war an bara? Eus!

Is there butter on the bread? Yes!

Tri flat yw terrys.

Three plates are broken.

Teyr mynysenn ha'n boes yw parys.

Three minutes and the food is ready.

Py eur yw hi lemmyn, mar pleg?

What time is it now, please?

Deg mynysenn dhe beder eur poran.

Ten minutes to four exactly.

17 MOY A NIVEROW - *MORE NUMBERS*

After counting the first twenty, **ugens**, the numbering starts on the second twenty, from twenty-one up to forty. Then it starts again with forty-one up to sixty, then sixty-one to eighty and finally eighty-one to one hundred.

21	onan warn ugens		31	unnek warn ugens
22	dew warn ugens		32	dewdhek warn ugens
23	tri warn ugens		33	trydhek warn ugens
24	peswar warn ugens		34	peswardhek warn ugens
25	pymp warn ugens		35	pymthek warn ugens
26	hwegh warn ugens		36	hwetek warn ugens
27	seyth warn ugens		37	seytek warn ugens
28	eth warn ugens		38	etek warn ugens
29	naw warn ugens		39	nownsek warn ugens
30	deg warn ugens		40	dew ugens

Notice that the linking word is **warn** 'on'. This is the only group of twenty in which this word is used. Subsequent groups of twenty have **ha** 'and' in its place.

41	onan ha dew ugens		51	unnek ha dew ugens
42	dew ha dew ugens		52	dewdhek ha dew ugens
43	tri ha dew ugens		53	trydhek ha dew ugens
44	peswar ha dew ugens		54	peswardhek ha dew ugens
45	pymp ha dew ugens		55	pymthek ha dew ugens
46	hwegh ha dew ugens		56	hwetek ha dew ugens
47	seyth ha dew ugens		57	seytek ha dew ugens
48	eth ha dew ugens		58	etek ha dew ugens
49	naw ha dew ugens		59	nownsek ha dew ugens
50	deg ha dew ugens		60	tri ugens

61	onan ha tri ugens		71	unnek ha tri ugens
62	dew ha tri ugens		72	dewdhek ha tri ugens
63	tri ha tri ugens		73	trydhek ha tri ugens
64	peswar ha tri ugens		74	peswardhek ha tri ugens
65	pymp ha tri ugens		75	pymthek ha tri ugens
66	hwegh ha tri ugens		76	hwetek ha tri ugens
67	seyth ha tri ugens		77	seytek ha tri ugens
68	eth ha tri ugens		78	etek ha tri ugens
69	naw ha tri ugens		79	nownsek ha tri ugens
70	deg ha tri ugens		80	peswar ugens

81	onan ha peswar ugens	91	unnek ha peswar ugens
82	dew ha peswar ugens	92	dewdhek ha peswar ugens
83	tri ha peswar ugens	93	trydhek ha peswar ugens
84	peswar ha peswar ugens	94	peswardhek ha peswar ugens
85	pymp ha peswar ugens	95	pymthek ha peswar ugens
86	hwegh ha peswar ugens	96	hwetek ha peswar ugens
87	seyth ha peswar ugens	97	seytek ha peswar ugens
88	eth ha peswar ugens	98	etek ha peswar ugens
89	naw ha peswar ugens	99	nownsek ha peswar ugens
90	deg ha peswar ugens	100	kans

In these larger numbers, put the thing numbered after the first part of the number, remembering to use **unn** in place of **onan** and the feminine forms, **diw** '2', **teyr** '3' and **peder** '4' where necessary: **unn hanaf warn ugens** '21 cups'; **unn venyn warn ugens** '21 women'; **tri den ha peswar ugens** '83 people'; **peder bro ha tri ugens** '64 countries'.

GERVA

arghantti, -ow *m.*	*bank*	**kan, -ow** *f.*	*song*
bargen-tir,	*farm*	**keur, -yow** *m.*	*choir*
bargenyow-t. *m.*		**martesen** *adv.*	*perhaps*
benyn, -es *f.*	*woman*	**mildir, -yow** *m.*	*mile*
bro, -yow *f.*	*country*	**pronter, -yon** *m.*	*preacher*
chapel, -yow *m.*	*chapel*	**skol, -yow** *f.*	*school*
dons, -yow *m.*	*dance*	**tavern, -yow** *m.*	*inn*
fos, -ow *f.*	*wall*	**teylu, -yow** *m.*	*family*
hanaf, -ow *m.*	*cup*		

DASWELES - *Review*

Yma tri den ha peswar ugens yn keur an chapel.	*There are eighty-three people in the chapel choir.*
Yma pymp tavern warn ugens y'n dre.	*There are twenty-five inns in the town.*
Yma deg den warn ugens y'n teylu bras na.	*There are thirty persons in that large family.*
A-dro dhe gans lyver yw gwerthys lemmyn.	*About a hundred books are sold now.*
Hanter kans mildir yw an fordh dhe Druru.	*The road to Truro is fifty miles.*
Hanter peswar warn ugens yw par dhe dhewdhek.	*Half of twenty-four is equal to twelve.*
Yma dewdhek flogh ha tri ugens y'n skol na. Re vyghan yw hi martesen.	*There are seventy-two children in that school. It is too small perhaps.*
Pymp chi ha peswar ugens yw chiow nowydh.	*Eighty-five houses are new houses.*
Yma dew gi ha dew ugens a-ji dhe'n gresenn.	*There are forty-two dogs in the centre.*
Teyr benyn warn ugens, peswar gour warn ugens hag unnek flogh yw etek den ha dew ugens warbarth.	*Twenty-three women, twenty-four men and eleven children is fifty-eight people altogether.*

DASWELES KEMMYSKYS - *Miscellaneous Review*

An donsyow bretonek ma yw brav.	*These Breton dances are grand.*
'Bro Goth' yw kan an vro.	*'Bro Goth' is the song of the country.*
Fatell yw pronter an chapel?	*What is the chapel preacher like?*
Nyns yw ev re dha, dell hevel.	*He isn't too good, it seems.*
Yma hwegh den warn ugens y'n kuntelles a-ji dhe hel an dre.	*There are twenty-six people in the meeting inside the town hall.*
Kemmer an ganstell, mar pleg!	*Take the basket, please!*
Fatla genes lemmyn, Gari?	*How are you now, Gary?*
Da lowr, meur ras, mes yma anwoes warnav, dell dybav.	*Well enough, thanks, but I've got a cold, I think.*
Py flogh yw mab Mrs Olver?	*Which child is Mrs Olver's son?*

Ottena! An maw moen na ryb an daras.	*There look! That thin boy next to the door.*
Pyth yw rag koen?	*What's for supper?*

Ny wonn hwath,
    pysk martesen.
	*I don't know yet,
	    fish perhaps.*

Dhe by eur yw li y'n ostel ma?	*At what time is lunch in this hotel?*
Dhe hanter dydh poran.	*At midday exactly.*
Py par aval yw hemma?	*What kind of apple is this?*
Aval 'Mamm-wynn An Gov' yw ev.	*It's a Granny Smith apple.*
Deves yw tanow war an woen.	*Sheep are scarce on the down.*
A wodhesta konvedhes hemma?	*Do you understand this?*
Na wonn! Arta, mar pleg.	*No! Again please.*
Nyns yw an bargen-tir ma pur vras.	*This farm is not very big.*
Fatell yw an gewer lemmyn?	*What is the weather like now?*
Oer, niwlek ha tewl yw hi.	*It is very cold, misty and dark.*
Yma peder kador warn ugens gesys a-ji dhe hel an eglos.	*There are twenty-four chairs left in the church hall.*
I yw pur feusik, dell dybav.	*They are very lucky, I think.*
Ty yw kar Mona, a nyns yw henna gwir?	*You are a relation of Mona isn't that true?*
Yw! My yw keniterow Mona.	*Yes! I am Mona's cousin.*

18 AN LE MAY MA TRAOW - *WHERE THINGS ARE*

There are a number of common words which show where a person or a thing is, words such as 'in', 'on', 'by' and so on. These are called prepositions (see the Glossary). Here are some examples:

ryb an amari	*by the cupboard*	
a-rag an amari	*in front of the cupboard*	
a-dryv an amari	*behind the cupboard*	
war² an amari	*on the cupboard*	
y'n amari **(yn + an = y'n)**	*in the cupboard*	
yn-dann² an voes	*under the table*	
orth an tan	*at the fire*	
der* an pras	*through the meadow*	
gans an teylu	*with the family*	

*The form **der** is used before vowels and the form **dre²** before consonants: **der an koes** 'through the wood'; **dre goes** 'through a wood'.

As stated in Part 16, in replying to questions of the kind 'Where is...?' there is no need in ordinary speech to repeat the whole phrase. This is shown in the examples below where the phrases **yma hi**, etc. are optional in the answer given.

EXAMPLES

Ple'ma an gath?	*Where is the cat?*
Ryb an fos (yma hi).	*Beside the wall (it is).*
Ple'ma Jori?	*Where is George?*
Orth an voes (yma ev).	*At the table (he is).*
Ple'ma an hanafow?	*Where are the cups?*
Y'n gegin (ymons i).	*In the kitchen (they are).*
Ple'ma an karr?	*Where is the car?*
A-rag an karrji (yma an karr).	*In front of the garage (is the car).*
Ple'ma an eskisyow?	*Where are the shoes?*
Yn-dann an gweli (ymons i).	*Under the bed (they are).*
Ple'ma an lowarth?	*Where is the garden?*
A-dryv an chi (yma ev).	*Behind the house (it is).*
Ple'ma Maria?	*Where is Mary?*
Orth an voes (yma hi).	*At the table (she is).*

Consider the two English statements:

1. *There is a cat in the garden*

2. *The cat is in the garden*

In the first statement no particular cat is intended. The noun 'cat' is indefinite and preceded by 'a', the indefinite article. In the English idiom, the verbal phrase 'there is' comes before the subject 'a cat'.

In the second statement a particular cat is in the mind of the speaker, the noun is definite, and preceded by the definite article 'the'. In the English idiom the verb 'is' follows the subject.

The same idea of one definite thing or of a number of definite things is also expressed by using pronouns such as **ev** 'he/it', **hi** 'she/it', **i** 'they', **hemma** 'this', **henna** 'that', **an re ma/na** 'these, those', etc.

Cornish also has different ways of expressing these two concepts. You have already used one, the **yma, eus, nyns eus** of Part 2, **Bosva**. This corresponds to statement 1 above. Statement 2 puts **usi** in place of **eus** as follows:

The question:

	positive	**usi?**	*is?/are?*
	negative	**a nyns usi?**	*is not?/are not?*

The answers:

	positive	**usi!**	*is/are (yes)*
	negative	**nag usi!**	*is not/are not (no)*

The statements:

	positive	**yma**	*is/are*
	negative	**nyns usi**	*is not/are not*

If the pronoun 'they' is the subject, then **usi** becomes **esons** and **yma** becomes **ymons**. The pronoun **i** 'they' can be added for extra emphasis or clarity: **esons i?, nyns esons i, ymons i.**

EXAMPLES

Usi an gath y'n lowarth?	*Is the cat in the garden?*
Usi! Yma hi ena.	*Yes! She is there.*
A nyns usi an boes war an voes hwath?	*Isn't the food on the table yet?*
Nag usi! Nyns usi ev ena hwath.	*No! It's not there yet.*
Usi an lyvrow omma?	*Are the books here?*
Esons i war an voes?	*Are they on the table?*
Esons/Nag esons.	*They are/They are not.*

GERVA

amari, -s *m.*	cupboard	**gorhel, -holyon** *m.*	ship
argh-lyvrow,	bookcase	**kath, -es** *f.*	cat
arghow-l. *f.*		**klokk, -ow** *m.*	clock
bleujenn, -ow *f.*	flower	**marghas, -ow** *f.*	market
bolla, -bollow *m.*	bowl	**melyn** *adj.*	yellow
bryjys *adj.*	boiled	**oy, -ow** *m.*	egg
dornla, -leow *m.**	handle	**a'n par ma/na**	of this/that kind
ensampel, -plow *m.*	example	**py lies**	how many (with
eskis, -yow *f.*	shoe		singular noun)
folenn, -ow *f.*	page, sheet	**tan, -yow** *m.*	fire
gaver, gever *f.*	goat	**ughel** *adj.*	high
glow *m.*	coal		

57

*Note that nouns which end in -**la** are derived from the word **le** 'place' and that the original sound is restored when the stress falls on it, as in the plural. The meaning 'place' is implied in these words: **dornla** = **dorn** 'hand' + **le** 'place', hence 'handle'.

DASWELES - *Review*

Ple'ma an lyver melyn?
Where is the yellow book?

War an voes (yma) martesen.
On the table (it is) perhaps.

Ple'ma an arghantti?
Where is the bank?

Yn kres an dre yma ev.
It's in the town centre.

Ple'ma an gador lemmyn?
Where is the chair now?

Orth an fos yma hi.
It's against the wall.

Ple'ma an bollys, mar pleg?
Where are the bowls, please?

Y'n amari ymons, dell dybav.
They are in the cupboard, I think.

Usi hwoer Peder y'n skol na?
Is Peter's sister in that school?

Usi! Yma hi ena gans Peder.
Yes! She's there with Peter.

Usi an lost a-rag an hel?
Is the queue in front of the hall?

Usi! Hag yma lost hir ryb an hel ynwedh.
Yes! And there is a long queue beside the hall too.

Eus lost rag an kyttrin?
Is there a queue for the bus?

Nag eus! Nyns eus nebonan ena.
No! There's no one there.

Eus kuntelles omma lemmyn?
Is there a meeting here now?

Eus! yma, dell hevel.
Yes! There is, it seems.

A nyns usi an lyver y'n arghlyvrow na?
Isn't the book in that bookcase?

Nag usi! Nyns usi ev ena.
No! It's not there.

A nyns usi an bleujennow genes?
Haven't you got the flowers?
(*literally* Aren't the flowers with you?)

Nag esons! Nyns esons.
No! They are not.

Ymons i gans an vamm.
Mother has them.
(*literally* They are with the mother)

Ple'ma an ki? Usi ev y'n lowarth?
Where is the dog? Is he in the garden?

Usi! Hag yma an gath ena ynwedh.
Yes! And the cat is there also.

Esons i ena warbarth ytho?
Are they there together then?

Nag esons! Yma an ki war an leur mes yma an gath y'n wydhenn.
No! The dog is on the ground but the cat is in the tree.

Kres oy yw melyn.	*The middle of an egg is yellow.*
Kemmer an dornleow, mar pleg.	*Take the handles, please.*
Ottomma gerva verr.	*Here's a short word list.*
An erva ma yw hir lowr, dell dybav.	*This word list is long enough, I think.*
Fatell yw an eskisyow ma ytho?	*How are these shoes then?*
Re vras yns.	*They are too big.*
Pur ughel yw tour an eglos, a nyns yw ev?	*The church tower is very high, isn't it?*
Ottena klokk an eglos!	*Look there, the church clock!*
Teyr eur poran yw hi.	*It's three o'clock exactly.*
Py folenn yw nessa?	*Which page is next?*
Folenn niver nownsek yw an nessa folenn.	*Page number nineteen is the next page.*
Pyth yw an bleujennow ma?	*What are these flowers?*
Lili yns.	*They are lilies.*
An keur yw parys lemmyn, dell hevel.	*The choir is ready now, it seems.*
Yma dew dhen ha dew ugens y'n kuntelles. Hemm yw niver da rag kuntelles a'n par ma.	*There are forty-two people in the meeting. This is a good number for a meeting of this kind.*
Oyow bryjys yw da rag hansel.	*Boiled eggs are good for breakfast.*

19 MEUR A po NEBES - *LOTS OF or NOT MANY*

MEUR 'much' or 'many' is followed by **a**² 'of' and an appropriate noun, singular or plural. The preposition **a** mutates by softening as shown.

Meur a² win yw re	*Much wine is too much*

Yma meur a² voestiow da **y'n dre**	*There are many good restaurants* *in town*

PALS 'many' follows a plural noun:

Broyow pals yw boghosek	*Many countries are poor*

LIES 'many' has already been mentioned (Part 18). It is used with a singular noun:

Lies karr yw re skav, dell dybav	*Many cars are too fast, I think*

NEBES meaning 'few' comes before a plural noun:

Nebes tus yw kevoethek	*Few people are rich*

NEBES meaning 'a little, some' comes before an appropriate singular noun.

Ottomma nebes keus ragos!	*Here is some cheese for you!*

GERVA

boesti, -ow *m.*	*café, restaurant*	**nebes** *m./adj.*	*few, little*
boghosek *adj.*	*poor*	**niwl, -ow** *m.*	*mist*
fenester, -tri *f.*	*window*	**ors, -es** *m.*	*bear* (animal)
gell *adj.*	*brown*	**orses, -ow** *f.*	*she bear*
gwel, -yow *m.*	*open field*	**oyl** *m.*	*oil*
kommol *coll.*	*clouds*	**pals** *adj.*	*many, numerous*
kommolenn, -ow *f.*	*a cloud*	**plasenn, -ow** *f.*	*disc, record*
lavrek, -vrogow *m.*	*trousers**	**yntra**	*between*
ledan *adj.*	*wide*	**ynter**	(before vowels)
lies *adj.*	*many*	**ynys, -ow** *f.*	*island*
meur *m./adj.*	*much, many*		

* Note that the Cornish word is singular, the English one plural.

DASWELES - *Review*

Nebes fordhow y'n ynys yw ledan lowr mes meur a fordhow ena yw re gul.	*Few roads on the island are wide enough but many roads there are too narrow*
Yma meur a orses gell yn Amerika.	*There are lots of brown bears in America.*
Nyns eus meur a gommolennow lemmyn.	*There are not many clouds now.*
Yma meur a wydhennow ha meur a vleujennow yn lowarth an chi bras na.	*There are many trees and many flowers in the garden of that big house.*
Pyskadoryon bals y'n porth ma yw boghosek.	*Many fishermen in this harbour are poor.*
Yma kanoryon bals yn keur an chapel.	*There are many singers in the chapel choir.*
Tus pals yw re dew.	*Many people are too fat.*
Lies ostel yw gwag, dell hevel.	*Many hotels are empty, it seems.*
A nyns eus lies aval gesys?	*Aren't there lots of apples left?*
Lies gerva yw re hir, dell dybav.	*Many word lists are too long, I think.*

DASWELES KEMMYSKYS - *Miscellaneous Review*

Plema'n tri faper?	*Where are the three papers?*
War an voes ymons	*They are on the table.*
Plema'n gever ytho?	*Where are the goats then?*
Y'n pras a-dryv drehevyans an bargen-tir ymons martesen.	*They are in the field behind the farm building perhaps.*
Yma an vamm-wynn orth an fenester gans an tas-gwynn.	*Grandmother is at the window with grandfather.*
Oyow bryjys yw bryntin, meur ras.	*Boiled eggs are fine, thanks.*
Yma dewdhek lyver ha dew ugens y'n argh-lyvrow.	*There are fifty-two books in the bookcase.*
Pyth yw an ynysow ma?	*What are these islands?*
Ynysow Syllan yns.	*They are the Isles of Scilly.*
Yma hwetek den ha peswar ugens y'n eglos warbarth gans an pronter.	*There are ninety-six people in the church together with the parson.*

61

An dhiw gador warn ugens yw parys a-ji dhe'n hel.	The twenty-two chairs are ready inside the hall.
Py eur yw hi lemmyn, mar pleg?	What time is it now please?
Trydhek mynysenn wosa diw eur poran yw hi.	It's thirteen minutes after two o'clock exactly.
Dhe by eur yth yw an tren dhe Aberplymm?	At what time is the train to Plymouth?
Dhe beder eur marnas kwarter yw ev.	It's at a quarter to four.
A-dro dhe unn eur yw hi lemmyn, dell dybav.	It's about one o'clock now I think.
Yma an plasennow y'n amari byghan.	The records are in the small cupboard.
Dornleow an darasow yw plos.	The door handles are dirty.
Lavrek an maw na yw re hir ha re ledan.	That boy's trousers are too long and too wide.
Pur goth yw an tavern ma.	This inn is very old.
Ev yw moen lowr, sur.	He is thin enough, certainly.
Nyns eus platow lowr.	There aren't enough plates.
Hwi yw pur lowen, dell vydh usys.	You are very happy, as usual.
Ni yw pur doemm, sur!	We are very hot, sure.
Skorr an gwydh yw terrys, a nyns yns i?	The branches of the trees are broken aren't they?
Nos dha ytho!	Good night then!
An yeth frynkek yw kewsys y'n pow ma, a nyns yw hi?	The French language is spoken in this country, isn't it?
Piw yw honna, an venyn voen na orth an voes?	Who is that, that slim woman at the table?
Tamsin yw hi, myrgh Mr ha Mres Angell.	She's Tamsiyn, Mr and Mrs Angell's daughter.
Py chambour yw an nessa dhe'n lowarth a-rag?	Which bedroom is nearest to the front garden?
Pyth yns i, mar pleg, an puskes ma?	What are they, please, these fish?
Brithyli yns.	They are mackerel.

20 ERGHI - GWRA HEMMA! *COMMAND - DO THIS!*

It is often necessary to tell someone to do something, although this is usually tempered by a 'please' or a 'will you?'.

Kemmer an lyver ma, mar pleg!
Take this book, please!

Igor e! Folenn ugens	*Open it! Page twenty*
Meur ras. Dege e lemmyn!	*Thank you. Shut it now!*
Ro an lyver dhe Sou, mar pleg!	*Give the book to Sue, please!*
Pys e, po hi, a igeri	*Ask him, or her, to open*
an lyver dhe folenn ugens	*the book at page twenty*
ha lenn an kynsa linenn!	*and read the first line!*
Gwra an keth tra gans nebonan	*Do the same thing with someone*
arall!	*else!*

The imperative form of the verb, the form used in giving an order, is usually the stem of the word. See 'stem' in the Glossary.

In speaking to a group of people, or in some circumstances to the public at large, the plural form is used. This is simply made by adding **-ewgh** to the singular form: **kemmer!** 'take!', singular and **kemmerewgh!** 'take', plural. Sometimes there is a difference in the vowel of the stem as: **igor!** 'open!', singular and **igerewgh!** 'open!', plural. This will be noted as it occurs.

A few common imperatives are irregular and these too will be noted as they occur. In the vocabulary the verbal noun is given in brackets and can be taken to mean the same as the English noun in '-ing', e.g. **kemmeres** 'taking, the act of doing so'.

To make a negative imperative, telling someone not to do something, simply put **na²** before the verb: **Na ge!** 'Don't go!'; **Na gemmerewgh an lyvrow!** 'Don't take the books!'.

63

Imperative:

singular	plural			
dege!	degeewgh!	*shut!*	(degea)	(shutting)
deus!	dewgh!	*come!*	(dos)	(coming)
gwra!	gwrewgh!	*do!*	(gul)	(doing)
igor!	igerewgh!	*open!*	(igeri)	(opening)
ke!	kewgh!	*go!*	(mos)	(going)
kemmer!	kemmerewgh!	*take!*	(kemmeres)	(taking)
lavar!	leverewgh!	*say! tell!*	(leverel)	(saying, telling)
lenn!	lennewgh!	*read out!*	(lenna)	(reading out)
pys!	pysewgh!	*ask! request!*	(pysi)	(asking, requesting)
ro!	rewgh!	*give!*	(ri)	(giving)
skrif!	skrifewgh!	*write!*	(skrifa)	(writing)

lavar dhymm!   *tell (to) me!*
ro dhymm!   *give (to) me!*
pysi neppyth diworth nebonan   *ask someone for something*
pysi nebonan a² wul neppyth   *ask someone to do something*

GERVA

bysi *adj.*	*busy, important*		**lavar, -ow** *m.*	*saying, phrase*
diworth *prep.*	*from*		**linenn, -ow** *f.*	*line*
e (= **ev**) *pron.*	*him, it*		**po** *conj.*	*or*
kynsa *adj.*	*first*		**tra*, -ow** *f.*	*thing, affair*

*The word **tra** 'thing' is one of several in Cornish which have a double gender, that is to say, in some circumstances it is treated as feminine and in others as masculine.

As feminine - it mutates after **an** 'the' and after **unn** 'one'. A following adjective is mutated: **tra vras** 'a big thing', **an dra vyghan** 'the little thing'.

As masculine - accompanying numerals are masculine: **peswar tra** 'four things'. Referring pronouns are masculine: **An dra ma yw plos**. **Ev yw du**. 'This thing is dirty. It's black'.

DASWELES - *Review*

Dege an daras, mar pleg, yeyn yw hi!	*Shut the door, please, it's cold!*
Gwra e lemmyn!	*Do it now!*
Lenn an lavarow!	*Read out the phrases!*
Ro an arghans dhe Beder!	*Give the money to Peter!*
Kemmerewgh an re ma!	*Take these!*
Skrifewgh hanow an lyver war gynsa linenn an folenn!	*Write the name of the book on the first line of the page!*
Pys e diworth Margh!	*Ask Mark for it! (ask it from Mark)*
Pys Helen a ri e dhe Margh!	*Ask Helen to give it to Mark!*
Lavar dhymm, pyth yw hemma?	*Tell me, what is this?*
Gwrewgh e warbarth!	*Do it together!*
Igor an fenester po dege an daras! Re wynsek yw hi!	*Open the window or close the door! It's too windy!*
Lennewgh an lavar warbarth!	*Read out the sentence together!*
Ke dhe'n fenester, mar pleg!	*Go to the window, please!*
Dewgh orth an tan! Oer yw hi!	*Come to the fire! It's very cold!*
Kemmerewgh oll dorn nebonan!	*Everyone take someone's hand!*

DASWELES KEMMYSKYS - *Miscellaneous Review*

Kres tre yw le bysi, dell vydh usys, mes kres an dre ma yw gwag.	*A town centre is usually a busy place but this town centre is empty.*
Nyns eus par dhe'n gour ma, dell dybav.	*This man has no equal, I think.*
An diogyon gernewek yw an kynsa a-ji dhe'n varghas.	*The Cornish farmers are the first inside the market.*
Lavarow lowr yw lowr.	*Enough words are enough.*
Meur a lavarow yw flows.	*Much speech is nonsense.*
Eus arghans lowr genes, Tom?	*Have you enough money, Tom?*
Nag eus, Maria, ro dhymm nebes peunsow, mar pleg!	*No, Mary, give me a few pounds please!*
Myttin da, Yowann. Fatla genes?	*Good morning, John. How are you?*
Da lowr, meur ras, mes yma anwoes poes warnav.	*Well enough, thanks, but I have a heavy cold.*

Pyth yw an blasenn na? Piw yw an kaner?	*What is that record?* *Who is the singer?*
Dornla an ganstell ma yw terrys.	*The handle of this basket is broken.*
A wodhesta konvedhes an lavar ma?	*Do you understand this expression?*
Na wonn! Arta, mar pleg!	*No! Again, please!*
Piw yw pronter an eglos ma?	*Who is the vicar of this church?*
Mr Le'ti yw an pronter omma.	*Mr Laity is the vicar here.*

21 MY YW ha NYNS OV - *I AM and I AM NOT*

A normal sentence, when affirmative and in which one thing is being identified with another or when a description is being added, has the form:

My yw Peder   *I am Peter*

Morwenna yw yowynk   *Morwenna is young*

This has been set out in Part 5 **Hevelepter** and Part 6 **Studh**. In these sentences the linking word is **yw** 'is', the 3s. present of the verb **bos** 'to be' and there is a slight emphasis on the subject, **My** or **Morwenna** in the examples, as though the statements were replies to the questions **Piw yw Peder?** 'Who is Peter?' and **Piw yw Morwenna?** 'Who is Morwenna?'.

The other persons of this tense are as shown in the table:

ov	*I am*	**on**	*we are*
os	*you* (s) *are*	**owgh**	*you* (pl) *are*
yw	*he/she/it is*	**yns**	*they are*

These inflected forms are used in questions, in negative statements and in sentences in which the complement is put first for emphasis.

Question   **Osta lowen?**   *Are you happy?*
Reply   **Ov** or **Nag ov**   *I am* or *I am not*

These direct replies are the equivalent of the English 'Yes!' or 'No!'.

Complement first:

Lowen osta?   *Are you happy?*
               (literally *Happy are you?)*
Lowen ov   *I am happy*
               (literally *Happy am I*) (not sad)

Negative:

Nyns ov lowen   *I am not happy*

GERVA

dell lavarav	*as I say*	**ke, -ow** *m.*	*hedge*
devedhys *adj.*	*come, arrived*	**kevoethek** *adj.*	*rich, powerful*
goes *m.*	*blood*	**koweth, -a** *m.*	*friend* (m.)
gwann *adj.*	*weak*	**kowethes, -ow** *f.*	*friend* (f.)
gweth *adj.*	*worse*	**krev** *adj.*	*strong*
(an) **gwettha**	*(the) worst*	**lew, -es** *m.*	*lion*
gyllys *adj.*	*gone, departed*	**lewes, -ow** *f.*	*lioness*
hwans, -ow *m.*	*desire, want*	**lyverji, -ow** *m.*	*bookshop*
yma hwans	*I want*	**na(g)** *conj.*	*nor* (adds **-g**
dhymm a²			before all vowels)
eus hwans dhis a²?	*do you want?*	**seth, -ow** *m.*	*jar, vase*

DASWELES - *Review*

Drehevyans an skol ma yw koth.	*This school building is old.*
Nyns ov koth na nyns ov yowynk.	*I am not old nor am I young.*
Kowethes Maria os, dell dybav.	*You are a friend of Mary's, I think.*
Nyns yw an boesti ma onan da.	*This restaurant is not a good one.*
On ni parys lemmyn?	*Are we ready now?*
Py lies owgh hwi oll warbarth?	*How many are you altogether?*
Yns i ensamplow da?	*Are they good examples?*
A nyns yns i kernewek?	*Aren't they Cornish?*

DASWELES KEMMYSKYS - *Miscellaneous Review*

Fatell yw an mebyl y'n chi na?	*What is the furniture like in that house?*
Py arghantti yw an nessa?	*Which bank is the nearest?*
Feusik on, sur.	*We are lucky, certainly.*
Yma unn chi a-dryv an sinema;	*There is a certain house behind the*
chi Mr Pollglas yw ev.	*cinema; it's Mr Polglas's house.*
Kemmer tri hwegynn!	*Take three sweets!*
Piw yw an gwettha flogh?	*Who is the worst child?*
Margh yw, dell dybav.	*Mark is, I think.*
Py eur yw hi, mar pleg?	*What time is it, please?*
Eth eur poran yw hi.	*It's exactly eight o'clock.*
Fatla genes an myttin ma?	*How are you this morning?*
Nyns ov yn poynt da. Yma anwoes	*I'm not well. I have a heavy cold.*
poes warnav.	

Na gewgh, mar pleg.	Don't go, please.
An re na yw boghosek. Tiogyon gernewek yns.	Those (people) are poor. They are Cornish farmers.
Berrheans lyver yw dhe les	The abridgement of a book is useful.
Eus pluvenn rudh genes, mar pleg?	Have you a red pen, please?
Ro dhymm plat!	Give me a plate!
Arta mar pleg!	Again, please!
Plat, onan bras!	A plate, a big one!
Pyth yw henna - an dra dhu na?	What's that - that black thing?
Nyns yw an kerdh re hir.	The walk isn't too long.
Yns i hwerydh, an dhiw vowes na?	Are they sisters, those two girls?
Nag yns!	No! (they aren't).
Yma deg stamp gesys y'n lyver-stamp ma.	There are ten stamps left in this stamp-book.
Na lavar ger! A wodhesta konvedhes?	Don't say a word! Do you understand?
Broder Androw yw pronter yn unn eglos.	Andrew's brother is a vicar in a certain church.
Oll an draow ma yw parys.	All these things are ready.
Py par bargen-tir yw henna?	What kind of farm is that?
Bargen-tir deves yw ev.	It's a sheep farm.
Igor daras an gegin, mar pleg!	Open the kitchen door, please!
Yma meur a dus a-ji dhe'n hel.	There are lots of people inside the hall.
Re boeth yw hi dhe hanter-dydh.	It's too hot at midday.
Nebes geryow yw lowr.	A few words are enough.
Pur sygh yw an lowarth.	The garden is very dry.
Dohajydh da dhis, Me. Kewer deg , a nyns yw hi?	Good afternoon to you, May. Nice weather, isn't it?
Trydhek den ha dew ugens a-ji dhe'n kyttrin yw re, dell hevel.	Fifty-three people in the bus are too many, it seems.
Yma an vamm orth an daras. Igor e ytho!	Mother is at the door. Open it then!

69

22 HEVELEPTER ha DIHEVELEPTER -
SIMILARITY and DIFFERENCE

HAVAL 'similar' is usually followed by the preposition **orth** 'at' but **dhe²** 'to' is sometimes used: **Liw an mor yw haval orth/dhe liw an ebrenn** 'The colour of the sea is similar to the colour of the sky'.

An enyval ma yw haval
orth margh

This animal is similar
to a horse

AN KETH means 'the same', 'identical' and it is followed by the word **ha** 'and'. Compounds of **keth** are also followed by **ha**, for instance **kettoth ha** 'the same speed as' or 'as soon as'; **kettermyn ha** 'the same time as'; **kehys ha** 'the same length as'.

Yw hemma an keth plat
ha'n huni kyns?

Is this the same plate
as the one before?

ARALL is used to indicate 'another one of the same kind'. It has a plural form, **erell** used only after plural nouns:

An plat ma yw plos, ro dhymm
onan arall, mar pleg!

This plate is dirty, give me
another one please!

Yma ensamplow erell
war folenn 72

There are other examples
on page 72

but

Lies den arall yw kamm
war an dra ma

Many other people are wrong
on this matter

KEN means 'another kind of':

Ottomma ken euryor

Here's another (kind of) watch

DIHAVAL is the opposite of **haval** (see above):

An gewer hedhyw yw dihaval
diworth an gewer de

The weather today is different
from the weather yesterday

The word **(an) huni** stands for the English 'the one' as a pronoun referring to something already mentioned: **an huni bras** 'the big one'. When it refers to something feminine in gender the mutation of the adjective takes place: **an desenn na, an huni vras** 'that cake, the big one', the word **tesenn** being feminine. You will also hear **an onan** used in this sense but **huni** is preferable.

GERVA

arall *sing. adj.*	other, another	**ken** *adj*	other
nebonan arall	someone else	**keth** *adj.*	same
erell *pl. adj.*	other, others	**an keth**	the same
re erell	other ones	**an keth tra**	the same thing
bryntin *adj.*	splendid	**an keth tra ma/na**	this/that very
dell leverir	as is said, one says		(same) thing
diek *adj.*	lazy	**kettermyn ha**	at the same time
dihaval *adj.*	unlike	**kettoth ha**	as soon as
ebrenn *f.*	sky	**kyns** *adj.*	former
enyval,-es *m.*	animal	**mor, -yow** *m.*	sea
euryor, -yow *f.*	watch timepiece)	**nes** *adj.*	nearer
gokki *adj.*	silly	**ober, -ow** *m.*	work, job
gwell *adj.*	better	**ogas (dhe)** *adv.*	near (to)
(an) gwella *adj.*	(the) best	**peub** *pron*	each, every
(an) huni *pron.*	(the) one	**plu, -yow** *f.*	parish
kamm *adj.*	wrong, bent	**pub** *adj.*	each, every
kemmyn *adj.*	common	**stevell,-ow** *f.*	room

LIWYOW - *Colours*

liw, yow *m.*	colour	**gwyrdh** *adj.*	green (apart from plants)
du *adj.*	black		
gell *adj.*	brown	**loes** *adj.*	grey
glas *adj.*	blue (and *green* of plants)	**melyn** *adj.*	yellow
		rudh *adj.*	red
gwynn *adj.*	white, fair		

Leurlenn an chambour yw haval orth huni an hel; melyn ha gwyrdh yns i.

The bedroom carpet is like the one in the hall; they are yellow and green.

An enyval na yw haval orth davas mes nyns yw ev davas.

That animal is like a sheep but it isn't a sheep.

Na lavar an keth tra arta!

Don't say the same thing again!

Nyns yw hemma an keth lyver ha huni Yowann.

This isn't the same book as John's.

Ke yn kettermyn ha Maria!

Go at the same time as Mary!

Yma an ganstell arall yn-dann an voes ena. Kemmer hi!

The other basket is under the table there. Take it.

A nyns usi an tavern nowydh ogas dhe'n huni arall?

Isn't the new pub near the other one?

Nyns yw an traow ma pur haval orth an re erell, yns i?

These are not very similar to the others, are they?

Plema'n benynes erell lemmyn?

Where are the other women now?

Y'n stevell arall ymons.

They are in the other room.

Ken termyn, ken hwedhel!

Another time, another story!

Kemmer ken hwegynn ytho!

Take another (kind of) sweet then!

Hemm yw kamm. An lavar ma yw dihaval diworth an lavar arall.

This is wrong. This sentence is different from the other sentence.

Broyow erell yw gwell, dell hevel.

Other countries are better, it seems.

Yma kommol y'n ebrenn ha dihaval yns diworth an re erell.

There are clouds in the sky and they are different from the others.

An yethow keltek

Yma a-ji dhe'n teylu keltek hwegh yeth yn dew deylu vyghan.

Gwydhelek, Albanek ha Manowek yw an teyr yeth a-ji unn teylu byghan.

Bretonek, Kernewek ha Kembrek, an teyr yeth ma yw an teylu byghan arall.

Bretonek ha Kernewek yw diw hwoer, dell leverir, ha Kembrek yw an geniterow dhe'n dhiw arall.

Kernewek yw kewsys omma a-ji Kernow ha hanow lies tre yw Kernewek.

Ottomma ensamplow: *Treveglos* yw **trev** hag **eglos**; *Trevean* yw **tre** ha **byghan**. *Tywardreath* yw **ti** ha **war** ha **treth**, sowsnekhes ('anglicized'). *Ninnis* yw **an** hag **ynys**. Yma hanow teylu *Angel* **an** ha **gell**.

Yma ensamplow pals a'n re ma.

23 AN TERMYN TREMENYS - *PAST TIME*

Ev yw hir *he is tall*   **Ev o hir** *he was tall*

In speaking of past time the verb **yw** 'is' becomes **o** 'was'. It is the 3rd person singular of the Imperfect tense of the verb **bos** 'be' and, like **yw**, does not change when the statement is an affirmative one even when the subject is a plural noun.

An gwydh o glas   *The trees were green*

The word **o** is used when talking about a state rather than an action.

An vugh o byghan   *The cow was small*

The demonstrative pronouns **hemma, homma** 'this', **henna, honna** 'that' drop the **-a** before **o** just as they do before **yw**:

Hemm o pur dha   *That was very good*
Henn o gwir   *That was true*

In negative statements, in questions and in statements in which the complement precedes for emphasis, it is necessary to use the inflected forms of this imperfect tense. These are set out in the table below. Replies to questions repeat the verb of the question in an appropriate person.

en	*I was*	**en**	*we were*
es	*you* (s) *were*	**ewgh**	*you* (pl) *were*
o	*he/she/it was*	**ens**	*they were*

Notice that the same form, **en**, is used for both 'I was' and 'we were'. To avoid ambiguity the appropriate pronoun can be added.

Examples

En vy diek?	*Was I lazy?*	**Es!**	*You were!*
Esta klav?	*Were you ill?*	**Nag en!**	*I was not!*
O hi kowethes?	*Was she a friend?*	**O!**	*She was!*
Nyns en ni toemm	*We were not warm*		
Ewgh hwi drog pes?	*Were you displeased?*	**Nag en!**	*We were not!*
Nyns ens i hwerydh	*They were not sisters*		
Fol en vy	*I was foolish*		

74

Both the present and the imperfect of **bos** have a long form which is used to show location and position.

These forms are simply made by adding the syllable **es-** to the short form, the exceptions being the third person singular when the present is **yma** in affirmative statements and **usi** or **eus** elsewhere, as we have already learnt, and **esa** in the imperfect.

esov	*I am*	**eson**	*we are*
esos	*you are* (s)	**esowgh**	*you are* (pl)
yma/usi/eus	*he/she/it is*	**ymons/esons**	*they are*

esen	*I was*	**esen**	*we were*
eses	*you were* (s)	**esewgh**	*you were* (pl)
esa	*he/she/it was*	**esens**	*they were*

It is a general rule in Cornish that when the verb begins an affirmative statement it is preceded by the verbal particle **y**[5] (**yth** before a vowel or **h**). The word **yma** which we have used frequently is considered to incorporate this particle already. For the fifth mutation see the table on page v.

It is possible however to put an adverb or an adverbial phrase before this particle: **Dhe unn eur poran y'n nos yth esa tros euthek** 'At one o'clock exactly in the night there was a frightful noise'.

Here are some examples of sentences using this long form.

Yth esov yn chi Karol.	*I am in Carol's house*
Nyns esons genes, sur	*They are not with you, certainly.*
Esesta war an treth?	*Were you on the beach?*
Yth esen vy yn gorsav an hyns-horn	*I was in the railway station*
Nyns esesta ganso	*You weren't with him*
Nyns esa an bel ena	*The ball was not there*
Yth eson y'n lowarth	*We are in the garden*
Esowgh hwi orth an voes?	*Are you at the table?*
Yth esen ni y'n dre	*We were in town*
Esewgh hwi war an treth?	*Were you on the beach?*
Nag esen!	*(No) We were not!*
Yth esens i yn-dann an lawlenn yn mysk an traow erell	*They were under the umbrella amongst the other things.*

Notice that although a speaker can make statements like **My yw lowen** 'I am happy' and **Hi o mowes** 'She was a girl', where an adjective or a noun is the complement, Cornish does not use, for example, *My yma y'n chi for 'I am in the house' (**Yth esov y'n chi**) or *Hi esa genes for 'She was with you' (**Yth esa hi genes**). These 'positional' statements with **yma** and **esa** and their personal, inflected forms have to have the construction shown in the examples above, using the verbal particle **y(th)**.

GERVA

bugh, -es *f.*	cow	**gorsav an kyttrin**	*bus station*
drog pes *adj.*	*displeased*	**hwoer, hwerydh** *f.*	*sister*
glawlenn, -ow *f.*	*umbrella*	**klav** *adj.*	*ill*
gorsav, -ow *m.*	*station*	**pel, -yow** *f.*	*ball*
gorsav an hyns-horn	*railway station*	**pes da** *adj.*	*pleased*
		treth, -ow *m.*	*beach*

DASWELES - *Review*

My o lowen ena mes nyns o Morwenna lowen martesen	*I was happy there but Morwenna was not happy perhaps .*
Yth esen vy y'n karr Jori.	*I was in George's car.*
An vugh o gwynn ha gell.	*The cow was white and brown.*
Yth esa an vugh y'n pras gans an re erell.	*The cow was in the meadow with the others.*
Nyns esens y'n pras bras.	*They weren't in the big meadow.*
O ev pes da gans hemma? Nag o!	*Was he pleased with this? No!*
Esa ev y'n lowarth ytho?	*Was he in the garden then?*
Nyns ewgh parys, dell dybav.	*You were not ready, I think.*
Nyns esewgh a-ji dhe'n drehevyans.	*You were not inside the building.*
A nyns ens i pes da gans henna?	*Weren't they pleased with that?*
A nyns esens i yn gorsav an kyttrin?	*Weren't they in the bus station?*
Esta skwith gans an oberennow?	*Were you tired with the exercises?*
Esesta y'n Gresenn Gernewek?	*Were you in the Cornish Centre?*
Glas o an del y'n koes.	*The leaves in the wood were green.*
Y'n koes yth esa del gell war an leur.	*In the wood there were brown leaves on the ground.*

Kamm en ni.	*We were wrong.*
Yth esen ni yn skath vras Mr Tommas.	*We were in Mr Thomas's big boat.*
A nyns esa an fleghes warbarth yn gorsav an hyns-horn?	*Weren't the children together in the railway station?*
Esens, sur.	*They were, certainly.*
Hwi o drog pes y'n prys na.	*You were displeased on that occasion.*
Yth esewgh yn Truru y'n prys na.	*You were in Truro on that occasion.*

DASWELES KEMMYSKYS - *Miscellaneous Review*

Yth esa diw venyn warn ugens y'n kuntelles.	*There were twenty-two people in the meeting.*
An donsyow kernewek yw da, a nyns yns i?	*The Cornish dances are good, aren't they?*
Pys glawlenn diworth an vodrep!	*Ask Auntie for an umbrella!*
Na gewgh gans tus kemmyn!	*Don't go with common people!*
An gweder o terrys.	*The mirror was broken.*
Py ostel yw an gwella yn Manow?	*Which hotel is best in the Isle of Man?*
Fatell o an gewer ytho?	*How was the weather then?*
Kosel o ha toemm, pur deg o hi.	*Calm and warm, it was very fine.*
Nyns esa meur a vebyl nowydh y'n chi.	*There wasn't much new furniture in the house.*
Nebes fleghes o gokki.	*A few children were silly.*
Gyllys o meur a arghans ha nyns o devedhys arghans lowr.	*A lot of money had (was) gone and not enough money had (was) come.*
Yw hi fur ytho?	*Is she wise then?*
Nag yw, dell leverir.	*She is not, as they say.*
Ro dhymm bara hag amanenn, dell vydh usys, mar pleg!	*Give me bread and butter as usual, please!*
Nyns esa kommolenn y'n ebrenn.	*There wasn't a (single) cloud in the sky.*
Eus oyl lowr yn jynn an karr?	*Is there enough oil in the engine of the car?*

24 PERGHENNIETH - *POSSESSION*

To mark ownership, possession, English uses words like 'my', 'your' and so on. These are called 'possessive adjectives'. In Cornish these words are as follows.

my	ow^3	**ow ewnter**	*my uncle*
your (s)	dha^2	**dha ewnter**	*your uncle*
his/its	y^2	**y ewnter**	*his uncle*
her/its	hy^3	**hy ewnter**	*her uncle*
our	agan	**agan ewnter**	*our uncle*
your (pl)	agas	**agas ewnter**	*your uncle*
their	aga^3	**aga ewnter**	*their uncle*

Some of these words cause mutations:

dha^2 and **y^2** cause second mutation which has already been used with **an** 'the' and in other places.

ow^3, **hy^3** and **aga^3** cause third, breathed mutation, which has already been used with the numbers **tri^3** and **teyr^3** '3'. It is repeated here for reference:

$$\textbf{k > h,} \qquad \textbf{p > f,} \qquad \textbf{t > th}$$

No mutation follows **agan, agas**.

Examples

		bread	*house*	*desk*	*bed*	*car*	*son*	*spade*	*father*
		bara	**chi**	**desk**	**gweli**	**karr**	**mab**	**pal**	**tas**
your	dha^2	*vara*	*ji*	*dhesk*	*weli*	*garr*	*vab*	*bal*	*das*
his	y^2	*vara*	*ji*	*dhesk*	*weli*	*garr*	*vab*	*bal*	*das*
my	ow^3	bara	chi	desk	gweli	*harr*	mab	*fal*	*thas*
her	hy^3	bara	chi	desk	gweli	*harr*	mab	*fal*	*thas*
their	aga^3	bara	chi	desk	gweli	*harr*	mab	*fal*	*thas*

It is a useful exercise to try putting these possessive adjectives with English words, just to get the hang of it: ow faint (paint), y dhoor (door), etc.

GERVA

bregh, -ow *f.*	*arm*	**kesva, -ow** *f.*	*board, organisation*
bythkweth *adv.*	*ever, never (with neg.)*	**kota, -ow** *m.*	*coat*
		le *adj.*	*less*
dell glywav	*as/so I hear*	**(an) lyha** *adj.*	*(the) least*
fordh-a-dro, *f.*	*roundabout*	**mil², -yow** *m.num.*	*thousand*
fordhow-a-dro	*(road)*	**pan²** *adv.*	*when*
goedh, -ow *f.*	*goose*	**peldroes** *f.*	*football game*
gwerther, -oryon *m.*	*seller, salesman*	**pott, -ow** *m.*	*pot*
horner, -oryon *m.*	*ironmonger*	**sim, -es** *m.*	*monkey*
kay, -ow *m.*	*platform, quay*	**tarow, terewi** *m.*	*bull*

*pan² means 'at the time when'. **Pan** is always followed by the verb: **Pan o Yowann maw** and not *Pan Yowann o maw.

It is not the word used to ask the question 'when?': 'When will she be here?' nor is it used in a relative sense as in the English sentence 'On the day when (= on which) he was born, there was a thunderstorm.'

The negative is **pan na²** (**nag** before parts of **bos** and **mos** which start with a vowel: **Pan nag esov yn ow chi, yth esov yn ow lowarth** 'When I am not in my house, I am in my garden').

DASWELES - *Review*

Ow hi yw kloppek.	*My dog is lame.*
Dha gota yw plos, dell dybav.	*Your coat is dirty, I think.*
Nyns yw nowydh y ji.	*His house is not new.*
Nyns yw ev y ji nowydh.	*It is not his new house.*
Yw hy howethes Myrna ytho?	*Is her friend Myrna then?*
Agan stevell y'n ostel o re vyghan.	*Our room in the hotel was too small.*
Agas tas yw ow howeth.	*Your father is my friend.*
Aga fleghes yw klav, dell glywav.	*Their children are ill, I hear.*
Agan kesva yw onan dha.	*Our association is a good one.*
Nyns o ow boes parys.	*My food was not ready.*
Dha gyttrin yw gyllys lemmyn.	*Your bus is gone now.*

An wydhenn ma yw marow. Hy del yw gell.	*This tree is dead. Its leaves are brown.*
A nyns esa delenn las gesys?	*Wasn't there a single green leaf left?*
Nag esa!	*No!*
Pan en maw, ow theylu o boghesek, sur.	*When I was a boy. my family was poor, certainly.*
Pan esa drehevyans ena nyns esa golow lowr yn agan chi.	*When there was a building there, there wasn't enough light.*
Pan nag o kevoethek, lowen o ev.	*When he was not rich, he was happy.*

DERIVAS BERR

Ottomma hwedhel teylu Margh Lawson.

Y das o horner yn Lannstefan. Y dhew vroder o gwerthoryon rag an tas. An gwerthji o onan bras yn Stret an Eglos.

Yth esa gwerthjiow erell y'n keth stret yn kres an dre, mes nyns ens pur vras. Byghan ens, dell hevel.

Gwreg Margh o benyn a-dhiworth Aberplymm mes ny wonn vy piw o hy thas hi. Nyns o an teylu kevoethek mes nyns ens i boghosek.

Pan o Margh maw yth esa pymp den y'n keth chi warbarth, an tas, an vamm ha'n tri maw.

Tas Margh ha'y vamm yw marow lemmyn mes yma an dhew vab erell hwath yn Lannstefan, aga thre.

25 HWARVOSOW TREMENYS - *EVENTS IN PAST TIME*

Here is a short story about Peter.

Peder a brenas eskisyow nowydh y'n dre.
Ev a worras an eskisyow ma yn sagh.
Ena ev eth dhe-dre arta. Ev a dhiskwedhas an eskisyow dhe Varia, y
wreg. Hi a leveris, "Brav yns!".
Peder a wiskas an eskisyow nowydh Dy' Sadorn nessa.

Translation:

Peter bought new shoes in town.
He put these shoes in a bag.
Then he went home again. He showed the shoes to Mary, his wife.
She said, "They're fine!"
Peter wore the new shoes the next Saturday.

This little story is told, as most are, as one happening occurring after another at a past time. The various events are presented like this:-

a brenas	*bought*	} all
a worras	*put*	} of
eth	*went'*	} these
a dhiskwedhas	*showed*	} forms
a leveris	*said*	} are
a wiskas	*wore*	} verbs

The word **a²** shows that an action is to follow.
This word **a²** softens the next letter; **prenas > a brenas**.
The verbal noun ending is dropped (**prena > pren**).
The ending **-as** shows that the action is in the past and marks the preterite tense.
Sometimes this ending is **-is**. This will be pointed out when it occurs.
In the word **eth** 'went', there is no **a²** in front and no special ending.
The person doing the action (the subject), Peter in this case, is named before the **a brenas** phrase and the verb remains singular even when the subject is plural.

81

My a werthas an karr koth	*I sold the old car*
An tas a wolghas an ki	*Father washed the dog*
Ni a esedhas ena	*We sat there*
An keur a ganas	*The choir sang*

If the word **re**² is put before the verb instead of **a**² then the meaning is the English present perfect tense, 'have done', 'has done'. This word is only used in affirmative statements:

My re werthas an karr koth	*I have sold the old car*	
An tas re wolghas	*Father has washed*	
an ki	*the dog*	
Ni re esedhas ena	*We have sat there*	

Sentences with this pattern of noun, **a**² + verb are called nominal sentences because they begin with and slightly emphasise the noun or pronoun subject. The other type of Cornish sentence construction is called a verbal sentence and will be dealt with below.

In narratives when the words of a speaker are given directly the verb **medhes** 'said' or, less usually, 'says' is used with a prefixed **yn**. It is not used otherwise.

yn-medhav	*I said/say*
yn-medh ev/Peder/hi/Maria	*he/Peter/she/Mary said/says*
yn-medhons	*they said/say*
"Ha lemmyn ni yw parys," **yn-medh Tamsyn**	*"And now we are ready,"* *said Tamsyn*
"Deus omma!" yn-medhav	*"Come here!" I said*

We have seen above that the past tense of a verb for the third person singular is made by adding **-as** (sometimes **-is**) to the stem of the verb. The complete table of this past tense (the preterite) is as follows:

PRENA *TO BUY*

prenis	*I bought*	**prensyn**	*we bought*
prensys	*you* (s) *bought*	**prensowgh**	*you* (pl) *bought*
PRENAS	*he/she bought*	**prensons**	*they bought*

These 'inflected' forms, made by adding various endings to the stem
pren-, are used in the following cases:

1. In questions introduced by **a²** or by **a ny²**.
2. In negative statements introduced by **ny²**.
3. In statements where the verbal phrase is to be stressed and is placed
   at the head of the sentence. The verbal particle is **y⁵**.

Examples

Positive statement (nominal sentence with the pronoun subject first to give it a
slight emphasis):

My a brenas jynn-amontya   *I bought a computer*

or (verbal sentence with slight emphasis on the action)

**Y prenas an tas
   jynn-amontya**

*Father bought
   a computer*

Question (verbal sentence):

**A brensys jy
   an radyo na?**

*Did you buy
   that radio?*

Reply (verbal sentence):

Prenis or **Na brenis.**   = *yes* or = *no*

Negative statement (verbal sentence):

Ny brensyn an boes y'n eur na   *We didn't buy the food then*

83

GERVA

de *m. adv.*	*yesterday*	**kinyow, -yewow** *m.*	*dinner*
didhanus *adj.*	*amusing*	**kok, -ow** *m.*	*fishing boat*
ena *adv.*	*there, then*	**kowl** *m.*	*soup*
hedhyw *adv.*	*today*	**pows, -yow** *f.*	*coat, gown*
hweg *adj.*	*sweet, nice*	**radyo, -yow** *m.*	*radio*
jynn -ow *m.*	*engine, machine*	**sagh, seghyer** *m.*	*sack, bag*
jynn-amontya *m.*	*computer*	**y'n eur ma** *adv.*	*now*
karr, kerri *m.*	*car*	**y'n eur na** *adv.*	*then*
ki, keun *m.*	*dog*	**ynwedh** *adv.*	*as well, also*

Many verbal nouns are also the stem and the endings will be added directly to this: **gweres** (**-as**) 'help', 3s. preterite **gweresas** 'helped'.

Verbs with verbal nouns ending in **-ya** are very common. They keep the y- in the 3s. preterite and in all parts of the verb except those which have an -s-, an -i- or another -y- in the ending or in which there is no separate ending: **red-ya** (**-as**) 'read':

redis	*I read*	**redsyn**	*we read*
redsys	*you* (s) *read*	**redsowgh**	*you* (pl) *read*
REDYAS	*he/she read*	**redsons**	*they read*
red!	*read!* (s)	**redyewgh!**	*read* (pl)

Note also that the stem vowel -a- of verbs like **kara** will become -e- when the added ending contains an -i-, -y- or -owgh. So the Preterite (Past) tense of **kara** 'love' is:

keris	*I loved*	**kersyn**	*we loved*
kersys	*you loved*	**kersowgh**	*you loved*
KARAS	*he/she loved*	**karsons**	*they loved*

In this and in future vocabularies the verbs will be listed separately. The verbal noun comes first with the verbal noun ending hyphenated for clarity. Then the form of the preterite ending will be given, thus:

diskwedh-es (**-as**), show
esedh-a (**-as**), sit
golgh-i (**-as**), wash
gorr-a (**-as**), put
gweres (**-as**) help
gwerth-a (**-as**), sell
gwisk-a (**-as**), wear, dress
kan-a (**-as**), sing

lenn-a (**-as**), read aloud, recite
lever-el (**-is**), say
mos/mones* (**eth**), go
neuv-ya (**-as**), swim
pren-a (**-as**), buy
red-ya (**-as**), read
treyl-ya (**-as**), turn, translate
    (**yn** to, into)

*The verb **mones** has a short and a long form of the verbal noun but there is no difference in meaning. Sometimes the use of the long form makes for greater clarity, avoiding confusion with **bos** 'be'. **Mos/mones** is an irregular verb and will be given in full later.

DASWELES - *Review*

A wolghsys jy an hanafow an myttin ma?	*Did you wash the cups this morning?*
Golghis, sur!	*Yes, certainly!*
Ytho ny wolghsys hemma.	*Well you didn't wash this one.*
Maria a wolghas henna, dell dybav.	*Mary washed that one, I think.*
Golgh e arta, mar pleg!	*Wash it again, please!*
Dy' Sadorn y prenas Wella ki.	*(On) Saturday Wella bought a dog.*
Ev re brenas keun kyns.	*He has bought dogs before.*
Piw a leveris henna?	*Who said that?*
A boensys jy pub dydh?	*Did you run every day?*
Poen lemmyn ytho!	*Run now then!*
An keur a ganas kan gernewek mes ny gensyn gans an keur.	*The choir sang a Cornish song but we did not sing with the choir.*
An vamm re worras an kinyow war an voes lemmyn. Kynsa yma kowl onyon.	*Mother has put the dinner on the table now. First there is onion soup.*
Y'n eur na y hwiskas hi pows las.	*At that time she wore a blue dress.*
Martyn eth dhe'n treth mes nyns* eth dhe neuvya.	*Martin went to the beach but he didn't go to swim.*
Y'n eur na yth eth ev dhe skol an eglos.	*He then went to the church school.*

* Note that **ny** becomes **nyns** before **eth** just as it does before the various parts of **bos** 'be'. Similarly **re** becomes **res**: **Hi res eth** 'She has gone'.

DERIVAS BERR

Yethow Kernow ha Breten Vyghan

Yeth Breten Vyghan yw haval orth yeth Kernow ha tus Breten Vyghan yw haval orth tus Kernow ynwedh.

An ger kernewek **yeth** yw an keth ger ha'n huni bretonek *yezh* ha'n ger **brav** yw an keth huni ha'n ger bretonek *brav*.

Mes yn lies ger an lytherenn **d** yn Bretonek re dreylyas dhe **s** yn Kernewek. Ensampel da yw an ger **tus**. Hemm yw *tud* y'n yeth vretonek.

Ottomma onan arall, **lagas** yw an keth ger ha *lagad* yn Bretonek. Pan eth tus diworth Kernow war an mor dhe Vreten Vyghan aga yeth koth eth ynwedh mes gyllys yw hi ken yeth lemmyn.

26 HWARVOSOW Y'N EUR MA - *PRESENT EVENTS*

Pub dydh y redyav an paper-nowodhow. Y'n keth termyn y red ow gwreg hy faper hyhi. A redydh jy paper-nowodhow pub dydh?

Every day I read the newspaper. At the same time my wife reads her paper. Do you read a newspaper every day?

In this short passage the intention is to say what habitually happens and the tense used is the present/future because the action is considered to extend to future time and is not confined to what is immediately happening.

The present/future tense of the regular verb is:

prenav	*I buy*	**prenyn**	*we buy*
prenydh	*you* (s) *buy*	**prenowgh**	*you* (pl) *buy*
PREN	*he/she buys*	**prenons**	*they buy*

As can be seen, this present/future tense has its own special endings to indicate the person involved. These endings are added to the stem of the verb (see the Glossary). The 3rd person singular usually consists of this stem only: **pren**.

In the vocabularies the form of the 3s. will be given when, as rarely happens, it differs from the stem.

Sentence structure is exactly the same as that described in Part 25. This is repeated here by way of revision.

Affirmative sentences are usually the nominal type (see Part 25), that is one in which the subject, noun or pronoun, singular or plural, comes before the verb and is linked to it by the particle **a**[2]:

An flogh a bren hwegynnow	*The child buys sweets*
An benynes a esedh orth an fenester	*The women sit at the window*
Ni a neuv y'n mor	*We swim in the sea*

Negative sentences or questions or those in which the verbal phrase comes first, are verbal sentences and the inflected forms of the verb, as given above, must be used but note that in these sentences if the noun subject is plural, then the verb remains singular:

Ny bren an flogh hwegynnow.	*The child does not buy sweets.*
A bren an flogh hwegynnow?	*Does the child buy sweets?*
Gans y arghans y pren an flogh hwegynnow.	*With his money the child buys sweets.*
Gans aga arghans y pren an fleghes hwegynnow.	*With their money the children buy sweets.*
Y'n gwerthji na y prenons aga hwegynnow.	*In that shop they buy their sweets.*
Ny weresav y'n lowarth.	*I don't help in the garden.*
A welydh jy an eglos?	*Do you see the church?*
Ena y tiskwedhyn an skeusennow.	*Then we show the photographs.*
War an voes y hworrons i an boes.	*On the table they put the food.*

GERVA

acheson, -ys *m.*	*reason*	**gwedrenn, -ow** *f.*	*glass, tumbler*
a-dal *prep.*	(+ noun) *opposite*	**gwedrennas, -ow** *f.*	*glassful*
a-dal dhe²	(+ pronoun) *opposite*	**hanow, henwyn** *m.*	*name*
bakken *m.*	*bacon*	**howl** *m.*	*sun*
bewin *m.*	*beef*	**howlsplann** *m.*	*sunshine*
bre, -ow *f.*	*hill*	**koynt** *adj.*	*strange*
byttegyns *adv.*	*nevertheless*	**lester, -tri** *m.*	*vessel* (dish or bo
daffar *m.*	*kit, gear*	**nans -ow** *m.*	*valley*
desedhys *adj.*	*situated*	**ny vern**	*it doesn't matter*
drog yw genev	*I'm sorry*	**pennseythun,**	*weekend*
esel, -i *m.*	*member, limb*	**-yow** *f.*	
ewn *adj.*	*correct, straight*	**puptra** *pron.*	*everything*
garth, -ow *m.*	*yard, court*	**yn hwir!** *excl.*	*really!*

ev-a, yv (-as)	*drink*	**mir-es (-as) orth**	*look at*
kews-el (-is)	*speak*	**tenn-a (-as)**	*pull*
kuntell (-as)	*collect*	**yskynn-a (-as)**	*ascend*
met-ya (-yas)	*meet*		
orth	*with*		

A verb may take a preposition to express a particular sense: **mires** 'look', **mires orth** 'look at', **leverel dhe** 'speak to'.

DASWELES - *Review*

An tren a as an gorsav dhe eth eur hanter poran.	*The train leaves the station at half past eight exactly.*
My a wolgh an lestri gans dowr poeth.	*I wash the dishes with very hot water.*
Ny yv ev korev mes gwin hepken.	*He does not drink beer but only wine.*
A esedhons i orth an tan pub gorthugher?	*Do they sit at the fire every evening?*
Ena y hworrav ow hota war an gador.	*Then I put my coat on the chair.*
A ny weresydh jy dha vamm y'n gegin?	*Don't you help your mother in the kitchen?*
Kolan a vir orth an lyver heb redya unn ger.	*Colin looks at the book without reading one word.*
Eseli an gowethas a esedh yn chi an pronter.	*The members of the society sit in the parson's house.*
Hi a vet orth Pol rag li.	*She meets Paul for lunch.*
A bal Mighal yn y lowarth lemmyn? Na bal ev!	*Does Michael dig in his garden now? No! (He does not dig).*
Ni a glyw an glaw orth fenester an chambour.	*We hear the rain against the window of the bedroom.*
Piw a dhysk kernewek y'n dre ma?	*Who learns Cornish in this town?*
Tri po peswar den, dell dybav.	*Three or four people, I think.*
Tus a dheu dhe weles an eglos koth.	*People come to see the old church.*
Jago a wisk y gota nowydh, my a wel.	*James wears his new coat, I see.*

DASWELES KEMMYSKYS - *Miscellaneous Review*

Agan boes dhe'n (= dhe + an) prys ma yw bewin.	*Our food for this meal is beef.*
Drog yw genev, dha wedrenn yw gwag. Kemmer an wedrennas a win ma!	*I'm sorry, your glass is empty. Take this glassful of wine!*
Ny vern, mes meur ras!	*It doesn't matter, but thanks!*

My a worta Tamsin orth daras an eglos.

I wait for Tamsin at the door of the church.

Pyth yw an daffar ma?

What is this gear?

Fatell yw an gewer? Eus howlsplann?

How is the weather? Is there (any) sunshine?

Y'n hwedhel na puptra o koynt.

In that story everything was strange.

"Nyns en vy feusik," yn-medh Hykka.

"I wasn't lucky," said Richard.

Ple'ma ow fluvenn, mammik?

Where's my pen, mummy?

War an leur yn-dann dha weli yn dha jambour, dell vydh usys!

On the floor under your bed in your bedroom, as usual!

DERIVAS BERR

Gevell Essa *Saltash's Twin*

Plougastell Daoulas yw tre yn Breten Vyghan ha par dhe Essa yw hi war lies fordh.

Yma ena pons bras a-dreus dhe avon vras hag yma sita vras, Brest, a-dal Plougastell.

Tus Plougastell a dh'aga *(dhe + aga)* ober yn Brest war an keth pons ma.

Lies den yn Plougastell a woer konvedhes Bretonek mes ny gewsons i an yeth ma. Styr an hanow yw **Plu + Kastell**.

27 VERBOW DHE LES - *USEFUL VERBS*

The words 'do', 'will', 'can', 'go' and 'come' are used in English in one form or another in almost everything we say and in Cornish they are equally common. The table below sets out the present and past of the equivalent Cornish verbs. Since the 3rd person singular is the form used most commonly in affirmative statements, this is given in its mutated form also.

The verbs **gul** 'do', 'make', **mynnes** 'be willing' and **galloes** 'be able' are what is called 'auxiliary verbs' used in 'periphrastic constructions' (see the Glossary):

My a wra lenna hwedhel dhe'n fleghes pub gorthugher
I read to the children every evening

Hi a vynnas mos gans Morwenna
She wished to go with Morwenna

Toni a yll esedha ryb Richard
Tony can sit beside Richard

GUL *TO DO, TO MAKE*

Gul is frequently used to add emphasis to the statement just as in English: **My a wra gweres y'n chi** 'I do help in the house', **Maria a wrug kewsel** 'Mary did speak'. It is also taken to indicate a simple future: **Hi a wra glaw a-vorow** 'It is going to rain tomorrow'. **Gul** is irregular in its forms.

Present

gwrav	*I do*	**gwren**	*we do*
gwredh	*you* (s) *do*	**gwrewgh**	*you* (pl) *do*
GWRA	*he/she does*	**gwrons**	*they do*
(a wra)			

Past (=Preterite)

gwrug	*I did*	**gwrussyn**	*we did*
gwrussys	*you* (s) *did*	**gwrussowgh**	*you* (pl) *did*
GWRUG	*he/she did*	**gwrussons**	*they did*
(a wrug)			

In the 2s. of both the present and the past tenses the verb is usually shortened in ordinary conversation and the alternative pronoun ending **-ta** joined on: **A wre'ta klywes an gan?** 'Do you hear the song?' **A wruss'ta esedha gans Mighal?** 'Did you sit with Michael?'

MYNNES *TO BE WILLING*

Mynnes is a regular verb like **prena**. It is used to indicate intention, willingness.

Present

mynnav	*I will*		**mynnyn**	*we will*
mynnydh	*you* (s) *will*		**mynnowgh**	*you* (pl) *will*
MYNN	*he/she will*		**mynnons**	*they will*
(a vynn)				

Past (= Preterite)

mynnis	*I was willing*		**mynnsyn**	*we were willing*
mynnsys	*you* (s) *were willing*		**mynnsowgh**	*you* (pl) *were willing*
MYNNAS	*he/she was willing*		**mynnsons**	*they were willing*
(a vynnas)				

A vynn'ta kemmeres an bluvenn ma?	*Will you have this pen?*
Mynnav! Ro hi dhymm, mar pleg.	*I will! Give it to me, please.*
A vynn'ta skrifa dha hanow, mar pleg?	*Will you write your name, please?*
Na vynnav! Drog yw genev.	*I will not! I'm sorry.*
A vynn'ta leverel dhymm an acheson?	*Will you tell me the reason?*
Mynnav! An bluvenn ma yw gwag.	*I will. This pen is empty.*

This short dialogue shows how to ask someone to do something.

The key words are **mynnydh** 'you will' and **mynnav** 'I will'. To make a question the word **a²** comes in front as usual, softening the next letter: **mynnydh > a vynnydh?**

Together with **ta** 'you' joined to the verb in place of **jy**, the phrase usually becomes shortened to **a vynn'ta?**.

GALLOES *TO BE ABLE*

Galloes 'to be able to' (Part 25) is also regular but it does change its internal vowel in some persons:

The word **galloes** is used in connection with the circumstances which will allow an action to take place. The verb **godhvos** (**godhes** is the 2s. present) refers to the innate ability or understanding of a skill.

Present

gallav	*I can*	**gyllyn**	*we can*
gyllydh	*you* (s) *can*	**gyllowgh**	*you* (pl) *can*
GYLL	*he/she can*	**gyllons**	*they can*
(a yll)			

Past (= Preterite)

gyllis	*I could*	**gyllsyn**	*we could*
gyllsys	*you* (s) *could*	**gyllsowgh**	*you* (pl) *could*
GALLAS	*he/she could*	**gallsons**	*they could*
(a allas)			

A wodhesta neuvya?	*Can you swim?*
	(Do you know how to swim?)
Gonn	*Yes, I know how to*
Na wonn	*No, I don't know how to*
A yll'ta kuntell an lyvrow?	*Can you collect the books?*
	(Have you the time/opportunity to?)
Gallav, sur	*I can, certainly*
Na allav	*No I can't*

With this word also the commonly used form for a question is **A yll'ta?** 'can you?' and the reply will be either **Gallav** 'I can' or **Na allav** 'I cannot'.

MONES/MOS *TO GO*

Mones is irregular. It does not require the particle **a**[2] before the 3s.

Present

av	*I go*	**en**	*we go*
edh	*you* (s) *go*	**ewgh**	*you* (pl) *go*
A	*he/she goes*	**ons**	*they go*

Past (= Preterite)

yth	*I went*	**ethen**	*we went*
ythys	*you* (s) *went*	**ethewgh**	*you* (pl) *went*
ETH	*he/she went*	**ethons**	*they went*

An dowr a yn nans dhe'n mor (not *a a)
The water goes down to the sea

Nebonan arall eth yn le Karl (not *a eth)
Someone else went in place of Charles

DONES/DOS *TO COME*

Present

dov	*I come*	**deun**	*we come*
deudh	*you* (s) *come*	**dewgh**	*you* (pl) *come*
DEU	*he/she comes*	**dons**	*they come*
(a dheu)			

Past (= Preterite)

deuth	*I came*	**deuthen**	*we came*
deuthys	*you* (s) *came*	**deuthewgh**	*you* (pl) *came*
DEUTH	*he/she came*	**deuthons**	*they came*
(a dheuth)			

An gwyns a dheu a'n mor
The wind comes from the sea

Jenefer a dheuth gans hy gour
Jenifer came with her husband

GERVA

dowr, -ow *m.*	*water*	**yn-bann** *adv.*	*upwards*
ganso *prep.*	*with him, it*	**yn le*** *prep.*	*in place (of)*
hanafas, -ow *m.*	*cupful*	**yn-mes (a²)** *prep.*	*out (of)*
hwel, -yow *m.*	*work*	**yn-nans** *adv.*	*downwards*
koffi *m.*	*coffee*		

*****yn le** 'in place of' can have a possessive adjective put before the noun: **yn ow le** 'in my place'.

DASWELES - *Review*

An vowes a wra hy ober omma.	*The girl does her work here.*
My a vynn esedha yn y le.	*I will sit in his place.*
Ev a yll gorra y draow ena.	*He can put his things there.*
Ni a dhe Druru gans ow thas.	*We go to Truro with my father.*
Maria a wrug henna, dell glywav.	*Mary did that, I hear.*
Nebonan a allas gweres.	*Someone was able to help.*
Peub a dheuth gans arghans lowr. Da o.	*Everyone came with enough money. It was good.*
Ny vynnas Lowena mones gans hy hwoer.	*Lowena did not wish to go with her sister.*
A ny allas an venyn gwiska hy hota?	*Could the woman not wear her coat?*
A yll an fleghes neuvya omma?	*Can the children swim here?*

DASWELES KEMMYSKYS - *Miscellaneous Review*

Fatell o an gewer yn Itali?	*How was the weather in Italy?*
Poeth o, sur, pur boeth.	*It was hot, certainly, very hot.*
Py par gwerther yw Jago?	*What sort of salesman is James?*
Py gour yw dha hwegron?	*Which man is your father-in-law?*
Ottena! An den berr, tew.	*See over there! The short, fat person.*
Piw o hy howethes wir?	*Who was her true friend?*
Ni oll warbarth eth yn-nans dhe'n treth rag neuvya.	*We all went down to the beach together in order to swim.*
Pyth yw hemma a-dryv an amari?	*What is this behind the cupboard?*

Paper-nowodhow koth yw, sur.	It's surely an old newspaper.
Berrheans an lyver o re verr, dell dybav.	The abridgement of the book was too short, I think.
My a brenas dewdhek oy nowydh y'n bargen-tir.	I bought twelve new eggs at the farm.
Py eur o pan dheuth hi tre arta?	What time was it when she came home again?
Nebes geryow yw an gwella.	A few words are the best.
Nyns esa meur a win gesys rag kinyow.	There was not much wine left for dinner.
Yth esa hwans dhymm a vones.	I wanted to go.
Ynter an garrek ha'n mor yth esen vy.	I was between the rock and the sea.
A nyns owgh hwi yeyn orth an daras ena?	Aren't you cold by the door there?
Gorr oyl a-ji dhe'n jynn; gwag yw, dell hevel.	Put some oil in the engine; it's empty it seems.
Nyns yw an hwedhel 'Mil Nos ha Nos' unn hwedhel mes lies hwedhel yn unn lyver.	The story 'A Thousand and One Nights' is not one story but many stories in one book.
Fatell o an gewer y'n eur na? Oer o, pur oer.	How was the weather at that time? It was cold, very cold.
Yth esa toll yn to hy chi ha ledan o an keth toll na.	There was a hole in the roof of her house and that same hole was wide.
An glaw a dheuth a-ji der an toll.	The rain came in through the hole.
Py boesti yw an gwella y'n dre ha py boesti yw an gwettha?	Which restaurant is the best in the town and which restaurant is the worst?
Boesti an tavern 'An Margh Wynn' yw an gwella, dell dybav, ha'n boesti a-ji dhe'n varghas yw an gwettha, dell glywav.	The restaurant of 'The White Horse' is the best, I think, and the restaurant in the market is the worst, I hear.
Ottena! Yma y wreg ganso lemmyn.	Look! There's his wife with him now.
Hwel, ena hanafas a goffi yw brav.	Work, then a cup of coffee is fine.

28 DHYMM ha DHIS - *TO ME and TO YOU*

The word **dhe²** 'to' is a preposition very commonly used in Cornish:

An keur a ganas dhe'n fleghes   *The choir sang to the children*
An keur a ganas dhedha   *The choir sang to them*

Most common prepositions can have endings added to them to indicate the person or thing they apply to:

	dhe²	*to*		
dhymm	*to me*		**dhyn**	*to us*
dhis	*to you* (s)		**dhywgh**	*to you* (pl)
dhodho	*to him/it*		**dhedha**	*to them*
dhedhi	*to her/it*			

	gans	*with*		
genev	*with me*		**genen**	*with us*
genes	*with you* (s)		**genowgh**	*with you* (pl)
ganso	*with him/it*		**gansa**	*with them*
gensi	*with her/it*			

	war²	*on*		
warnav	*on me*		**warnon**	*on us*
warnas	*on you* (s)		**warnowgh**	*on you* (pl)
warnodho	*on him/it*		**warnedha**	*on them*
warnedhi	*on her/it*			

	heb	*without*		
hebov	*without me*		**hebon**	*without us*
hebos	*without you* (s)		**hebowgh**	*without you* (pl)
hebdho	*without him/it*		**hebdha**	*without them*
hebdhi	*without her/it*			

	yn	*in*		
ynnov	*in me*		**ynnon**	*in us*
ynnos	*in you* (s)		**ynnowgh**	*in you* (pl)
ynno	*in him/it*		**ynna**	*in them*
ynni	*in her/it*			

		rag	*for*

ragov	*for me*	**ragon**	*for us*
ragos	*for you* (s)	**ragowgh**	*for you* (pl)
ragdho	*for him/it*	**ragdha**	*for them*
rygdhi	*for her/it*		

		a²	*from, of*

ahanav	*from me*	**ahanan**	*from us*
ahanas	*from you* (s)	**ahanowgh**	*from you* (pl)
anodho	*from him/it*	**anedha**	*from them*
anedhi	*from her/it*		

		orth	*at*

orthiv	*at me*	**orthyn**	*at us*
orthis	*at you* (s)	**orthowgh**	*at you* (pl)
orto	*at him/it*	**orta**	*at them*
orti	*at her/it*		

Remember that the 3rd person singular pronouns can mean 'it': **ynno** 'in it'; **warnedhi** 'on it', **hebdho** 'without it', etc.

To add extra emphasis to these and other expressions, the suffixed pronouns can be employed. For instance, **ragov** means 'for me' but with an added pronoun it becomes **ragov vy** 'for *me*'. These pronouns added after a word are here given in full:

vy	*me*	**ni**	*us*
jy	*you*	**hwi**	*you*
ev	*him/it*	**i**	*them*
hi	*her/it*		

Note that after a verb the form **jy** is often replaced by **ta** which is written with the verb as one word: **osta** = **os jy** 'are you?'.

Examples

ragov vy	*for me*	**hebon ni**	*without us*
genes jy	*with you* (s)	**orthowgh hwi**	*at you* (pl)
ynno ev	*in it/him*	**dhedha i**	*to them*
warnedhi hi	*on it/her*		

These suffixed pronouns can themselves be doubled to increase emphasis further:

evy	*me*		**nyni**	*us*
tejy	*you* (s)		**hwyhwi**	*you* (pl)
eev	*him/it*		**ynsi**	*them*
hyhi	*her/it*			

Examples

Yma an vowes ganso eev   *The girl is with **him***

My a vynn esedha gansa ynsi   *I will sit with **them***

Note that the preposition **dhe**[2] 'to' has several special forms to which these suffixed pronouns are attached. They are:

dhymmo *to me*	**dhymmo vy** *to me*	**dhymmo evy** *to ME*
dhiso *to you*	**dhiso jy** *to you*	**dhiso tejy** *to YOU*

GERVA

a-hys *adv.*	*along*		**gour, gwer** *m.*	*man, husband*
als, -yow *f.*	*cliff*		**hoelan** *m.*	*salt*
baner, -yow *m.*	*flag*		**lo, -yow** *f.*	*spoon*
bownder, -yow *f.*	*lane*		**loas, -ow** *f.*	*spoonful*
chymbla, -blow *m.*	*chimney*		**nyhewer** *m./adv.*	*last night*
diwedhes *adj.*	*late*		**skol, -yow** *f.*	*school*
dyskador, -yon *m.*	*teacher*		**stret, -ow** *m.*	*street*
dyskadores, -ow *f.*	*teacher*		**sugra** *m.*	*sugar*
euthek *adj.*	*frightful*			

dysk-i (-as)	*learn, teach*		**klyw-es (-as)**	*hear, perceive,*
gas-a (-as)	*leave*			*sense, feel*
gort-os, gorta (-as)	*wait for*		**pal-as (-as)**	*dig*
gwel-es (-as)	*see*			

The ending **-es** when added to a masculine noun denotes a female of the same kind: **lew** 'lion', **lewes** 'lioness'; **mer** 'mayor', **meres** 'mayoress'.

The ending **-as** added to the name of a container denotes the capacity of that container, the English '-ful': **kalter** 'kettle', **kalteras** f. 'a kettleful'. The derived noun keeps the gender of the original word.

DASWELES - *Review*

Henna a dhiskwedhas an folenn dhedha.	*That person showed the paper to them.*
Ny worrsons i aga hanstell warnedhi (an voes).	*They did not put their basket on it (the table).*
A ganas Margh genowgh?	*Did Mark sing with you?*
My a welas tarow y'n pras.	*I saw a bull in the field.*
Yth esa bughes ynno ynwedh.	*There were cows in it too.*
Kemmer an kowl ma, yma bollas ragos.	*Take this soup, there is a bowlful for you.*
Hebdhi nyns ov lowen.	*Without her I am not happy.*
Nyns eth Morwenna hebov.	*Morwenna did not go without me.*
A leversys jy hemma ragon?	*Did you say that for us?*
Rygdhi y hwrug ev an dra.	*For her he did the thing.*
Gwra an hwel gansa!	*Do the work with them!*
Ro e dhymmo vy, mar pleg!	*Give it to me, please!*
Ny dhiskwedhsyn an golow dhedha.	*We did not show them the light.*
Lavar dhymm piw yw an re ma!	*Tell me who those people are!*

DASWELES KEMMYSKYS - *Miscellaneous Review*

Nos dha dhywgh hwi oll, nos dha!	*Good night to you all, good night!*
Eus nebes koffi gesys ragov?	*Is there a little coffee left for me?*
Nag eus. Yma te hepken.	*No. There is tea only.*
Usi an saghasow a avalow a-ji dhe'n karrji? Esons!	*Are the bags of apples inside the garage? They are!*
Pyth yw an dra ma yn Kernewek?	*What is this object in Cornish?*
Glawlenn yw.	*It's 'glawlenn' (umbrella).*
Py hwel eus dhodho?	*What work has he got?*
Dyskador yw, dell glywav.	*He is a teacher, I hear.*
Nyns yns aga hota* ynsi, sur.	*They are not their coats, certainly.*
Ny wonn kovedhes. Arta mar pleg, ha lenta.	*I don't understand. Again please, and slower.*
Hy thas-gwynn o pronter yn Eglos Pow Sows.	*Her grandfather was a parson in the Church of England.*
Ott! Chymbla an chi na yw gyllys gans an gwyns krev.	*Look! The chimney of that house has gone with the strong wind.*
Tasik, tasik! Ple'ma agan ki?	*Daddy, daddy! Where is our dog?*
Piw yns i, an re na a-rag gwerthji an horner?	*Who are they, those (people) in front of the ironmonger's shop?*
Ny wonn. Mes na gews dhedha! Tus kemmyn yns, dell hevel, ha nyns yns agan parow, sur.	*I don't know. But don't speak to them! They are common people, it seems and they are not our equals for sure.*
Pub avon omma yw keltek ha pub menydh ynwedh.	*Every river here is Celtic and every mountain too.*
Bregh an gador ma yw terrys.	*The arm of this chair is broken.*
On ni diwedhes? On, dell dybav.	*Are we late? We are, I think.*
Yma bownder verr ha kul ynter an dhew bras vras.	*There is a short, narrow lane between the two big fields.*
Yntra naw den ev yw an lyha oll.	*Among nine people he is the least of all.*
Re dhiwedhes os, ow howeth, ha nyns eus hanafas a goffi ragos.	*You are too late, my friend, and there is no cup of coffee for you.*

*aga hota = 'their coat' = 'their coats'. Cornish asumes that they have only one coat each. Similarly **aga fenn** 'their head' = 'their heads' in English.

29 HWARVOSOW OW PESYA - *CONTINUING ACTION*

Yma Jerri ow koska lemmyn   *Jerry is sleeping now*

When an action is going on at the time of speaking, it can be indicated by using the word **ow**[4] and the verbal noun, **koska** in the example. This translates the English '-ing' as in 'sleeping'.

Ow changes certain following letters: **b > p**; **d > t**; **g > k**. This is the fourth mutation, 'hardening'. See also the table on page v.

ow pywa (bywa) 'living'; **ow tybri** (dybri) 'eating'; **ow karma** (garma) 'shouting'.

Ow becomes **owth** before vowels and **h**-: **owth eva** 'drinking'; **owth holya** 'following'.

This construction is called 'the present participle construction'.

Note that the commonly used verbs **mynnes** 'be willing' and **galloes** 'be able' are not used in this way.

The 3s. of **bos** is used in its long form, **yma** when the statement is positive, whether or not the subject is plural. As the examples show, the verb starts the sentence.

In negative statements and in questions the form to use is **usi** with definite subjects and **eus** with indefinite ones and in the plural, when no noun subject is expressed, **esons** 'they are'.

In the past tense (imperfect) the form of **bos** is, again, the long form.

For other persons, e.g. 'I am', 'I am not', etc., the appropriate forms are used: **Yth esov ow tybri ow hoen** 'I am eating my supper'; **Nyns eson ow megi** 'We are not smoking'.

These tenses are repeated here for reference:

102

Present

esov	*I am*	eson	*we are*
esos	*you* (s) *are*	esowgh	*you* (pl) *are*
yma (usi, eus)	*he/she/it is*	ymons (esons)	*they are*
yma Maria	*Mary is*		
yma an kokow	*the fishing boats are*		

Imperfect

esen	*I was*	esen	*we were*
eses	*you were*	esewgh	*you were*
esa	*he/she/it was*	esens	*they were*
yth esa Maria	*Mary was*		
yth esa an kokow	*the fishing boats were*		

Remember that these long forms of **bos** 'be' cannot be used, as the short forms can, with the subject first:

My yw skwith   *I am tired*

and

Yth esen ow tybri   *I was eating*
(but not *My esa ow tybri)

Examples: **Yma** + *noun (singular or plural)*

Yma an avon ow resek yn krev.	*The river is running strongly.*
Yma krys ow kregi war benn an gweli.	*There is a shirt hanging on the end of the bed.*
Yma an fleghes ow tyski Kembrek.	*The children are learning Welsh.*
Yma an gowethas owth omguntell.	*The society is meeting.*
Yma ki owth hartha a-ves.	*There is a dog barking outside.*
Nyns usi an flogh ow koska lemmyn.	*The child is not sleeping now.*
Nyns eus karr ow tos.	*There is no car coming.*
Nyns usi hy harr ow tos.	*Her car is not coming.*
Eus gwyns ow hwytha?	*Is there a wind blowing?*
Usi an keur ow kana?	*Is the choir singing?*

Remember that these expressions mean that something is happening (or not happening) at the time of speaking.

103

If there is no separate noun subject, the inflected forms of the verb are used. A pronoun subject may be expressed:

Esowgh hwi ow redya warbarth?	*Are you reading together?*
A nyns esen ni ow kweres?	*Weren't we helping?*
Nyns esons ow kwari yn ta.	*They are not playing well.*
Esos jy ow kasa lemmyn?	*Are you leaving now?*
Nyns esowgh ow mires orthiv.	*You are not looking at me.*

Examples - affirmative statements

Yth esov ow powes y'n lowarth.	*I am resting in the garden.*
Yth esos ow synsi an lovan.	*You are holding the rope.*
Yma ev ow palas gans an bal derrys.	*He is digging with the broken spade.*
Yth eson ow terri bleujennow.	*We are picking flowers.*
Yth esowgh hwi ow nesa an gresenn.	*You are approaching the centre.*
Ymons owth oberi gans aga thas.	*They are working with their father.*
Yth esens ow kolghi an lestri plos.	*They were washing the dirty dishes.*
Yth esa an maw ow megi.	*The boy was smoking.*

Examples - negative statements

Nyns esov ow skrifa travydh.	*I am not writing anything.*
Nyns esos jy ow serri, esos jy?	*You are not getting angry, are you?*
Nyns esen ni ow redya.	*We were not reading.*
Nyns usi an yeynell owth oberi.	*The refrigerator is not working.*
Nyns eus nebonan ow kelwel.	*There is no one calling.*
Nyns eson ni ow megi.	*We are not smoking.*
Nyns esowgh ow sevel hwath.	*You are not standing yet.*
Nyns esons ow tos.	*They are not coming.*
Nyns esen vy ow kana.	*I was not singing.*

Examples - questions

Esos jy ow koslowes?	*Are you listening?*
Usi an goel ow lenwel?	*Is the sail filling?*
Eus flogh ow kewsel?	*Is there a child speaking?*
Esons i ow kerdhes gensi?	*Are they walking with her?*
Usi an gerens ow keskewsel?	*Are the parents talking together?*
Esewgh hwi ow kewsel orti?	*Were you speaking to her?*

Examples - replies

Esov! or **Nag esov!**	*I am!* or *I am not!*
Usi! or **Nag usi!**	*It is!* or *It is not!*
Eus! or **Nag eus!**	*There is!* or *There is not!*
Esons! or **Nag esons!**	*They are!* or *They are not!*
Esens! or **Nag esens!**	*They were!* or *They were not!*
Esen! or **Nag esen!**	*I was!* or *I was not!* or *We were!* or *We were not!* (depending on context)

Note that English uses forms in '-ing' with two meanings. Compare the following statements: 'Grandmother likes sitting at the fire' and 'Grandmother is sitting at the fire'. In the first statement the word 'sitting' names the thing that Grandmother likes and it is a noun. In the second statement the same word sitting' describes Grandmother and it is an adjective. In Cornish the two meanings are expressed in completely different ways: **An vamm-wynn a gar esedha** 'Grandmother likes sitting' in contrast to **Yma an vamm-wynn owth esedha** 'Grandmother is sitting'.

GERVA

dien *adj.*	*complete*	**kollell, kellylli** *f.*	*knife*
dyskans, -ow *m.*	*lesson*	**krys, -yow** *m.*	*shirt*
glesin, -yow *m.*	*lawn, grass*	**marghas, -ow** *f.*	*market*
goel, -yow *m.*	*sail*	**travydh** *pron.*	*anything* (with neg.) *nothing*
gorthyp. -ybow *m.*	*answer*		
kar, kerens *m.*	*close relative, parent*	**yeynell, ow** *f.*	*refrigerator*
		yn ta *adv.*	*well*

aswonn (-is)	*know, recognise*	**kosk-a (-as)**	*sleep*
		kreg-i (krogas)	*hang*
byw-a (-as)	*live, exist*	**lenw-el (-is)**	*fill* (a^2) *with*
dybr-i, deber, (-is)	*eat*	**meg-i (mogas)**	*smoke*
ev-a, yv (-as)	*drink*	**nes-a (-as)**	*approach* (**dhe**[2])
garm-a, (-as)	*shout*	**ober-i (-as)**	*work*
goslow-es (-as)	*listen* (**orth**) *to*	**omguntell (-as)**	*meet together*
gwari (-as)	*play*	**powes (-as)**	*rest*
harth-a (-as)	*bark*	**res-ek (-as)**	*run*
hwyth-a (-as)	*blow*	**serr-i (sorras)**	*make/be angry*

kerdh-es (-as)	walk	sev-el (-is)	stand, erect, set up
keskews-el (-is)	converse	terr-i (torras)	break
klapp-ya (-yas)	chatter		

In the review below the two usages are shown.

DASWELES - *Review*

My a gar dybri dyenn kernewek.	I love eating Cornish cream.
Yth esov ow tybri li y'n gegin.	I am eating lunch in the kitchen.
Joy a vynn skrifa dhodho.	Joy will write to him.
Yma hi ow skrifa dhodho y'n chi.	She is writing to him in the house.
Joy re skrifas dhodho mes nyns eus gorthyp hwath.	Joy has written to him but there is no reply yet.
Yma an baner owth yskynna.	The flag is going up.
My a allas yskynna an vre heb gweres.	I was able to ascend the hill without help.
Yma ev ow kuntell an tokynyow.	He is collecting the tickets.
Y ober yw kuntell an tokynyow.	His work is collecting the tickets
Lowena a gar gwiska hy hota du.	Lowena likes wearing her black coat.
Nyns usi hi ow kwiska hy hota du.	She is not wearing her black coat.

DASWELES KEMMYSKYS - *Miscellaneous Review*

Gorr an kellyli war an voes!	Put the knives on the table!
Morwenna yw lowen. Hy fenn-bloedh yw hedhyw.	Morwenna is happy. Her birthday is today.
Py mappa yw an gwella ragon?	What map is the best for us?
Py par gorthyp yw henna?	What sort of answer is that?
Fatell o an gewer ragowgh y'n Alban?	How was the weather for you in Scotland?
Esedh y'n trysa desk!	Sit in the third desk.
Y'n seythves dydh an dra o dien.	On the seventh day the matter was complete.
Kan an kynsa salm warn ugens!	Sing the twenty-first psalm!
Kikti Mr Bates yw an peswara gwerthji yn Stret an Eglos.	Mr Bates' butcher's shop is the fourth shop in Church Street.
Hi a lennas an nawves dyskans.	She read the ninth lesson.

An dohajydh ma ymons i ow metya orth aga howetha.

A nyns esens i ow synsi an dornleow?

A vynn'ta dybri an aval ma?

Na vynnav, meur ras!

A yll'ta gweles an mor hwath?

Gallav!

Ottomma an ganstell mes nyns eus travydh ynni.

Ottena an kok mes nyns eus den ynno.

Lemmyn y prenyn brithylli y'n varghas.

A vynnowgh hwi mones genen dhe'n dons?

Ev a wrug lestrier a brenn derow.

I re werthas an sinema koth.

An losow yw byw hwath.

Marilynn vyghan a welas sim y'n wydhenn.

Kemmer an diwes ma ragos.

Ny garav an venyn na namoy.

An ebrenn o loes gans kommol ha hi a wrug glaw.

Ty a yll lenwel an hanaf a dhowr.

Yv hanafas anodho!

Jori a asas y gi yn-mes a'n chi.

Ny yllydh jy esedha war an glesin. Re lyb yw ev.

Dyw genes! Dha weles skon.

Nyns yw ow harr gwerthys hwath.

Hy fows wyrdh yw nowydh.

An re na a glapp flows.

Ny aswonnav an gour na.

Yth esa kestenenn hir yn kres an glesin.

Piw yw hy hweger ytho?

Mir orth an bluvek blos na!

Gorta diw vynysenn, mar pleg!

This afternoon they are meeting their friends.

Weren't they holding the handles?

Will you eat this apple?

No thanks!

Can you see the sea yet?

I can (= yes).

Look here's the basket but there's nothing in it.

There is the fishing boat but there's no one in it.

Now we buy mackerel in the market.

Will you go with us to the dance?

He made a dresser of oak wood.

They have sold the old cinema.

The plants are alive still.

Little Marilyn saw a monkey in the tree.

Take this drink for you (= yourself).

I don't like that woman any more.

The sky was grey with clouds and it rained.

You can fill the cup with water.

Drink a cupful of it!

George left his dog outside the house.

You can't sit on the lawn. It's too wet.

Goodbye! See you soon.

My car is not sold yet.

Her green dress is new.

Those (people) talk nonsenes.

I don't know that man.

There was a tall chestnut tree in the middle of the lawn.

Who is her mother-in-law, then?

Look at that dirty cushion!

Wait two minutes, please!

30 GRASSA - *GRATITUDE*

Saying 'Thank you'.

The commonest way of saying 'thank you' has already been mentioned:

Meur ras!	*Thanks!*
Meur ras dhis!	*Thank you!* (to one person)
Meur ras dhywgh!	*Thank you!* (to more than one person).

You may want to mention what the thanks are for. So:

Meur ras dhis a'n te   *Thank you for the tea*

Here use the word **a²** 'of, from'.

If someone is to be thanked for doing something, then the present participle is used as in Part 29:

Meur ras dhis ow tos (dos)   *Thank you for coming*
Meur ras dhywgh hwi ow   *Thank you for helping*
  kweres (gweres) **gans an hwel**   *with the work*

There are other ways of expressing gratitude:

Aswonnav gras dhis a'n boes   *Thank you for the food*
which is literally 'I acknowledge thanks...

This is rather more formal than just **meur ras dhis**:

Synsys meur ov dhis a'n   *I am much obliged to you for the*
  gweres   *help*

Pandra *'what thing?'*

Pandr'a wre'ta Sadornweyth?   *What do you do on Saturdays?*

The word **pandra** 'what, what thing' can be used independently standing alone, whereas **py** 'what, which' is accompanied by a noun.

Pandra can be followed by a verb and the final **-a** drops before the particle **a²** and is replaced by an apostrophe as in the example.

Examples

> **Pandr'a dhybris Peder**
>   **y'n boesti chenek na?**

> *What did Peter eat*
>   *in that Chinese restaurant?*

> **Pandr'a redyas an flogh?**

> *What did the child read?*

This word can be used as an exclamation, just as 'what!' can be in English:

> **Pandra! A nyns eus**
>   **arghans gesys?**

> *What! Isn't there*
>   *any money left?*

Another exclamative is the word **ass²** which is put before a verb, usually **yw** 'is' or **o** 'was'. It can be translated by 'How!'.

> **Ass yw da an boes ma!**

> *How good this food is!*

> **Ass o kamm y lavar!**

> *How wrong his words were!*

> **Ass wrons i kana!**

> *How they do sing!*

GERVA

dyenn *m.*	*cream*	**mappa, -ow** *m.*	*map*
dyenn-rew *m.*	*ice-cream*	**na fors!** *interj.*	*it doesn't matter!*
		penn-bloedh *m.*	*birthday*
gorthyp, -ybow *m.*	*answer, reply*	**synsys** *adj.*	*held, beholden*
gras, -ow *m.*	*thanks*	**tokyn, -yow** *m.*	*ticket*
gweres, -ow *m.*	*help*	**uskis** *adj.*	*quick, immediate*
aswonn (-is)	*acknowledge*		
dehwel-es (-is)	*return*	**kar-a (-as)**	*love*
dybr-i deber (-is)	*eat*	**klapp-ya (-yas)**	*chatter*
		syns-i (-is)	*hold, seize*

DASWELES - *Review*

Meur ras dhis a'n gweres.
Thank you for the help.

Pandr'a wrug hi gans an paper-nowodhow?
What did she do with the newspaper?

Ny wrav ow oberenn uskis.
I do not do my exercises quickly.

Ass yw ewnter Ralf feusik!
How lucky uncle Ralph is!

Yma hwans dhymm a weles an eglos vryntin na.
I want to see that fine church.

Fatell o an gewer yn Sen Ostell?
How was the weather in St. Austell?

Awelek o, pur awelek, heb mar.
It was windy, extremely windy, without a doubt.

My a wra henna arta.
I shall do that again.

Py par yeth yw honna?
What kind of language is that?

Ass os gokki, Kernewek yw hi.
How silly you are, it's Cornish.

Pandr'a wredh jy gans an toll yn to an karrji?
What shall you do with the hole in the roof of the garage?

Aswonnav gras dhywgh hwi ow kuntell an arghans ragon.
I thank you for collecting the money for us..

Pandra! A nyns yw henna noy Mr Peters?
What! Isn't that Mr Peters' nephew?

Pandr'a evons i? Gwin rudh?
What do they drink? Red wine?

Ro dhymm gwedrennas anodho, mar pleg!
Give me a glassful of it, please!

Ny wren ni kewsel dhedha.
We don't speak to them.

A wrewgh hwi dannvon lytherow heb stampow?
Do you send letters without stamps?

Pan wra hi ergh, yeyn yw an gewer.
When it snows, the weather is cold.

110

DASWELES KEMMYSKYS - *Miscellaneous Review*

Piw a yll bos salow?	*Who can be safe?*
Bleujennow an eythin yw melyn ha rudh.	*The flowers of the gorse are yellow and red.*
Yma hwans dhymm a dhybri oyow bryjys rag hansel.	*I want to eat boiled eggs for breakfast.*
Ugens mildir yw dhe Lannstefan.	*It is twenty miles to Launceston.*
Yma meur a fenestri y'n drehevyans na.	*There are lots of windows in that building.*
Gorr dha dhaffar y'n garth!	*Put your gear in the yard!*
My re viras orth y vregh. Shyndys yw, dell hevel.	*I have looked at his arm. It is injured, it seems.*

DERIVAS BERR

An Bennseythun Gernewek *The Cornish Weekend*

Le an Bennseythun kernewek y'n vlydhen mil, naw kans, pymthek ha peswar ugens yw Aberfal. An le ma yw desedhys ogas dhe'n mor ha brav yw.

Ty a lever, martesen, "Ny wonn konvedhes Kernewek lowr hwath". Ny vern! Yma dyskadoryon dha ha dyskadoresow da ena. Ty a yll dyski gansa.

Kewgh genen dhe'n Bennseythun vrav!

111

Numbers which show the order of things, 'first', 'second' and so on are called 'ordinal numbers.

1st	**kynsa**	**1a**	
2nd	**nessa**	**2a**	
3rd	**trysa/tressa**	**3a**	
4th	**peswara**	**4a**	
5th	**pympes**	**5es**	
6th	**hweghves**	**6ves**	
7th	**seythves**	**7ves**	
8th	**ethves**	**8ves**	
9th	**nawves**	**9ves**	
10th	**degves**	**10ves**	
11th	**unnegves**	**11ves**	
⬇		⬇	and then go on adding -**ves** to the
⬇		⬇	cardinal number up to **20ves**
19th	**nownsegves**	**19ves**	
20th	**ugensves**	**20ves**	
⬇		⬇	Then carry on changing the first
⬇		⬇	part of the number as above
21st	**kynsa warn ugens**	**21ens**	
22nd	**nessa warn ugens**	**22ens**	
30th	**degves warn ugens**	**30ens**	etc. up to **40ves** then:
41st	**kynsa ha dew ugens**	**41ens**	
50th	**hanterkansves**	**50ves**	
51st	**unnegves ha dew ugens**	**51ens**	
100th	**kansves**	**100ves**	

These ordinal numbers come before the noun: **an trysa dydh** 'the third day'; **an tressa salm warn ugens** 'the twenty-third psalm'; **hemm yw an tri ugensves penn-bloedh** 'this is the sixtieth anniversary'.

There is no special form used for the feminine nor is there any mutation.

GERVA

a-ugh* *prep.*	above	**hwath** *adv.*	still, yet
askloes *pl.*	chips	**isel** *adj.*	low
bresel, -yow *f.*	war, strife	**kig** *m.*	meat
bronn, -ow *f.*	hill	**kiger, -oryon** *m.*	butcher
desk, -ow *m.*	desk	**kikti, -ow** *m.*	butcher's shop
dien *adj.*	full, complete	**koloven, -yow** *f.*	column
diworth *prep.*	from	**krev** *adj.*	strong
dres *prep.*	over, beyond	**leun (a²)** *adj.*	full (of)
edhen, ydhyn *f.*	bird	**losow** *coll.*	plants
es *adj.*	easy, comfortable	**losowenn -ow** *f.*	a plant
fest *adv.*	very	**losow-kegin** *coll.*	vegetables
fest da	very good	**losowenn-gegin** *f.*	vegetable
fos, -ow *f.*	wall	**losowennow-**	vegetables
fylm, -ow *m.*	film	**kegin** *pl.*	
ger, -yow *m.*	word	**lyther,-ow** *m.*	letter
gwerthji, -ow *m.*	shop	**nevra** *adv.*	ever (with
gwyns, -ow *m.*	wind		negative) *never*
gwynsek *adj.*	windy		
haneth *adv.*	this evening,	**park, -ow** *m.*	field, park
	tonight	**park kerri** *m.*	car park
		selsik *coll.*	sausages
heb *prep.*	without	**selsigenn, -ow** *f.*	sausage
heb mar *adv.*	certainly	**tredan** *m.*	electricity

*The preposition **a-ugh** takes personal endings:

	a-ugh	*above*	
a-ughov	*above me*	**a-ughon**	*above us*
a-ughos	*above you* (s)	**a-ughowgh**	*above you* (pl)
a-ughto	*above him/it*	**a-ughta**	*above them*
a-ughti	*above her/it*		

dannvon (-as)	send	**lenw-el (-is) a²**	fill (with)
diwedh-a (-as)	finish	**ober-i (-as)**	work
drehedh-es (-as)	reach	**pellgews-el (-is)**	telephone
gwel-es (-as)	see	**treyl-ya (-yas)**	turn, translate
kews-el (-is)	speak	**treylya yn**	translate into

113

DASWELES - *Review*

Hi re dhrehedhas hy hansves penn-bloedh.	*She has reached her hundredth birthday.*
Ny dhiwedhis vy an trysa lyver hwath.	*I have not finished the third book yet.*
An degves ger y'n ugensves linenn yw 'kath'.	*The tenth word in the twentieth line is 'kath' (cat).*
Ev a redyas y hanow y'n peswara koloven war an pympes folenn a'n paper-nowodhow.	*He read his name in the fourth column on the fifth page of the newspaper.*
Hanterkansves penn-bloedh diwedh Nessa Bresel an Norvys o ha seytegves pennbloedh ha tri ugens diwedh Kynsa Bresel an Norvys.	*It was the fiftieth anniversary of the end of the Second World War and the seventy-seventh anniversary of the end of the First World War.*
Ottena! kommol loes a-ugh an koes.	*Look! Grey clouds above the wood.*
Yma Breten Vyghan dres an mor.	*Brittany is over the sea.*
My re welas ydhyn pals y'n lowarth haneth.	*I have seen many birds in the garden this evening.*
Fest da o an boes y'n ostel na.	*The food in that hotel was very good.*
Piw a bellgewsis orthis haneth?	*Who telephoned you this evening?*

114

DASWELES KEMMYSKYS - *Miscellaneous Review*

Pandr'a synsis ev yn y dhorn?

Diskwedh e dhymm, mar pleg!

Eus gever y'n gwel? Eus!

Py lies? Peder gaver.

Py eur o hi pan dheuth hi tre?

Deg mynysenn wosa hwegh eur.

Gorr glow war an tan. Oer yw hi.

Yma meur a arghans dhodho.

Kevoethek yw ev.

Nyns yw hemma an keth sagh ha'n kynsa huni.

Yma hwans dhymm a yskynna an vre ughel na.

Nyns ov gwerther da.

I a vynnas mos y'n eur na pan nag ens pes da gans ow hows.

Ny yllowgh gwari peldroes y'n pras na.

Ni a gar hwedhel didhanus.

Py liw yw an sethow na?

Melyn yns.

Ny welyn an baner kernewek a-ugh tour an eglos y'n dre ma.

What did he hold in his hand?

Show it to me, please!

Are there any goats in the field? Yes!

How many? Four goats.

What time was it when she came home?

Ten minutes after six.

Put coal on the fire. It's cold.

He has much money.

He's rich.

This is not the same bag as the first one.

I want to ascend that high hill.

I am not a good salesman.

They wished to go then when they were not pleased with what I said.

You cannot play football in that field.

We love an amusing story.

What colour are those jars?

They are yellow.

We do not see the Cornish flag above the church tower in this town.

32 PY DYDH YW EV? - *WHAT DAY IS IT?*

The days of the week are:

Dy' Sul	*Sunday*	**Dy' Yow**	*Thursday*
Dy' Lun	*Monday*	**Dy' Gwener**	*Friday*
Dy' Meurth	*Tuesday*	**Dy' Sadorn**	*Saturday*
Dy' Mergher	*Wednesday*	**Dy'**	*is short for* **dydh**

The months of the year are:

mis Genver	*January*	**mis Gortheren**	*July*
mis Hwevrer	*February*	**mis Est**	*August*
mis Meurth	*March*	**mis Gwynngala**	*September*
mis Ebryl	*April*	**mis Hedra**	*October*
mis Me	*May*	**mis Du**	*November*
mis Metheven	*June*	**mis Kevardhu**	*December*

Dates are thus expressed:

an 1a a vis Meurth   *1st March*

an 24a a vis Kevardhu   *24th December*

The word for 'year' is **blydhen, blydhynyow** *f.*, so **an vlydhen** 'the year'.

An vlydhen yw mil, naw kans, pymthek ha peswar ugens
The year is one thousand, nine hundred and ninety-five

The four seasons are:

Gwenton	*Spring*	**Kynyav**	*Autumn*
Hav	*Summer*	**Gwav**	*Winter*

As ordinary nouns these are:

gwenton -yow *m,.* **hav -ow** *m,.* **kynyav -ow** *m.*, **gwav -ow** *m.*

GERVA

a-dreus dhe[2] *prep.*	*across, athwart*	**herwydh** *prep.*	*according to*
a-dro dhe[2] *prep.*	*about, concerning*	**kernewek** *adj.*	*Cornish*
a-dryv dhe[2] *prep.*	*behind*	**Kernewek** *m.*	*Cornish language*
arvor, -yow *m.*	*shore, coast*	**kroust** *m.*	*picnic meal, crib*
bloedh *m.*	*year of age*	**loer, -yow** *f.*	*moon*
bys, -yes *m.*	*finger*	**lytherva, -ow** *f.*	*post-office*
bys *prep.*	*until*	**lyverva, -ow** *f.*	*library*
bys vykken *adv.*	*for ever*	**rev, -ow** *f.*	*oar*
dalleth *m.*	*beginning*	**splann** *adj.*	*splendid, shining*
diwotti, -ow *m.*	*inn, pub*	**skwith** *adj.*	*tired*
fals *adj.*	*false*	**taves, -vosow** *m.*	*tongue, language*
genys *adj.*	*born*	**tir, -yow** *m.*	*land*
a veu genys	*was born*	**yagh** *adj.*	*healthy*

klyw-es (-as)	*hear, smell, sense in general*	**poen-ya (-yas)**	*run hard*
		rev-ya (-yas)	*row* (a boat)
pareus-i (-as)	*prepare*	**splann-a (-as)**	*shine*

Certain adverbial phrases can be converted into prepositional expressions by adding **dhe**[2]:

a-dreus	*adv.*	*across*	**a-dreus dhe'n avon**	*across the river*
			a-dreus dhedhi	*across it (f.)*
a-dro	*adv.*	*around*	**a-dro dhe'n chi**	*around the house*
			a-dro dhodho	*around it (m.)*
a-ji	*adv.*	*inside*	**a-ji dhe'n eglos**	*inside the church*
			a-ji dhedhi	*inside it (f.)*
a-ves	*adv.*	*outside*	**a-ves dhe'n karrji**	*outside the garage*
			a-ves dhodho	*outside it (m.)*

Other phrases govern the noun directly but pronouns through **dhe**[2]:

a-barth	*for the sake of*	**a-barth Jori**	*for George's sake*
		a-barth dhodho	*for his sake*
a-dal	*opposite*	**a-dal an chi**	*opposite the house*
		a-dal dhodho	*opposite it (m.)*
a-dryv	*behind*	**a-dryv an gwydh**	*behind the trees*
		a-dryv dhedha	*behind them*

117

| **a-hys** | *along* | **a-hys an treth** | *along the beach* |
| | | **a-hys dhodho** | *along it (m.)* |

Nouns ending with the suffix **-va** which gives the idea of the place where something is or where something happens, are always feminine and make a plural with **-ow**: **lytherva vras** (bras) 'a big post-office', **lythervaow bras** 'big post offices'.

DASWELES - *Review*

Mis Genver yw oer, mis Est yw poeth, dell vydh usys.	*January is cold, August is hot, usually.*
Yma deg dydh warn ugens yn mis Metheven hag unnek dydh warn ugens yn mis Gortheren.	*There are thirty days in June and thirty-one days in July.*
Henn yw unn jydh*(dydh) ha tri ugens warbarth.	*That is sixty-one days altogether.*
Yma tri mis yn Gwenton	*There are three months in Spring.*
Py dydh yw an pympes warn ugens a vis Kevardhu?	*What day is the twenty-fifth of December?*
Dy' Mergher yw an degves, dell dybav.	*Wednesday is the tenth, I think.*
Y'n vlydhen mil, naw kans ha pymp ha dew ugens Nessa Bresel an Norvys a dhiwedhas.	*In the year nineteen hundred and forty-five the Second World War ended.*
Py dydh yw ev hedhyw?	*What day is it today?*
Dy' Gwener an nownsegves a vis Genver y'n vlydhen mil, naw kans, pymthek ha peswar ugens yw.	*It is Friday the nineteenth of January in the year one thousand, nine hundred and ninety-five.*

*dydh, *day*; an jydh, *the day*; unn jydh *one day*; but **dew dhydh**, *two days*.

DASWELES KEMMYSKYS - *Miscellaneous Review*

Ow hwegron a oberas y'n karrji war y garr koth.	*My father-in-law worked in the garage on his old car.*
Y nith, Hylda, a glywas Bretonek kewsys yn Montroules.	*His niece, Hilda, heard Breton spoken in Morlaix.*
Dohajydh da dhywgh hwi oll.	*Good afternoon to you all.*

118

A vynnowgh hwi kewsel kernewek genen?	*Will you speak Cornish with us?*
An maw a dennas an lovan mes re wann o ev.	*The boy pulled the rope but he was too weak.*
Ny yll ev gul an ober na namoy.	*He cannot do that work any more.*
Ple'ma ow fluvennow, an huni dhu ha'n huni rudh?	*Where are my pens, the black one and the red one?*
Yma hwans dhymm a brena brithili.	*I wish to buy mackerel.*
Yth eson ow nesa dhe gres an dre.	*We are approaching the town centre.*

33 DA YW GANS ha DROG YW GANS -
APPROVAL and DISAPPROVAL

The phrases **da yw genev** and **drog yw genev** are widely used to convey approval and disapproval respectively.

Da yw genev redya	*I like to read*
Da yw gans Loveday kana	*Loveday likes to sing*
Da yw genes mires orth	*You like to watch*
an bellwolok	*the television*
Drog yw ganso eva gwin	*He doesn't like to drink wine*
Da yw gensi dybri boes da	*She likes to eat good food*
Da yw genen kerdhes	*We like to walk*
Da yw genowgh donsya	*You like to dance*
Drog yw gansa oberi y'n lowarth	*They do not like to work in the garden*

In all these expressions the leading elements are **da yw** 'it is good', **drog yw** 'it is bad'. The person who is expressing approval or disapproval is indicated by **gans** 'with'. **Gans** can be changed to show a particular person as in the examples.

The thing that pleases, the subject of the sentence, is expressed by a verbal noun, e.g. **kana** 'singing'. Notice that the English versions of these expression uses 'to' before the verbal noun. This is not translated in the Cornish, that is, we do not say *Da yw genev dhe dhonsya but **Da yw genev donsya**.

Negative and interrogative forms are freely used as in the examples below. Saying **drog yw gans**... is not quite the same as saying **nyns yw da**... which is a less definite way of expressing dislike.

Da yw genev neuvya	*I like swimming*
Da yw gans an fleghes gwari	*The children like to play*
Drog yw genev bos a-ves	*I don't like being out*
nosweyth	*at night*
Drog yw gans Loveday	*Loveday doesn't like*
dybri boes frynkek	*eating French food*
Nyns o da ganso gortos re bell	*He didn't like waiting too long*
	= He wasn't keen on waiting too long
Drog o ganso gortos re bell	*He disliked waiting too long*

120

There are a number of handy expressions which can be constructed in the same way. Use **gwell** for 'preferable', **kas** for 'hateful', **poes** ('heavy') for 'reluctant':

Gwell yw gans Jori kewsel Kernewek	*George prefers to speak Cornish*
Kas yw gans pubonan esedha re hir	*Everyone hates sitting too long*
Poes o gansa bos unnver gensi	*They were reluctant to agree with her*
Yw gwell genes jy kavoes dha dokyn lemmyn?	*Do you prefer to have your ticket now?*
Nyns o re boes gansa esedha rag aga the, dell hevel	*They weren't too reluctant to sit down for their tea, it seems*

Remember that the thing, action and so on which is pleasant or unpleasant, is the subject of the sentence, and is expressed by a verbal noun in most cases. **Gans** indicates the person involved.

GERVA

a-ves *adv.*	*outside*	**trigys** *adj.*	*settled, resident, occupying*
herwydh *prep.*	*according to*		
kas *m.*	*hate*	**tu, -yow** *m.*	*side, direction*
pellgowser, -ow *m.*	*telephone*	**unnver** *adj.*	*in agreement*
pellwolok *f.*	*television*	**usadow** *m.*	*use, usage*
pubonan *pron.*	*everyone*	**herwydh usadow**	*as usual*
pupprys *adv.*	*always*	**yet, -tow** *f.*	*gate*
rudhvelyn *adj.*	*orange*	**yndella** *adv.*	*thus*
taklow *pl.*	*things, gear*	**ystynnans, -ow** *m.*	*extension, appendix*
gorfenn-a (-as)	*finish*	**trig-a (-as)**	*live, dwell*
gwari (-as)	*play*	**ystynn-a (-as)**	*extend*
kerdh-es (-as)	*walk*		

DASWELES - *Review*

Da yw gans Maria gwari gensi, herwydh usadow.	Mary likes playing with her, usually.
Kas yw genev kerdhes tre hebos.	I hate walking home without you.
Gwell o genen bos unnver ganso.	We prefered agreeing with him.
Drog yw genen triga yn mes a'n dre.	We don't like living out of town.
Poes yw gansa poenya re bell.	They are reluctant to run too far.
Ystynn dha dhorn dhymm, da yw genev synsi dha dhorn.	Hold out your hand to me, I like to hold your hand.
Poes o gans an fleghes gwari a-ves pan wrug hi glaw mes da o gansa gul henna pan wra hi ergh.	The children were reluctant to play outside when it rained but they like to do that when it snows.

DASWELES KEMMYSKYS - *Miscellaneous Review*

Ev a ystynnas an pellgowser dhymm.	He handed me the telephone.
Gorr an taklow yn stevell arall, mar pleg!	Put the gear in another room, please!
An pympes stevell war an tu na yw agan chambour nyni.	The fifth room on that side is our bedroom.
An ystynnyans yw berrheans an lyver dien, dell hevel dhymm.	The supplement is an abridgement of the whole book, it seems to me.
Ass yw honna drog! Yet an lowarth, daras an chi ha'n fenestri yw rudhvelyn aga liw.	How bad that is! The garden gate, the door of the house and the windows are orange in colour.
Pubonan a warias y'n stret y'n eur na. Ny warisons y'n lowarth.	Everyone played in the street then. They did not play in the garden.
Yma anwoes warnowgh oll, dell glywav.	You all have a cold, I hear.
Chiow bras ha tus kevoethek a drig ynna.	Big houses and rich people live in them.
Pys e a wortos a-ves!	Ask him to wait outside.
An gath vyghan a warias yn-dann an gweli.	The little cat played under the bed.
Pan splann an loergann war an arvor a-dreus an mor kosel, ass yw hi teg!	When the full moon shines on the shore across the calm sea, how beautiful it is!

122

Mir orth an bellwolok! Yndella ty a yll dyski meur.

Watch the television! In that way you can learn much.

Talan a veu genys Dy' Yow an nessa warn ugens a vis Hedra y'n vlydhen mil, naw kans ha seytek. Seytek bloedh ha tri ugens o ev yn mil naw kans pymthek ha peswar ugens. Ev yw yagh hwath.

Talan was born on Thursday the twenty-second of October, nineteen hundred and seventeen. He was seventy-seven years old in nineteen hundred and ninety-five. He is still fit.

Hwedhel Agan Taves I

The Story of Our Language I

Y'n vlydhen mil hag eth kans nyns o agan taves kernewek byw. Nyns esa den ow klappya Kernewek, dell hevel.

Mes y'n vlydhen mil, naw kans pymthek ha peswar ugens yma tus ow klappya an keth yeth arta. Fatell yll homma bos gwir?

Yma a-dro dhe dhew kans blydhen ynter an dhiw vlydhen ma. Hwedhel agan taves yw hemma.

Da yw genen mos dhe dhalleth an dra ha ni a wra henna y'n rannow erell.

34 PERGHENNIETH - *POSSESSION*

Asking someone if they own something:

Eus karr dhis? *Have you a car?*

What is really being said in Cornish is 'Is there a car to you? and this is the pattern to use.

Eus chi dhis? *Have you a house?*

Eus ki dhis? *Have you a dog?*

To answer questions like this, say:

Eus! *There is! (= yes)*

adding if you like:

Yma karr dhymm *I have a car (= there is a car to me)*

Eus gerlyver dhis? *Have you a dictionary?*
Eus! Yma gerlyver dhymm *Yes! I have a dictionary*

All this can be put in the past:

Esa karr dhis? *Did you have a car?*

Word for word this is: *'Was there a car to you?'*

Reply:

Esa! *There was! (= yes)*

And add for emphasis:

Yth esa karr dhymm *I did have a car*

Esa sagh dhis? *Did you have a bag?*
Esa! Yth esa sagh dhymm *Yes! I did have a bag*

124

And of course this kind of question can be asked of other people:

Eus flogh dhedhi?	*Has she a child?*
Eus! Yma flogh dhedhi	*Yes! She has a child*
Esa kath dhedha?	*Did they have a cat?*
Esa! Yth esa kath dhedha	*Yes! They had a cat*

The question may merely be whether or not a person has something with them at the moment of speaking. In this case we use **gans** 'with' in place of **dhe** 'to'.

Eus ki ganso?	*Has he a dog with him?*
Eus! Yma ki ganso	*Yes! He has a dog with him*
Eus flogh gensi?	*Is there a child with her?*
Esa koweth genes?	*Did you have a friend with you?*
Esa! Yth esa koweth genev	*Yes! I had a friend with me*

It will have been noticed that in the questions asked so far, the question has been about an indefinite 'something': 'Has she a child?'.

By a slight change in words, by using the short form of **bos** in place of the long form, we can ask whether a particular, definite thing is the property of a person. We do this because the complement is regarded as being like an adjective:

Yw an bluvenn ma dhis?	*Is this pen yours?*
Word for word this is:	*Is this pen to you?*

The answer will be either:

Yw! An bluvenn yw dhymm	*It is (= yes). The pen is to me (= is mine)*

or:

Nag yw! Nyns yw an bluvenn dhymm	*It is not (= no). The pen is not to me (= is not mine)*

In speaking of the past the verb will change to **o** 'was'.

O an lyver dhe Yowann?   *Was the book John's?*

Word for word this is: *Was the book to John?*

The answer will be either:

O! An lyver o dhe Yowann   *Yes! It was John's book*

or

Nag o! Nyns o an lyver dhe   *No! The book was not John's*
Yowann

GERVA

ammeth *f.*	*agriculture*	**hogh, -es** *m.*	*pig*
bal, -yow *m.*	*mine*	**hyns, -yow** *m.*	*path*
bowji, -ow *m.*	*cowshed*	**igor** *adj.*	*open*
davas, deves *f.*	*sheep*	**kales** *adj.*	*hard*
dewweder *pl.*	*spectacles*	**kleudh, -yow** *m.*	*ditch*
dhe-ves *adv.*	*away* (motion)	**lent** *adj.*	*slow*
diwedh *m.*	*finish, end*	**medhyk, -ygyon** *m.*	*doctor*
esedhva, -ow *f.*	*sitting-room*	**melin, -yow** *f.*	*mill*
estyllenn, -ow *f.*	*shelf*	**nowodhow** *pl.*	*news*
fenten, -tynyow *f.*	*fountain, spring*	**pasti, -ow** *m.*	*pasty*
gerlyver, -vrow *m.*	*dictionary*	**perghenn, -ow** *m.*	*owner*
gover, -ow *m.*	*brook*	**pons, -yow** *m.*	*bridge*
gweli, -ow *m.*	*bed*	**rewl, -ow** *f.*	*rule*
gwlas, -ow *f.*	*country, land*	**rewler, -oryon** *m.*	*manager*
hager *adj.*	*ugly*	**skiber, -yow** *f.*	*barn*
heyl, -yow *m.*	*estuary*		

glan-he (-has)*	*clean*	**lamm-a (-as)**	*jump*
kell-i (kollas)	*lose*	**mag-a (-as)**	*rear, nourish*
kosk-a (-as)	*sleep*	**omglyw-es (-as)**	*feel, be aware*
kyrgh-es (-as)	*fetch*	**terr-i (torras)**	*break, pick*

126

* Many useful verbs are made from adjectives by adding a suffix **-he** to the adjective. The present future in these cases ends in **-ha** and the stress always falls on the syllable beginning with **-h**. Examples: **hir** adj. 'long'; **hirhav** 'I lengthen', **hirhydh** 'you lengthen', **hirha** 'he/she lengthens', **hirhyn** 'we lengthen', **hirhowgh** 'you lengthen', **hirhons** 'they lengthen'. The past tense is equally simple since the endings are the usual ones added to the syllable **-as-** in each person except the 1s and 3s: **hirhis** 'I lengthened', **hirhasys** 'you lengthened' **hirhas** 'he/she lengthened', **hirhasyn** 'we lengthened', **hirhasowgh** 'you lengthened', **hirhasons** 'they lengthened'. Again the syllable beginning with **-h-** takes the stress.

DASWELES - *Review*

Eus jynn-amontya dhis? Nag eus!	*Have you a computer? No!*
Eus kadoryow-bregh dhedhi? Eus!	*Has she got armchairs? Yes!*
Yma diw gador-vregh dhedhi.	*She has two armchairs.*
Nyns eus tigenn nowydh dhymm.	*I have not got a new wallet.*
Yma nebes pelyow dhe'n fleghes.	*The children have a few balls.*
Eus hanow dhe'n ki ma?	*Has this dog got a name?*
Esa le'ti dhe'n bargen-tir na?	*Had that farm a dairy?*
Nyns esa keow ledan dhe'n pras.	*The field did not have wide hedges.*
Eus esedhva vras dhe'n chi na?	*Has that house a large lounge?*
Eus! Yma onan pur vras dhodho.	*Yes! It has a large one.*
Eus kath gensi? Nag eus lemmyn.	*Has she a cat with her? Not now!*
Esa aga broder gansa?	*Did they have their brother with them?*
Yw an dhewweder ma dhis?	*Are these spectacles yours?*
Yns. I yw dhymm, meur ras.	*Yes. they are mine, thanks.*
Yw an wedrenn ma dhedhi? Yw!	*Is this her glass? Yes!*
A nyns yw an nessa karr dhe Vr Martyn?	*Isn't the next car Mr Martin's?*
Yw! Ev yw dhe Vr Martyn, dell dybav.	*Yes! It's Mr Martin's, I think.*
O an eskisyow dhedha? Ens!	*Were the shoes theirs? Yes!*
A nyns o an diwes na dhe Wella?	*Wasn't that Wella's drink?*
Nag o! Dhe Gerensa o.	*No! It was Karenza's.*
My a verrhas ow hows mes ny verrhasons aga hows ynsi.	*I cut short my speech but they did not cut short their speech.*

127

DASWELES KEMMYSKYS - *Miscellaneous Review*

Tasik! Tasik! Ottena! Ergh war an glesin!

Daddy! Daddy! Look! Snow on the lawn!

Aga chi yw gwerthys y'n eur ma.

Their house is sold now.

Dha weles Dy' Meurth martesen!

See you (on) Tuesday perhaps!

Niver an gorholyon y'n porth yw eth.

The number of ships in the harbour is eight.

Hedhyw yw an dewdhegves a vis Meurth, pennbloedh ow gwreg.

Today is the twelfth of March, my wife's birthday.

Ro dhymm an hoelan, mar pleg!

Give me the salt, please!

Ple'ma an gerlyver kernewek?

Where is the Cornish dictionary?

War drysa estyllenn an argh-lyvrow y'n esedhva yma, dell dybav.

On the third shelf of the bookcase in the lounge it is, I think.

Yth esa ke isel a-dal an chi.

There was a low hedge opposite the house.

Nyns esa tra arall a-dal dhodho.

There was nothing else opposite it.

Yth esa pastiow yeyn rag agan kroust. Bryntin!

There were cold pasties for our crib. Fine!

Yth esov ow mires orth an gorholyon ena.

I am looking at the ships there.

Hi a wiskas hy fows las.

She wore her blue dress.

Ny evav te na koffi herwydh usadow.

I don't drink tea or coffee usually.

Pan dhehwelydh tre, an teylu yw lowen.

When you return home, the family is happy.

Mona re gollas hy arghans.

Mona has lost her money.

An gath a gosk war an gweliow.

The cat sleeps on the beds.

Ena y lammas an vugh dres an ke.

Then the cow jumped over the hedge.

Mr Evans, an tiek, a vag deves ha hoghes.

Mr Evans, the farmer, breeds sheep and pigs.

Glanha an bord du ragov, mar pleg!

Clean the blackboard for me, please!

Ny gyrghsons aga thaklow gansa.

They did not bring their things with them.

An vodrep Me a dorras bleujennow yn hy lowarth.

Aunt May picked flowers in her garden.

Dowr an fenten a dhe'n gover.

The spring water goes to the brook.

Ny wra ev y hwel. Diek yw ev,

He does not do his work. He is lazy.

Ev yw diwedhes pupprys.

He is always late.

Ammeth yw tra vras yn Kernow.

Agriculture is a big affair in Cornwall.

35 OLL, NEBES po MANN - *ALL, A LITTLE or NOTHING*

OLL 'ALL'. The Cornish **oll** is used, in the main, in the same way as the English 'all'.

1. **Oll** can stand by itself as equivalent to a noun:

      Oll yw kellys   *All is lost*

2. **Oll** is connected to another word or words in a compound expression but there are some differences in the positioning of the corresponding words as between English and Cornish. Compare the expressions:

Oll an fleghes	*All (of) the children*
Oll ni or **Oll ahanan**	*All of us*
An dre oll	*The whole town*
Ragon ni oll	*For us all*
Hemma oll	*All this*

The grammatical distinction is that in the first set of Cornish statements the word **oll** is part of a possessive construction and in the second set it is in apposition to what precedes it.

Thus	**Oll an dus**	*All the people*
and	**An dus oll**	*The people, the whole lot*

Oll an dus a asas an
   kuntelles warbarth
	All the people left
	   the meeting together

Oll anedha a dreylyas
   a-dhistowgh
	All of them turned
	   straightaway

Oll ahanan a ganas
   y'n keur na
	All of us sang
	   in that choir

Kernowyon oll, keffrys
   koth ha yowynk
	Cornish people all, both
	   old and young

Meur ras dhywgh hwi oll	*Thank you all*

NEBES   'a few', 'a little', 'some' is used as follows:

1.   As a noun:

Nebes a lever yndella   *A few (people) say so*

2.   Before a noun in the plural to mean 'a few':

Nebes geryow yw gwella   *A few words are best*

3.   With the preposition **a**² and a pronominal ending:

Nebes ahanowgh hwi a vydh   *A few of you will be*
    dewisys   *chosen*

4.   Before a noun in the singular to mean 'a little':

Nebes leth yw gesys   *A little milk is left*

5.   With the preposition **a**² and a pronominal ending:

Nebes anodho o poder   *A little of it was rotten*

MANN *m*. 'nothing':

There are several ways of expressing the meaning 'none at all'.

1.   In a negative statement the noun is followed by the word **vydh** 'any' (= bydh) in this permanently mutated form:

Tra 'thing' + **vydh** = **travydh** 'anything'

The negative may be implied rather than explicitly stated:

Nyns eus karr vydh y'n fordh	*There is no car at all on the road*
A leveris ev travydh?	*Did he say anything?*
Ger vydh!	*(Not) a word*
A welsys jy an edhen na?	*Did you see that bird?*
Travydh!	*(I didn't see) anything!*

130

2. The word **mann** 'nothing' is used:

Ev a leveris mann   *He said nothing*

3   By making the statement negative and using the word **onan** 'one':

Ny dreylyas onan anedha   *Not one of them turned*
  a-dhistowgh   *straightaway*
Ny ganas onan ahanan   *None of us sang*
  y'n keur na   *in that choir*

COMPOSITION

To say that something is made of a certain material or to say that a specific number of a group is meant, the preposition **a**² 'of' is used:

Ev a welas ros a horn   *He saw a wheel of iron*
                                      (an iron wheel)
Yw an amari ma gwrys a   *Is this cupboard made of*
  brenn-derow?   *oak wood?*
Ugens a'n fleghes   *Twenty of the children*
  a wortas a-dhelergh   *waited behind*
Kans anedha a dhehwelis   *A hundred of them returned*

MORE PREPOSITIONS

The prepositions which have personal ending can be grouped according to the vowel which occurs in the ending of the first and second persons singular. This is most usually -o- as in the preposition **yn** 'in', 'on' (see Part 28).

Like **yn** are the following prepositions.

yn-dann²	'under'		
yn-dannov *under me*		**yn-dannon** *under us*	
yn-dannos *under you* (s)		**yn-dannowgh** *under you* (pl)	
yn-danno *under him/it*		**yn-danna** *under them*	
yn-danni *under her/it*			

131

	a-dhann[2]	'from under'	
a-dhannov	*from under me*	**a-dhannon**	*from under us*
a-dhannos	*from under you* (s)	**a-dhannowgh**	*from under you* (pl)
a-dhanno	*from under him/it*	**a-dhanna**	*from under them*
a-dhanni	*from under her/it*		

	a-ugh	'above'	
a-ughov	*above me*	**a-ughon**	*above us*
a-ughos	*above you* (s)	**a-ughowgh**	*above you* (pl)
a-ughto	*above him/it*	**a-ughta**	*above them*
a-ughti	*above her/it*		

Heb 'without' and **rag** 'for' also with **-o-** final, have been set out in Part 28, and **a-rag** 'in front of' is like **rag**.

Other prepositions in **-o-** are:

	ryb	'beside'	
rybov	*beside me*	**rybon**	*beside us*
rybos	*beside you* (s)	**rybowgh**	*beside you* (pl)
rybdho	*beside him/it*	**rybdha**	*beside them*
rybdhi	*beside her/it*		

	dres	'beyond', 'over'	
dresov	*beyond me*	**dreson**	*beyond us*
dresos	*beyond you* (s)	**dresowgh**	*beyond you* (pl)
dresto	*beyond him/it*	**dresta**	*beyond them*
dresti	*beyond her/it*		

	dre[2]	'through'	
dredhov	*through me*	**dredhon**	*through us*
dredhos	*through you* (s)	**dredhowgh**	*through you* (pl)
dredho	*through him/it*	**dredha**	*through them*
dredhi	*through her/it*		

	yntra/ynter	'between'	
yntredhov	*between me*	**yntredhon**	*between us*
yntredhos	*between you* (s)	**yntredhowgh**	*between you* (pl)
yntredho	*between him/it*	**yntredha**	*between them*
yntredhi	*between her/it*		

The prepositions **a²** 'of', 'from' and **war²** 'on' have been set out in Part 28 and have 1s. and 2s. endings in **-a-**. Like **war** are **diwar** and **a-dhiwar** 'from off'.

The prepositions **orth** 'at' and **diworth** 'from' have the same endings in **-i**. **Orth** is repeated here from Part 28 for ease of reference:

	orth	'at'	
orthiv	*at me*	**orthyn**	*at us*
orthis	*at you* (s)	**orthowgh**	*at you* (pl)
orto	*at him/it*	**orta**	*at them*
orti	*at her/it*		

	diworth	'from'	
diworthiv	*from me*	**diworthyn**	*from us*
diworthis	*from you* (s)	**diworthowgh**	*from you* (pl)
diworto	*from him/it*	**diworta**	*from them*
diworti	*from her/it*		

The prepositions **dhe²** 'to' and **gans** with have endings peculiar to themselves and have been set out in Part 28.

Some prepositions are made up of two parts. **Yn kever** 'about', 'regarding' is an example. It comes before a noun without mutation: **yn kever an hwedhel na** 'concerning that story'. If however it is to be followed by a pronoun, then the possessive adjectives are put before the second part of the preposition with any mutation which is appropriate: **yn ow hever, yn dha gever, yn y gever, yn hy hever, yn agan kever, yn agas kever, yn aga hever**, 'concerning me', etc. Other, similar, prepositions will be noted in the Vocabularies as they occur.

GERVA

a-barth dhe *prep.*	on behalf of	**howldrevel** *m.*	sunrise, the east
a-dhelergh *adv.*	behind, to the rear	**howlsedhes** *m.*	sunset, the west
a-dhistowgh *adv.*	immediately	**kalter, -yow** *f.*	kettle
distowgh *adv.*		**kansblydhen,**	century
a vydh	3s. of **bos** 'will be'	**-ynyow** *f.*	
ankor, -s *m.*	anchor	**leth** *m.*	milk
bedh, -ow *m.*	grave, tomb	**marow** *adj.*	dead
blew *coll.*	hair	**nown** *m.*	hunger
blewynn, -ow *m.*	a hair	**yma nown**	I am hungry
dans, dens *m.*	tooth	**dhymm**	
derwenn, -ow *f.*	an oak tree	**poder** *adj.*	rotten
dhe les	useful	**puber** *m.*	pepper
meur dhe les	very useful	**rewer, -oryon** *m.*	freezer
efan *adj.*	wide, spacious	**ros, -ow** *f.*	wheel
goel, -yow *m.*	sail	**skentel** *adj.*	clever
gols *coll.*	the hair of the head	**syghes** *m.*	thirst
		yma syghes	I am thirsty
govynn, -ow *m.*	question	**dhymm**	
gwrys *adj.*	made, done	**yeynell ,-ow** *f.*	refrigerator
gwynnrudh *adj.*	pink	**yn kever** *prep.*	about, regarding
bryj-on, bros	boil	**garm-a (-as)**	shout
(brojyas)		**goel-ya (-yas)**	sail
dri, dre (dros)	bring	**gorthyb-i (-is)**	answer
fisten-a (-as)	hurry	**govynn (-as)**	ask

DASWELES - *Review*

Ystynn dhymm nebes leth, mar pleg. Yma syghes dhymm.	*Pass me some milk, please. I'm thirsty.*
Oll ahanan a yll gorthybi dhe'n govynn na.	*All of us can answer that question.*
Oll an gerens (pl. of **kar**) yw marow lemmyn.	*All the near relations are dead now.*
Nebes a'n hynwyn yw kernewek, dell hevel.	*Some of the names are Cornish, it seems.*
A-barth oll ahanan, 'Meur ras!'	*On behalf of all of us, 'Thanks!'*
Yw oll ahanowgh parys?	*Are you all ready?*

134

Nyns eus denvydh omma kynth yw hi seyth eur lemmyn.	There's no one here although it's seven o'clock now.
Nyns yw onan ahanowgh krev lowr dhe sevel an men ma.	Not one of you is strong enough to lift this stone.
An pastiow da ma yw gwrys a vewin. An vamm a brenas an kig yn kikti Mr Ross, an kiger. Ev a werth an gwella bewin.	These good pasties are made of beef. Mother bought the meat in Mr. Ross' butcher's shop. He sells the best beef.
An bowjiow yw gwrys a brenn.	The cowsheds are made of wood.
An hwegynnow na o gwrys a sugra gwynnrudh	Those sweets were made of pink sugar.

DASWELES KEMMYSKYS - *Miscellaneous review*

Ass yns teg, pennow an menydhyow y'n howlsedhes, an howl rudh a-ughta.	How beautiful the tops of the mountains are in the sunset, the red sun above them.
Ny wonn konvedhes travydh yn y gever.	I don't understand anything about it.
Pandr'a leveris Maria yn kever Manow? Ny leveris hi ger yn hy hever.	What did Mary say about the Isle of Man? She didn't say a word about it.
An leth y'n badell a brojyas yn kettermyn ha'n dowr y'n galter.	The milk in the saucepan boiled at the same time as the water in the kettle.
Yma hwans dhymm a wovynn henna orth Jenefer po yn hy le nebonan arall.	I want to ask Jenifer that or in her place someone else.
An pyskador a dennas an ankor ha'n kok a woelyas a-dhistowgh.	The fisherman pulled the anchor and the boat sailed straight away.
I a balas kleudh down a-dro dhe'n park-kerri.	They dug a deep trench around the car park.
Fisten, fisten! Yma ergh ow tos!	Hurry, hurry! There's snow coming!
Piw a armas yndella?	Who shouted like that?
Kommol loes a dhre glaw.	Grey clouds bring rain.
Fatell o y worthyp? Ass o gokki!	How was his reply? How silly it was!
Ottomma! Ow gols. My re dennas diw vlewenn wynn diworto!	See here! My hair. I've pulled two white hairs from it!

135

Yowann a wovynnas orth an tiek, 'Py par gwydh yns i?' Ev a worthybis, 'Derow yns'.

John asked the farmer, 'What sort of trees are they?' He replied, 'They are oaks.'

Oll an fleghes a arm, 'Kernow bys vykken!' Pes da ov vy a henna.

All the children shout, 'Cornwall for ever!' I am pleased at that.

Yma peder ros dhe bub karr. Yma an pympes a-ji ynno.

Every car has four wheels. The fifth one is inside it.

Yma nown dhe'n vebyon (pl. mab). An vamm a vynn ri nebes boes dhedha. Mes eus boes lowr y'n yeynell? Eus. Yma meur a vara hag amanenn gesys hwath ynwedh.

The boys are hungry. Mother will give them some food. But is there enough food in the refrigerator? Yes! There is a lot of bread andbutter still left as well.

Esedh a-dhelergh, mar pleg. Nyns eus le gesys rybov.

Sit at the back, please. There's no place left beside me.

Ty a vydh meur dhe les omma owth oberi genen.

You will be very useful here working with us.

Hwedhel Agan Taves II
The Story of Our Language II

Yth esa unn yeth keltek kewsys yn Breten Veur kyns kres an pympes kansblydhen. Predennek kemmyn o an keth yeth na.

Ottomma nebes geryow keltek a'n termyn na gans aga far yn Kernewek kemmyn: *maros* - mor, *kadros* - kador, *dubros* dowr, *tigos* - ti/chi, *novijos* - nowydh, *monijos* - menydh, *roudos* - rudh, *devos* - dyw, *sindos* - an.

Haval yns orth agan geryow kernewek mes ty a yll gweles -*os* war benn an geryow koth ma.

Agan yeth nyni re gollas an -*os* kyns kres an hweghves kansblydhen. A'n termyn na ni a yll kewsel yn kever Kernewek koth, Bretonek koth ha Kembrek koth.

136

36 HA, KYNS HA WOSA - *WHILE, BEFORE and AFTER*

WHILE Although there is a word for 'while' in Cornish - **hedra** - it is much more usual to use the word for 'and' **ha** and the present participle construction as in this example:

Yth esen ow redya an paper-nowodhow ha my ow tybri

I was reading the newspaper while I was eating

which is literally 'and I eating'.

BEFORE AND AFTER   Two words most frequently used here are **kyns** 'before' and **wosa** 'after':

Golgh dha dhiwleuv kyns dybri dha voes!   *Wash your hands before eating your food*

Tas a gosk yn ta wosa oberi yn tiwysek   *Father sleeps well after working hard*

Kyns y vos dyskador, souder o   *Before he was a teacher he was a soldier*

Wosa agan gweles ev eth tre   *After seeing us he went home*

In the first two examples the words **kyns** 'before' and **wosa** 'after' are used with a verbal noun.

In the third example a possessive adjective, **y²** 'his', is used to give the meaning 'his being'.

In the last example a possessive adjective, **agan**, 'our', is used to give the literal meaning 'our seeing' and this is equivalent to the English 'seeing us'.

GERVA

a'y anvodh	*unwillingly, against his will*	**menydh, -yow** *m.*	*mountain*
a'y esedh	*he (is) seated*	**mogh** *pl.*	*pigs*
a'y sav	*he (is) standing*	**morthol, -ow** *m.*	*hammer*
a'y vodh	*willingly, with his agreement*	**pal, -yow** *f.*	*spade*
		pell *adj.*	*far*
		plos *adj.*	*dirty*
a'y wrowedh	*he (is) lying down*	**poll, -ow** *m.*	*pool, pit*
breus, -ow *m.*	*judgement, opinion*	**pow, -yow** *m.*	*country(side)*
		prysk *coll.*	*bushes*
bys vykken *adv.*	*for ever*	**pryskenn, -ow** *f.*	*bush*
diwleuv *dual*	*pair of hands*	**res yw**	*it is necessary*
diwysek *adj.*	*hard-working*	**rych** *adj.*	*rich*
dydhlyver, -vrow *m.*	*diary*	**serrys (orth)** *adj.*	*angry (with)*
euth *m.*	*terror, dread*	**soedh, -ow** *f.*	*work, office*
forn, -ow *f.*	*stove*	**soedhva, -ow** *f.*	*office* (place)
gwari, -ow *m.*	*game, play*	**soweth** *excl.*	*unfortunately*
gwithyas, gwithysi *m.*	*guardian*	**strel, -yow** *m.*	*mat, rug*
		Syllan *f.*	*Isles of Scilly*
gwithyas kres	*policeman*	**tamm, temmyn** *m.*	*piece, bit*
hal, -ow *f.*	*moor, marsh*	**tamm ha tamm**	*bit by bit*
hos, heyji *m.*	*duck*	**tasik** *m.*	*daddy*
kert, -ow *m.*	*lorry*	**tas-gwynn, tasow-wynn** *m.*	*grandfather*
keskows, -ow *m.*	*conversation*		
kornell, -ow *f.*	*corner*	**towlenn,-ow** *f.*	*programme, plan*
kweth, -ow *f.*	*cloth, garment*	**treweythyow** *adv.*	*sometimes*
lin, -yow *m.*	*line*	**tros, -yow** *m.*	*noise*
linenn, -ow *f.*	*line, thread*	**uvel** *adj.*	*humble*
lin *coll.*	*linen, flax*	**yeyn** *adj.*	*cold*
linenn, -ow *f.*	*a piece of linen, a flax plant*	**yowynk** *adj.*	*young*
		yn mysk *prep.*	*amongst* (like **yn kever**)
lynn, -ow *m.*	*lake*		

daskorr (-as)	return, restore	omwisk-a (-as)	dress oneself
dons-ya (-yas)	dance	omwolgh-i (-as)	wash oneself
gwith-a (-as)	guard	pleg-ya (-yas)	fold, bend,
jynnskrif-a (-as)	type		be pleasing to
keskews-el (-is)	converse	serr-i (sorras)	make/be angry,
liw-ya (-yas)	colour	serri orth	be angry with
meg-i (mogas)	smoke	tyl-i, tal (tylis)	pay, owe

DASWELES - *Review* (a + ow³ becomes a'm; a + y² becomes a'y²; ha + y² becomes ha'y² a + hy³ becomes a'y³ and ha + hy³ becomes ha'y³ ; a + aga³ becomes a'ga³ ; ha + aga³ becomes ha'ga³ and yn + aga³ becomes y'ga)

Yth esen a'm esedh hag i ow tonsya.	*I was sitting while they were dancing*
Yma Peder ow kolghi fos yn unn stevell ha'y wreg ow liwya fosow an stevell arall.	*Peter is washing a wall in one room while his wife is painting the walls of the other room.*
Yth esa an vamm a'y sav ha'n fleghes ow kwari.	*Mother was standing while the children were playing.*
Yma perghenn an boesti ow jynn- skrifa gans unn bys hag ev ow megi yn keth prys.	*The owner of the restaurant is typing with one finger while smoking at the same time.*
Yth esens i a'ga gorwedh y'ga gweli ha'n vamm ow pareusi aga hansel.	*They were lying in bed while mother was preparing their breakfast.*
Omwolgh ha my owth omwiska!	*Wash while I am dressing!*
Wosa redya an dowlenn my a geskewsis yn hy hever gans ow gour.	*After reading the programme I talked about it with my husband.*
An drehevyans o melin goth kyns y vos diwotti, herwydh y berghenn.	*The building was an old mill before it was a pub, according to its owner.*
Karol a lanhas an lestri kyns aga daskorr dhe'n lestrier.	*Carol cleaned the dishes before returning them to the dresser.*

DASWELES KEMMYSKYS - *Miscellaneous review* (y'gan = yn+agan; dh'y²/³ = dhe+y² *or* dhe+hy³)

An gewer yw hager war an heyl. Ny yll den gweles a-dreus dhodho.	*The weather is ugly on the estuary. A person cannot see across it.*
Mir orth an pons! Yma puskes y'n avon yn-danno.	*Look at the bridge! There are fish in the river under it.*

An hyns yw efan mes leun a dus yw ev.

Ke dhe-ves! Pur skwith ov.

Nevra ny vynn hi dehweles ha homm yw kales.

An tiek a dhros y vughes dhe'n skiber.

An rewler a worras an lytherow war an desk rybdho.

Yma euth dhymm. My a glywas tros ughel yn-mes y'n lowarth.

Ottena! A-dro dhe hanterkans hos war an lynn yn kres an hal.

Ymons i ow neuvya warbarth.

Res yw dhe Vr Richards mos dh'y soedhva pub dydh mes sowedh diwedhes yw ev treweythyow.

Ny welsons an kert orth an gornell.

Pow pell yw Ejyp ha tir bras yw ynwedh.

Usi an lytherva ogas dhe hel an dre? Usi!

An peswara drehevyans diworto yw ev a'n keth tu.

Goel Sen Pyran a vydh[a] pub blydhen dhe'n pympes a vis Meurth.

Tus pals a dhe'n eglos y'gan gwlas dhe'n jydh[b] na.

Ple'ma bedh Sen Pyran hedhyw? Piw a woer?

The road is wide but it is full of people.

Go away! I am very tired.

She will never wish to return and that is hard.

The farmer brought his cows to the barn.

The manager put the letters on the desk beside him.

I'm terrified. I heard a noise outside in the garden.

Look there! About fifty ducks on the lake in the middle of the moor.

They are swimming together.

Mr Richards must go to his office every day but unfortunately he is sometimes late.

They did not see the lorry at the corner.

Egypt is a distant country and it is large also.

Is the post office near the town hall? Yes!

It's the fourth building from it on the same side.

St Pyran's Day is on the fifth of March each year.

Many people go to church in our land on that day.

Where is St Pyran's grave today? Who knows?

---

[a] Note that the future tense of **bos**, **a vydh**, is also used to express an habitual action.

[b] The word **dydh** *m.* 'day' becomes **jydh** after an 'n' at the end of the previous word. So **an jydh** 'the day' and **unn jydh** 'one day'. The plural remains unchanged: **an dydhyow** 'the days'.

140

Hwedhel Agan Taves III

The Story of Our Language III

Wosa kelli pennow hy geryow *-os* ha re erell, an yeth Predennek koth a dreylyas hag yndella y sevis tamm ha tamm Kembrek koth ha Predennek koth a'n Howlsedhes.

Wosa mones tus pals a-dreus an mor yn kres an pympes kansblydhen hag arta orth penn an hweghves kansblydhen yth esa teyr rann a'n yeth Predennek koth.

Der an kansblydhynyow an teyr yeth a dheuth ha bos *(= became)* dihaval, Kembrek, Kernewek ha Bretonek.

Yma genen lyver ha'y hanow yn Latin yw *Vocabularium Cornicum,* henn yw Gerva Gernewek. Yma ynni lies ger a Gernewek koth ha rybdha aga far yn Latin.

Ottomma nebes ensamplow   anedha ha'ga *(ha'ga = ha+aga)* far yn Kernewek Kemmyn:

arluit	**arloedh**	*cuit*	**koes**
guirion	**gwiryon**	*diskient*	**diskians**
skuid	**skoes**	*menit*	**menydh**

An re nowydh re drelyas **-t** dhe **-dh** -po dhe **-s**, ha **-d** ha **-t** dhe **-s** ynwedh. An dhiw yeth arall, Kembrek ha Bretonek, re withas an lytherennow **-d** ha **-t** ma. Ty a wra gweles henna y'n nessa rann.

141

37 HEVELEBI TRAOW - *COMPARING THINGS;* DASWRIANS - *REPETITION*

Maria yw mar² hir avel Janet   *Mary is as tall as Janet*

In saying that two persons or things are equal in some respect, Cornish speakers use **mar²** for the first 'as' and **avel** for the second 'as'. The word **mar²**causes soft mutation. **Avel** does not cause mutation. (Remember however that **keth** 'same' is followed by **ha** and not by **avel**: **an keth ha** = *the same as*)

Avel can have personal endings just as some prepositions can. They are:

avelov	*as me*	**avelon**	*as us*
avelos	*as you* (s)	**avelowgh**	*as you* (pl)
avello	*as him/it*	**avella**	*as them*
avelli	*as her/it*		

Notice that the forms of the third person have **-ll-**.

If the second part of the comparison has a verb, then it is introduced by **dell²** 'as':

Nyns ov mar dha dell² o ev   *I am not as good as he was*

One person or thing may exceed another in some way. In English this is expressed by words like 'taller', 'shorter'.

Janet yw hirra es Lisa   *Janet is taller than Liza*

English adds the syllable '-er' to the adjective. In Cornish the same meaning is given by doubling the last consonant and adding **-a**. If the consonant is already double this remains.

Some final consonants are 'hardened' as well as being doubled, for example a final **-b** becomes **-pp-**, a final **-v** becomes **-ff-**. The vocabularies will give the comparative form of each adjective.

The second member of the comparison is introduced by the word **es** or **ages**. They have the same meaning, 'than'. There are personal endings to **es** and **ages** also.

(ag)esov	*than I*	(ag)eson	*than we*
(ag)esos	*than you* (s)	(ag)esowgh	*than you* (pl)
(ag)esso	*than he/it*	(ag)essa	*than they*
(ag)essi	*than she*		

Note that the forms of the third person have **-ss-**.

The words **moy** 'more' and **(an) moyha** are sometimes put before the adjective to make the comparison. This is necessarily so with awkward words like **a-varr** 'early', so **moy a-varr** 'earlier' and with past participles like **parys** 'ready', **an moyha parys** 'the most ready', **moy terrys** 'more broken'. In all other cases the regular comparative is preferable, e.g. **kernewekka** 'more Cornish'.

When the comparative adjective is used to denote the highest degree of the quality, it comes before its noun without any mutation.

Bronn Wennili yw an ughella
menydh yn Kernow

Brown Willy is the highest mountain in Cornwall

Some common adjectives have irregular comparison, just as in English.

da	*good*	gwell	*better*	**(an) gwella**	*(the) best*
drog	*bad*	gweth	*worse*	**(an) gwettha**	*(the) worst*
meur	*much, many*	moy	*more*	**(an) moyha**	*(the) most*
nebes	*little, few*	le	*less*	**(an) lyha**	*(the) least*
ogas	*near*	nes	*nearer*	**(an) nessa**	*(the) nearest*

DASWRIANS - *REPETITION*

In English the prefix 're-' can mean 'again' as in 're-do': 'I'll re-do the garden'. In Cornish the same meaning is given by prefixing **das²** or **as²** to a verb. **Das-** is more usual and mutates some letters as the vocabularies will show:

gul	*do, make*	**daswul**	*redo, remake*
leverel	*say*	**dasleverel**	*say again*

143

GERVA

a-wosa *adv.*	*afterwards*	kepar ha	*like, just as* (with
a'n par ma/na	*of this/that kind*		*noun/pronoun)*
bys (yn/dhe²) *prep.*	*up to*	kepar ha dell²	*just as* (with verb)
den bal, .	*miner*	krow, -yow *m.*	*hut*
tus bal *m*		medhyk, -ygyon *m.*	*doctor*
dihwans *adv.*	*eagerly*	mil, -yow *m.*	*thousand*
edhen, ydhyn *f.*	*bird*	milvil, -yow *m.*	*million*
gwivrenn, -ow *f.*	*wire*	mowes, -i *f.*	*girl*
hware *adv.*	*suddenly*	our, -yow *m.*	*hour* (duration)
kelorn, kelern *f.*	*bucket*	res yw	*it is necessary*

adj.	comp. adj.		adj.	comp. adj.	
brav	braffa	*finer*	koth	kottha	*older*
bryntin	bryntinna	*finer*	krev	kreffa	*stronger*
byghan	byghanna	*smaller*	kul	kulla	*narrower*
diwedh	diwettha	*later*	lowen	lowenna	*happier*
es	esya	*easier*	nowydh	nowyttha	*newer*
feusik	feusikka	*luckier*	oer	oerra	*colder*
fol	folla	*more foolish*	poeth	poettha	*hotter*
glan	glanna	*cleaner*	salow	salwa	*safer*
glyb	glyppa	*wetter*	skav	skaffa	*lighter*
hweg	hwekka	*sweeter*	trist	trista	*sadder*
isel	isella	*lower*	ughel	ughella	*higher*

The common word **tre** which was formerly **trev**, has the original meaning 'farmstead', 'settlement'. It now means either 'home' or 'town'. These are differentiated thus:-

HOME	**tre** or **yn tre** at home	**dhe-dre** homewards,	**a-dre** from home
TOWN	**y'n dre** in town	**dhe'n dre** to town	**a'n dre** from town

The word **kyn⁵** 'though' comes before a verb. If the verb starts with a vowel or with **h-**, then **kyn** becomes **kynth**:

Kyn hwelas an lyther, ny redyas ger anodho
Though he saw the letter, he did not read a word of it
Kynth o an gewer toemm, nyns eth hi dhe'n dre mes gortos tre
Though the weather was hot, she did not go to town but stayed home

diskwedh-es (-as)	*show*	goslow-es (-as) (orth)	*listen (to)*
diwisk-a (-as)	*undress*	gwesk-el (-is)	*strike*
doen, deg, dug	*bring, carry*	kar-a (-as)	*love*
dysk-i (-as) (dhe)	*teach (to)*	nij-a (-as)	*fly*
dysk-i (-as) (gans)	*learn (with, from)*	sen-i (sonas)	*ring, sound*
		syw-ya (-yas)	*follow*

DASWELES - *Review*

An re ma yw mar dha avel hemma, dell glywav.	*These are as good as this, I hear.*
Nyns yw an wivrenn mar hir avel an huni arall.	*The wire is not as long as the other one.*
Bys dhe'n eur ma nyns yw an gewer mar lyb dell o hi de.	*Until now the weather is not as wet as it was yesterday.*
Nyns ov mar dhrog avella, dell dybav.	*I am not as bad as they, I think.*
Yw Margh mar drist dell o ev Dy' Sul?	*Is Mark as sad as he was (on) Sunday?*
Hware yth omglywis mar lowen avel edhen.	*Suddenly I felt as happy as a bird.*
A nyns yw hy chi mar vyghan avel krow den bal?	*Isn't her house as small as a miner's hut?*
Puptra a vydh mar salow avel chi pronter.	*Everything will be as safe as a parson's house.*
Nyns on ni mar feusik avelli.	*We are not as lucky as her.*
Na gows mar fol!	*Don't talk so foolishly!*
Lowena o mar skav avelov ow tonsya.	*Lowena was as nimble as me (at) dancing.*
Dell glywav, an korev na yw kepar ha dowr toemm.	*As I hear, that beer is like warm water.*
Esta mar oer dell leverydh?	*Were you as cold as you say?*
Mar es yw dyski Kernewek avel dyski ken yeth.	*It's as easy to learn Cornish as to learn any language.*
Dew our diwettha o pan dheuth hi.	*It was two hours later when she came.*
Milvil yw moy es naw kans mil a gans mil.	*A million is more than nine hundred thousand by a hundred thousand.*
Yw korev a'n par na kreffa ages gwin?	*Is beer of that sort stronger than wine?*

Kolan a boenyas dihwans dh'y vamm mes lenta o es y hwoer.	Colin ran hard to his mother but he was slower than his sister.
Pandra! An gewer yw braffa lemmyn.	What! The weather is finer now.
Y'n Gwenton an eythin yw hwekka es dell yns i y'n Gwav	In the Spring the gorse is sweeter than it is in winter.

(Note that **eythin** is collective and is treated as a plural, hence **yns**)

Nyns yw an vebyon hirra ages aga hwerydh.	The boys are not taller than their sisters.
Hy gour o poessa agessi.	Her husband was heavier than she.
Keur an chapel yw brassa es keur eglos an blu martesen.	The chapel choir is bigger than the choir of the parish perhaps.
Py lies den yw furra ages Seleven?	How many people are wiser than Solomon?
Esedh orth an tan! Ty a vydh toemma ena.	Sit at the fire. You will be warmer there.
Py par ydhyn a nij ughella ages an kommol?	What kind of birds fly higher than the clouds?
Roger yw moy bysi es y goweth, Les.	Roger is busier than his friend, Les.
An dra ma yw an gwettha oll	This affair is the worst (of) all.
A nyns yw an lew an kreffa enyval y'n norvys?	Is not the lion the strongest animal in the world?
An brassa stevell yw an nessa stevell dhe'n wolghva.	The biggest room is the nearest room to the bathroom.
Gwari peldroes. Henn yw an gwella gwari!	Playing football. That is the best game.
Nag yw! Gwari rygbi yw gwell es gwari peldroes.	No! Playing rugby is better than playing football.
An tewa dyenn a vydh pup-prys melyn, mar velyn avel amanenn.	The thickest cream is always yellow, as yellow as butter.
Dr Treven o an furra medhyk y'n dre. Nyns esa medhyk furra agesso yn mysk an vedhygyon erell.	Dr Tremayne was the wisest doctor in the town. There was no doctor wiser than he amongst the other doctors.

DASWELES KEMMYSKYS - *Miscellaneous Review*

Yma hwans dhymm a wortos ow gwreg yn gorsav an kyttrin.	*I want to wait for my wife in the bus station.*
Puskes a neuv yn dowrow an avon ha'n mor.	*Fish swim in the waters of the river and the sea.*
Res yw dhe bubonan sywya an keth fordh ha'n huni gyns.	*Everyone must follow the same course as the one before.*
Kynth o an galter leun a dhowr bryjys, nyns esa lowr rag peswar hanafas a de.	*Although the kettle was full of boiled water, there was not enough for four cups of tea.*
Kyn hwra an eseli aga ober, nyns yw ev da gans peub anedha.	*Though the members do their work, not all of them are satisfied with it.*
Yth esen vy y'n dre hag a-wosa yn tre arta.	*I was in town and afterwards at home again.*
Yma an vamm ow tiwiska an yowynka flogh.	*Mother is undressing the youngest child.*
Henri a vynn esedha war an isella kador.	*Henry will sit on the lowest chair.*
Ny yll ev esedha war an ughella huni.	*He cannot sit on the highest one.*
An skoloryon, mebyon ha mowesi, a dhe'n keth skol y'n dre.	*The schoolchildren, boys and girls, go to the same school in town.*

38 Y WERES - *HELPING HIM*

Perl a wrug gweres an maw *Pearl helped the boy*
Perl a wrug y weres *Pearl helped him*

In this last statement the pronoun **y** 'his' takes the place of the noun **maw** in the first statement. When auxiliary verbs are used in a periphrastic sentence (see Glossary) the pronoun objects, 'me', 'you', 'him', 'her', 'us', 'you' 'them' become in Cornish the possessive pronouns 'my', 'your', 'his', 'her', 'our', 'your', 'their' before the verbal noun, so that the sentence given as an example is, word for word, 'Pearl did his helping'. These possessive adjectives cause mutations as described in Part 24.

Peder a wrug ow gweles	*Peter saw me*
Hi a vynn dha glywes (klywes)	*She will hear you*
Lowena a yll y skrifa	*Lowena can write it* (m.)
My a wra hy hudha (kudha)	*I shall hide it* (f.)
Yowann a vynnas agan toella	*John wished to deceive us*
Nebonan a wrug agas herdhya	*Someone pushed you*
Hwi a allas aga frena (prena)	*You were able to buy them*
Ny wrug Maria aga gweles ena	*Mary didn't see them there*

If the sentence is a question introduced by **piw**, **py**, **pyth**, **pandra**, etc., then the construction is as above:

Piw a vynn ow gweres?	*Who will help me?*
Py flogh a wra y dhyski?	*Which child will learn it?*
Pyth a wra y lanhe?	*What cleans it?*
Pandr'a yll y dhaskorr?	*What can return it?*

When these words denote the object, then the possessive adjective must still be used:

Piw a vynn'ta y weles?	*Whom will you see?*
Py chi a wrug Mr Potter y brena?	*What house did Mr Potter buy?*
Pandr'a yllons i y wul?	*What can they do?*

148

CONTRACTED FORMS OF THE POSSESSIVE ADJECTIVES

Certain possessive adjectives combine with **a²** 'of', **dhe²** 'to', **ha** 'and', **yn** 'in'. Several examples have occurred in the Reviews.

		my	*your* (s)	*his/its*	*her/its*	*our*	*your* (pl)	*their*
		'm (ow)	**'th⁵** (dha)	**y²**	**hy³**	**agan**	**agas**	**aga³**
a	*of*	**a'm**	**a'th⁵**	**a'y²**	**a'y³**	**a'gan**	**a'gas**	**a'ga³**
dhe	*to*	**dhe'm**	**dhe'th⁵**	**dh'y²**	**dh'y³**	**dh'agan**	**dh'agas**	**dh'aga³**
ha	*and*	**ha'm**	**ha'th⁵**	**ha'y²**	**ha'y³**	**ha'gan**	**ha'gas**	**ha'ga³**
yn	*in*	**y'm**	**y'th⁵**	**yn y²**	**yn hy³**	**y'gan**	**y'gas**	**y'ga³**

There is no mutation after **'m** as there is after its equivalent **ow**.

The form **th⁵** is followed by the fifth, mixed mutation:

b > v   d > t   g > h   go > wo   gro > wro   gru > wru   gw > w   m > v

(See also the table on page v.)

In the third person note that masculine and feminine forms appear to be the same in several cases but the mutations will distinguish them, e.g. **dh'y²** **das** 'to his father' but **dh'y³** **thas** 'to her father'.

There is no mutation after **agan** and **agas** but the normal 'breathed' mutation after **aga³**.

A possessive adjective is repeated before each noun to which it refers:
I yw ow mamm ha'm tas   *They are my mother and my father*

CONSECUTIVE ACTIONS

In the English statement

Pam came into the room and sat down and read a book

three actions are named as being performed one after another by the same person. The Cornish equivalent is:

Pam a dheuth y'n stevell hag esedha ha redya lyver

You will notice that the Cornish uses a verbal noun for the second and third actions, the person and tense having been shown by the first, inflected verb, **a dheuth**.

This is only done when the statement is affirmative, when the same person is involved and when there is no change of tense indicated. If there are such changes or if the actions are to be separately emphasised, then the subsequent actions must indicate this by use of inflected verbs. The conjunction is usually **ha(g)** but others occur e.g. **mes** 'but', **po** 'or'.

Consecutive actions linked:
> **Pam a dheuth y'n stevell hag esedha ha redya lyver**
> *Pam came into the room (and) sat down and read a book*

Consecutive actions separately emphasised:
> **Pam a dheuth y'n stevell hag a esedhas hag a redyas lyver**
> *Pam came into the room and sat down and read a book*

or **Pam a dheuth y'n stevell ha hi a esedhas ha hi a redyas lyver**
> *Pam came into the room and she sat down and she read a book*

Negative statement:
> **Pam a dheuth y'n stevell mes ny redyas hi lyver**
> *Pam came into the room but she did not read a book*

Consecutive actions with a change of tense:
> **Pam a dheuth y'n stevell hag yma hi ena hwath**
> *Pam came into the room and she is still there*

Consecutive actions with a change of person:
> **Pam a dheuth y'n stevell ha my a gewsis orti**
> *Pam came into the room and I spoke to her*

GERVA

bywnans, -ow *m.*	*life*	**mernans** *m.*	*death*
dasserghyans *m.*	*revival*	**sans, sens** *m.*	*saint*
gradh, -ow *m.*	*step, grade*	**sebon** *m.*	*soap*
gwari, -ow *m.*	*stage play*	**skeul, -yow** *f.*	*ladder*
heskenn, -ow *f.*	*saw*	**skubell, -ow** *f.*	*brush*
lugarn, lugern *m.*	*lamp*	**tansys, -yow** *m.*	*bonfire*
medhel *adj.*	*soft*	**tassans** *m.*	*patron saint*

byw-a (-as)	*live*	merw-el, merow (-is)	*die*
dassergh-i (-as)	*revive*	minhwerth-in	*smile*
drehev-el (-is)	*build, raise*	(minhwarthas)	
herdh-ya (-yas)	*push*	pes-ya, pys (-yas)	*continue*
hwerth-in	*laugh*	prev-i (provas)	*prove, test*
(hwarthas)		skub-a (-as)	*sweep*
hwil-as, hwila (-as)	*look for, try*	toell-a (-as)	*deceive*
kav-oes, kyv (-as)	*have, get*	tregh-i (troghas)	*cut*
kudh-a (-as)	*hide*		

DASWELES - *Review*

Plema'n boes, mar pleg? Meg a
  wra y bareusi.
*Where is the food, please? Meg is
  going to prepare it.*

Ny allav y drelya yn Sowsnek.
I can't translate it into English.

Piw a yll aga dannvon dhodho
  dh'aga frevi.
*Who can send them to him to test
  them?*

Ni a vynn y dhiwedha a-dhistowgh.
We will finish it straightaway.

Kemmer an wedrenn arta. Ny
  wrug Jenni hy lenwel a win.
*Take the glass again. Jenny didn't fill
  it with wine.*

A wre'ta agan aswonn? Drog yw
  genev! Ny wrav agas aswonn.
*Do you know us? Sorry! I don't know
  you.*

Ottomma an selsigennow
  ma! Re goth yns, sur.
  Piw a vynn aga
  dybri lemmyn?
*Look here, these sausages!
  They are too old, surely.
  Who will eat them
  now?*

A wra an venyn na ow hara? Ny
  wonn! Ny wonn!
*Does that woman love me? I don't
  know! I don't know!*

Pubonan a synsis an lovan ha'y
  thenna.
Everyone held the rope and pulled it.

Yma an tas ow palas y'n lowarth.
  Piw a vynn y weres?
*Father is digging in the garden. Who
  will help him?*

151

DASWELES KEMMYSKYS - *Miscellaneous Review*

Meur a draow yw gwerthys.

An awel o krev. Ny allas an gorholyon dos ogas dhe'n porth.

An tasow-wynn a esedhas warbarth yn-mes a'n diwotti ha klappya.

Yma an gath a'y growedh war an leur yn-dann an gador y'n esedhva.

Eus arghans lowr y'n arghantti rag prena karr nowydh?

Eus arghans lowr dhyn ynno?

Noy Mr Stevens yw moen ha'y nith yw tew.

Ro dhedhi hy eskisyow gell, mar pleg.

Dhe by eur yth yw an tren dhe Loundres an dohajydh ma?

Yma tren skav dhe dhiw eur marnas teyr mynysenn warn ugens.

Otta! An lavrek ma yw re verr ragov.

Res yw dhis prena lavrek nowydh ytho.

Yth esa syghes bras dhymmo vy hag yth evis gwedrennas a gorev a-dhistowgh.

Nebes podigow yw terrys, re erell yw plos. Ny yll den eva leth anedha.

Usi an amaris orth an fos? Ymons!

Nyns eus gesys kestenenn y'n koes, dell dybav.

Martesen onan goth hepken.

Syns dornla an daras ha trel e!

Many things are sold.

The wind was strong. The ships couldn't come near to the harbour.

The grandfathers sat together outside the pub and chatted.

The cat is lying on the floor under the chair in the sitting room.

Is there enough money in the bank to buy a new car?

Have we enough money in it?

Mr Stevens's nephew is slim and his niece is fat.

Give her her brown shoes, please.

At what time is the train to London this afternoon?

There is a fast train at twenty-three minutes to two.

Look! These trousers are too short for me.

You must buy new trousers then.

I had a great thirst and I drank a glassful of beer straightaway.

Some jugs are broken, others are dirty. No one can drink milk from them.

Are the cupboards against the wall? Yes!

There isn't a chestnut tree left in the wood, I think.

Perhaps an old one only.

Catch hold of the door handle and turn it!

152

Py lies mildir yw an fordh dhe Druru a Essa? | How many miles is the road to Truro from Saltash?

Kanow agan bro yw hwekka ages kanow broyow erell. | The songs of our land are sweeter than the songs of other lands.

Ni a dhybris li. Ena ni a gerdhas. Kerdh hir o dhe'n kerrek war an hal | We ate lunch. Then we walked. It was a long walk to the rocks on the moor.

Lost aga hi yw shyndys. | Their dog's tail is injured.

Poes o genen pysi Martyn a weres gans an hwel mes da o ganso agan gweres. | We were reluctant to ask Martin to help us with the work but he was glad to help us.

Golgh an badell vras kyns hy gorra yn amari an gegin. | Wash the big saucepan before putting it in the kitchen cupboard.

Jen a skubas strel daras an chi gans skubell gales ha strel an esedhva gans skubell vedhel. | Jane swept the door mat of the house with a hard brush and the lounge mat with a soft brush.

Ewnter Frank a droghas skorrennow gans heskenn hag ev a wrug aga gorra war an tansys yn y lowarth. | Uncle Frank cut branches with a saw and he put them on a bonfire in his garden.

An gwithyas-kres a yskynnas an skeul bys dhe fenester an ughella chambour. | The policeman went up the ladder as far as the window of the highest bedroom.

Na hwarth! My re gollas an sebon y'n dowr. Res yw dhymm y hwilas. | Don't laugh! I have lost the soap in the water. I must look for it.

Fatell yll hi bywa heb pellgowser yn hy chi? | How can she live without a telephone in her house?

An vamm-wynn re verwis a-dhistowgh. | Grandmother has died suddenly.

Wosa li y kevis vy pal ha mos yn-mes dhe balas y'n lowarth a-rag an chi. | After lunch I got a spade and went out to dig in the front garden.

153

Hwedhel Agan Taves IV

The Story of Our Language IV

Ni re gollas meur a'gan yeth. Martesen yma folennow koth a lyvrow koth yn lyverva. Yn lyverva an Vatikan martesen!

An Gernowyon goth a skrifas oberow pals, gwariow, yn ensampel.

Mes yma nebes oberow gesys dhyn hwath. Yma dhyn dew wari a'n oesow kres ha bardhonieth ynwedh. Yma tri gwari yn-dann hanow **An Ordinale**.

An kynsa gwari anedha yw *Origo Mundi*, hemm yw dalleth an bys, an nessa yw *Passio Domini*, hemm yw mernans Krist, ha'n trysa, *Resurrexio Domini*, hemm yw dasserghyans Krist.

Yma ynwedh gwari, **Bywnans Meriasek**. Meriasek yw tassans Kammbronn ha lemmyn yma genen **Bywnans Ke,** nowydh kevkys.

An bardhonieth yw Passhyon Agan Arloedh, hemm yw mernans ha dasserghyans Krist.

39 AN ACHESON - *THE REASON WHY*

The phrase which is usually used to begin the question 'why' is **prag y**[5] which causes fifth state mutation and is followed by a verb. Before a vowel **y** becomes **yth**. Examples 1 and 2:

1.	**Prag y harmas** (garma) **ev?**	*Why did he shout?*
2.	**Prag yth evas hi an te**	*Why did she drink the tea*
	toeth da?	*very quickly?*

The reason why is introduced either by **drefenn** 'because' and the verbal noun **bos** 'to be' with a possessive adjective before it (Example 3), or by a noun in the possessive construction after it (Example 4). You have already met this construction with **kyns** ha **wosa** in Part 36.

3.	**Prag y trigas Mighal tre?**	*Why did Michael stay home?*
	Drefenn y vos skwith	*Because he was tired*
4.	**Drefenn bos y wreg klav**	*Because his wife was ill*

Alternatively, to emphasise the subject, it may be put first and joined to the verbal noun by **dhe**[2] 'to'. Examples 5 and 6:

5.	**Drefenn ev dhe vos skwith**	*Because he was tired*
6.	**Drefenn y wreg dhe vos klav**	*Because his wife was ill*

If a verb other than **bos** is required in the reply, then the construction with **dhe**[2] is used. Example:

7.	**Drefenn ev dhe weres y**	*Because he helped his*
	wreg ow kolghi an lestri	*wife to wash the dishes*

The statements which provide these answers are 'open' in that there is nothing to indicate at what time the action occured. This has to be taken from the context. Example 7 could equally well be interpreted in another context as 'because he is helping' or 'will help'.

The question 'why not' is introduced by the phrase **prag na**[2] followed by an inflected verb. Example 8:

8   **Prag na vynnydh jy**
     gortos penn an gwari?
     Drefenn ow bos helergh
     ow tehweles tre

Why don't you wait for
*   the end of the play?*
Because of my being late
*   returning home*
*   (= I will be late)*

A negative answer is given by **drefenn na²** with an inflected verb.
Example 9:

9.   **Drefenn na² vynnav gortos**   *Because I don't want to wait*
      mar hir   *so long*

GERVA

alemma *adv.*	*from here/ now*	**ker,** *adj.* **kerra**	*dear, dearer*
alena *adv.*	*from there/then*		(both senses)
anfur *adj.*	*unwise*	**Kerneweger,**	*Cornish speaker*
anfurra	*more unwise*	**-oryon** *m.*	
apposyans, -ow *m.*	*examination*	**kert, -ow** *m.*	*lorry*
baban, -es *m.*	*baby*	**kloes, -yow** *f.*	*rack*
bardhonieth *m.*	*poetry*	**kons, -yow** *m.*	*pavement*
dargan, -ow *f.*	*forecast*	**kost, -ow** *m.*	*cost*
difun *adj.*	*awake*	**kowrvargh,**	*camel*
diwros, -ow *f.*	*bicycle*	**kowrvergh** m.	
furv, -ow *f.*	*shape, form*	**lows** *adj.* **lowsa**	*loose looser*
fyrfa *adj.*	*firmer*	**lywyer, -yoryon** *m.*	*driver*
fyrv	*firm*	**managh, menegh** *m.*	*monk*
ganow, -ow *m.*	*mouth*	**managhti, -ow** *m.*	*monastery*
garth-gwari,	*playground*	**olifans, -es** *m.*	*elephant*
garthow-g. *m.*		**ranndir, -yow** *m.*	*region, district*
gorher, -yow *m.*	*cover*	**seulabrys** *adv.*	*formerly*
gwas, gwesyon *m.*	*fellow*	**sewen** *adj.*	*successful*
gweythva, -ow *f.*	*factory*	**sewenna**	*more successful*
hegar (orth) *adj.*	*well disposed (to)*	**souder, -oryon** *m.*	*soldier*
hegarra	*better disposed*	**soweth** *interj.*	*alas*
helergh *adj.*	*late*	**taksi, -s** *m.*	*taxi*
jynn-ebrenn, *m.*	*aeroplane*	**toeth da**	*quickly*
jynnow-ebrenn		**trigva, -ow** *f.*	*address*
kamera, -s *m.*	*camera*	**tynn** *adj.*	*tight, intense*
kay, -ow *m.*	*quay, platform*	**tynna**	*more intense*

appos-ya (-yas)	*examine*	lesk-i (loskas)	*burn*
dargan-a (-as)	*forecast*	perth-i (porthas) kov a[2]	*remember*
gwayt-ya (-yas)	*expect*	sewen-i (-as)	*succeed, prosper*
hwarvos, hwer (hwarva)	*happen*	skoedh-ya (-yas)	*support*
kampoell-a (-as)	*mention*	tyb-i (-is)	*think*

Another preposition which, being made up of two parts, takes a possessive adjective as its object, is **warlergh** = **war** + **lergh** 'on the track of', 'behind', 'after'. So **war ow lergh** 'after, behind me', **war aga lergh** 'after, behind them', etc. It can be used as **wosa** is (Part 36): **warlergh hy bos omma genen** 'after she was here with us'.

DASWELES - *Review*

Prag y prenas Pol an korev?	*Why did Paul buy the beer?*
Drefenn ow bos heb arghans.	*Because I was without money.*
Prag y teuthons i ena?	*Why did they come then?*
Drefenn bos hwans dhedha a'gan gweles.	*Because they wanted to see us.*
Prag y targanas an gwas kewer deg hag yma hi ow kul glaw?	*Why did the fellow forecast fine weather and it's raining?*
Drefenn ev dhe vos gokki, sur.	*Because he was silly, certainly.*
Prag y hworfennowgh agas ober dhe beder eur pub Dy' Gwener?	*Why do you finish your work at four o'clock every Friday?*
Drefenn bos hwans dhyn a vones tre moy a-varr.	*Because we want to go home earlier.*
Prag y tybydh yndella?	*Why do you think so?*
Drefenn nag eus ken fordh dhe dybi.	*Because there is no other way to think.*
Prag nag esosta ow skoedhya dha goweth?	*Why are you not supporting your friend?*
Drefenn nag ov mar anfur dhe wul henna y'n prys ma.	*Because I am not so unwise (as) to do that this time.*
Prag y tregh ev an skorrennow na?	*Why does he cut those branches?*
Drefenn ev dh'aga leski war an tansys.	*Because he burns them on the bonfire.*
Prag na worr Hykka y basti y'n forn?	*Why doesn't Dick put his pasty in the oven?*
Drefenn ev dh'y dhybri yeyn.	*Because he eats it cold.*

DASWELES KEMMYSKYS - *Miscellaneous review*

Yma fleghes ow kwari yn garth-gwari an skol vyghan. Re anedha yw bysi. Yma re erell a'ga sav orth fos an keth skol.

There are children playing in the playground of the little school. Some of them are busy. Others are standing against the wall of the same school.

Prag yma an re ma ow sevel yndella? Martesen drefenn aga bos skwith. I re worfennas aga gwari ynsi.

*Why are these standing in this way? Perhaps because they are tired. They have finished **their** game.*

'Osta lywyer an karr ma, syrr?' yn medh an gwithyas kres.

'Are you the driver of this car, Sir?' the policeman said.

'Ov!' Mr Karn a worthybis. 'Pandr'a hwer?'

'I am!' Mr Carne replied. 'What's afoot?'

'Yma diwros war an fordh ena ha gour shyndys a'y wrowedh war an leur', an gwithyas kres a leveris. 'Res yw dhis gortos deg mynysenn, mar pleg. Ni a vynn y worra dhe'n klavji a-dhistowgh.'

'There's a bicycle on the road there and a man lying injured.' replied the policeman. 'You must wait ten minutes, please. We will take him to hospital immediately.'

'My a vynn agas skoedhya y'n dra ma,' Mr Karn a leveris. 'A allav vy agas gweres?'

'I will support you in that,' Mr Carne said. 'Can I help you?'

An glaw yw tynna es dell o de. Nyns o an dhargan gwir, my a dyb.

The rain is more intense than it was yesterday. The forecast was not true, I think.

Yma jynn-ebrenn ughel a-ugh an kommol. A yll'ta y glywes?

There's an aeroplane high above the clouds. Can you hear it?

Gallav mes ny allav y weles.

I can but I cannot see it.

Ro dhymm dha drygva ha'th hanow, mar pleg.

Give me your name and address, please.

Oll ahanowgh yw Kernewegoryon mes nebes ahanowgh yw gwell ages re erell.

All of you are Cornish speakers but some of you are better than others.

Igor gorher an badell! Pyth eus yn-danno?

Open the lid of the saucepan. What's beneath it?

Piw a appos an lywyoryon-taksi y'n ranndir ma?

Who examines the taxi drivers in this district?

158

Esowgh hwi ow kwaytya kerdh an olifanses ha'n kowrvergh ha'n enyvales erell dre gres an dre? Soweth, gyllys yns. I eth alemma seulabrys dhe deyr eur poran. Pan o Pamela difun, hi a wolghas an lestri ha'ga gorra y'n gloes.	*Are you waiting for the procession of the elephants and the other animals through the town centre? A pity, they are gone. They went from here at three o'clock exactly. When Pamela was awake, she washed the dishes and put them in the rack.*

Hwedhel Agan Taves V
The Story of Our Language V

My re gampoellas **An Ordinale**. Hemm yw gwari sans hag ynno yma tri gwari, onan rag pub dydh a dri dydh.

Piw a skrifas an gwariow ma? Ny wonn. Herwydh pub den skiansek neb managh yn Managhti Glasneth a wrug aga skrifa. Gyllys yw an managhti lemmyn. Nyns eus ena yn y le travydh marnas fosow isel. Yth esa an managhti ogas dhe Bennrynn.

Y'n dydhyow na tus pals o Kernewegoryon. A'n gwariow ma ni re gavas meur a'gan yeth. Ottomma ensampel diworth an kynsa gwari. Pan welas Faro tus Israel yn kres an Mor Rudh ev a leveris:

(Kernewek Kres)	(Kernewek Kemmyn)
My a vyn aga sywa	My a vynn aga sywya
dhe'n mernans aga gorra	dhe'n mernans aga gorra
kekyffrys byan ha bras	kekeffrys byghan ha bras.
Ny fynnaf, certan gasa	Ny vynnav sertan gasa
onan vyth ol the vewa	onan vydh oll dhe vywa.

Hemm yw studh an lavarow ha haval yns dh'agan lavarow dell yllydh gweles. A wodhesta konvedhes an bardhonieth ma?

159

SKEUL AN YETH - OBERENNOW
Oberennow rag Lyver 1
Exercises for Book 1

This booklet of exercises is intended to be used alongside the course book, **Skeul an Yeth**, and a cassette accompanies the exercises. It is recommended that each exercise should be used in the following way.

♦ The introductory explanation together with the examples is played.
♦ The first item is played and the 'pause' button applied while the student attempts an answer.
♦ The model answer is played and the 'pause' button is applied while the student repeats the model answer.
♦ The model answers are written down.

However the material may be used in any other way which suits the requirements of the student or the teacher.

RANN 1 KORTESI
Oberenn 1.1
Put the following greetings into Cornish, e.g.:
Hullo Yowann - how are you?
Fine thanks, and you?
Dydh da Yowann - fatla genes?
Yn poynt da, meur ras - ha ty?
Repeat the model answers:
1. *Good evening Patrick. Good evening Michael. This is Paul.*
2. *Good evening Paul. How are you?*
3. *Well enough, thanks.*
4. *Good night everybody.*
5. *Good night Mark.*
6. *Good-bye John.*
7. *Good bye everybody.*

RANN 2 BOSVA
Oberenn 2.1
Make statements by putting **yma** in place of **eus** in the following questions, e.g.:
Eus karrji ryb an chi?
Yma karrji ryb an chi.
Repeat the model answers:

1. Eus pluvek ena?
2. Eus eglos y'n le?
3. Eus karr a-ji an karrji?
4. Eus pluvenn ryb an lyver?

Oberenn 2.2
Make questions by putting **eus** in place of **yma** in the following statements, e.g.:
Yma leow gesys omma.
Eus leow gesys omma?
Repeat the model answers:
1. **Yma aval genes.**
2. **Yma jynn-skrifa ena.**
3. **Yma moes a-ji an chi.**
4. **Yma lyver gesys omma.**

Oberenn 2.3
Make a statement by putting **ottomma** before the following word, e.g.:
Eglos. Ottomma eglos.
Repeat the model answers:
1. **Karrji**   2. **Avalow**   3. **Moes**

Oberenn 2.4
Make a statement by putting **ottena** before the following word, e.g.:
Kador. Ottena kador.
Repeat the model answers:
1. **Lyver**   2. **Pluvek**   3. **Pluvennow**

RANN 3 DIBLANSNETH
Oberenn 3.1
Make the following words definite by putting **an** before them, e.g.:
Gweder. An gweder.
Repeat the model answers:
1. **Pras**   2. **Sinema**   3. **Lestrier**

Oberenn 3.2
Make the following feminine words definite by putting **an** before them, e.g.:
Kador-vregh. An gador-vregh.
Repeat the model answers:
1. **Leurlenn** 2. **Goen**   3. **Tesenn**

Oberenn 3.3
Change the meaning of the following phrases from 'this' to 'that', e.g.
An brithel ma.   **An brithel na.**
Repeat the model answers:
1. **An arr ma**

2. An vowes ma
3. An genter ma

RANN 4 ANDHIBLANSNETH
Oberenn 4.1
Put the following into Cornish, e.g.:
A mirror. **Gweder**
Repeat the model answers:
  1. A girl   2. A meadow 3. A stamp

Oberenn 4.2
Change the following phrases from meaning 'a something' to meaning 'a certain something', e.g. **lestrier. unn lestrier.**
Repeat the model answers:
  1. Pluvenn   2. Tesenn   3. Sinema

Oberenn 4.3
Complete the following sentences by translating the key word, e.g.:
Yma *someone* **ena. Yma neponan ena.**
Repeat the model answers:
  1. Eus *something* gesys?
  2. Eus *something* war an voes?
  3. Yma *someone* a-ji an karr.

RANN 5 HEVELEPTER
Oberenn 5.1
Make the following statements negative, e.g.
An drehevyans na yw ostel.
Nyns yw an drehevyans na ostel.
Repeat the model answers:
  1. An dra ma yw prenn, dell hevel.
  2. Honn yw Maria.
  3. An eglos ma yw bryntin.
  4. An re ma yw losow.

Oberenn 5.2
Reply to the following questions positively and then negatively, e.g.:
Yw hemma eythin? Yw/Nag yw.
Repeat the model answers:
  1. Yw hemma kenter?
  2. Yw an voes ma derow?
  3. Yw an diwes ma gwin frynkek?
  4. Yw an re ma mebyl?

Oberenn 5.3
Answer the questions by translating the key word, e.g.:
Pyth yw hemma? *(a pen)* **Pluvenn yw.**

Repeat the model answers:
  1. Pyth yw henna? *(a nail)*
  2. Pyth yw henna? *(a mirror)*
  3. Pyth yw henna? *(a church)*
  4. Pyth yw an re ma? *(apples)*

RANN 6 STUDH
Oberenn 6.1
Translate into Cornish, e.g.:
The pens are new.
An pluvennow yw nowydh.
Repeat the model answers:
  1. The church is old, I think.
  2. The things are ready, certainly.
  3. These children are lucky.
  4. The girl is happy now.
  5. The furniture is sold, it seems.
  6. This road is narrow.

Oberenn 6.2
Make these negative statements positive, e.g.:
Nyns yw hemma brav. Hemm yw brav.
Repeat the model answers:
  1. Nyns yw an maw ma fol.
  2. Nyns yw an losow ma byw.
  3. Nyns yw an den na gwann.
  4. Nyns yw an gegin kul.
  5. Nyns yw an avalow ma hweg.
  6. Nyns yw henna da.

Oberenn 6.3
Make these statements negative, e.g.:
An re ma yw parow.
Nyns yw an re ma parow.
Repeat the model answers:
  1. Honn yw Fiona.
  2. An drehevyans na yw Hel an Dre.
  3. An re na yw gwerthys.
  4. An gwin ma yw hweg.
  5. An gweder ma yw dhe les
  6. An jynn-skrifa yw parys lemmyn.

Oberenn 6.4
Translate the questions, e.g.:
Is that chair light? **Yw an gador na skav?**
Repeat the model answers:
  1. Is the wine ready?
  2. Is the furniture sold.
  3. Are the things useful?
  4. Is that person foolish?
  5. Is that building a church?

6. *Is the girl happy now?*

Oberenn 6.5
Make the following statements into negative questions, e.g.:
An fordh ryb an eglos yw kul.
A nyns yw an fordh ryb a eglos kul?
Repeat the model answers:
1. **An lyver ma yw dhe les.**
2. **Hel an Dre yw nowydh.**
3. **An vowes yw salow lemmyn.**
4. **An re ma yw parys.**
5. **An den ma yw feusik.**
6. **An gweder yw gwerthys.**

RANN 7 DASWRIANS
Oberenn 7.1
Answer that you understand/you do not understand these questions, e.g.:
Eus aval gesys? A wodhesta konvedhes?
Gonn/Na wonn.
Repeat the model answers:
1. **Yw an bluvenn ma koth?**
   A wodhesta konvedhes?
2. **Yw an chi na nowydh?**
   A wodhesta konvedhes?
3. **Eus karr a-rag an chi lemmyn?**
   A wodhesta konvedhes?

Oberenn 7.2
Translate into Cornish, e.g.:
The child is weak **An flogh yw gwann.**
Repeat the model answers:
1. *Which apple is sweet?*
2. *Which ones are useful?*
3. *Which cushion is that?*
4. *Which wine is ready?*
5. *Which children are happy?*
6. *Which stamp is Welsh?*

Oberenn 7.3
Introduce the key word into the sentence to complete it, e.g.:
An gewer yw *(very cold)*.
An gewer yw oer.
Repeat the model answers:
1. **An gewer yw** *(very hot)*.
2. **Hi a wra** *(rain)*.
3. **Hi a wra** *(snow)*.
4. **An gewer yw** *(bright)*.
5. **Hi yw** *(misty)*.

6. **Hi yw** *(very windy)*.

Dasweles
Listen to the conversation.
Dohajydh da, Peder. Fatla genes?
Da lowr, da lowr, mes yma anwoes warnav.
An gewer yw sygh mes yeyn lemmyn.
Homm yw da genes, a nyns yw?
Yw, sur. Eus karr genes y'n dre.
Nag eus. Yma an karr y'n karrji lemmyn.

RANN 8 GOROW HA BENOW
Oberenn 8.1
Make the following masculine words definite by adding **an** 'the'., e.g.: **Tas. An tas.**
Repeat the model answers:

1. **Gour**	2. **Brithel**	3. **Kenderow**
4. **Le**	5. **Noy**	6. **Gorthugher**
7. **Tus**	8. **Tiogyon**	9. **Pyskadoryon**

Oberenn 8.2
Make the following feminine words definite by adding **an** 'the', e.g.:
Mamm. An vamm.
Repeat the model answers:

1. **Nos**	2. **Keniterow**	3. **Modrep**
4. **Nith**	5. **Kenter**	6. **Kador**
7. **Kegin**	8. **Gwreg**	9. **Hwoer.**

Oberenn 8.3
Make questions from these statements, e.g.::
Yma mowes y'n gegin.
Eus mowes y'n gegin?
Repeat the model answers:
1. **An gewer yw teg.**
2. **Yma ke ryb an koes.**
3. **An le'ti ma yw nowydh.**
4. **Yma anwoes war an den na.**
5. **An tiek na yw feusik.**
6. **Nyns eus pluvek war an gador.**

Oberenn 8.4
Translate the sentences.
Repeat the model answers:
1. *Grandmother is old now.*
2. *Father has a cold.*
3. *The weather is warm.*
4. *Mother is a Cornishwoman.*
5. *This family is happy.*
6. *It's snowing now.*

RANN 9 DESKRIFA TRAOW

Oberenn 9.1

Add the key word to the sentences. (All the nouns are masculine), e.g.:

Yma koes ena (bras). **Yma koes bras ena.**

Repeat the model answers:
1. **Ottena drehevyans (nowydh).**
2. **Eus aval ena? (byghan).**
3. **Yowann yw maw, dell dybav (fol).**
4. **Kernow yw pow, sur (keltek)**
5. **Yma gweder omma (byghan)**
6. **Nyns yw chi, dell hevel (nowydh).**

Oberenn 9.2

Add the key word to the following sentences. (All the nouns are feminine), e.g.:

Homm yw kador (byghan).
Homm yw kador vyghan.

Repeat the model answers:
1. **Eus benyn ena? (koth)**
2. **Lannstefan yw tre (bras)**
3. **Pyth yw hemma? Kador yw. (kembrek)**
4. **Leurlenn yw honna. (brav)**
5. **Ottena an eglos. (teg)**
6. **Yma moes omma. (byghan)**
7. **An Tamer yw avon. (down)**

Oberenn 9.3

Put the key word into the sentences. (All the nouns are plural), e.g.:

Tus yns (gwann). **Tus wann yns.**

Repeat the model answers:
1. **An re ma yw tus. (kernewek)**
2. **An re na yw tus. (bretonek)**
3. **Yma pyskadoryon ena. (brav)**
4. **Pyskadoryon yns. (da)**
5. **Ottena benynes. (koth)**
6. **Benynes yns. (kembrek)**
7. **A nyns yw an re na fleghes? (byghan)**
8. **Fleghes yns. (lowen)**
9. **Pluvennow yns. (byghan)**
10. **Eus chiow ena? (bras)**

Oberenn 9.4

Supply the questions to which these sentences are the answers, e.g.:

An tas-gwynn yw. **Piw yw henna?**

Repeat the model answers:
1. **Tus koth yns.**
2. **Mr Karn yw.**
3. **Flogh fol yw.**
4. **Benyn gembrek yw**
5. **Pyskadoryon yns.**
6. **An vamm yw.**

Oberenn 9.5

Put each word into a question introduced by **fatell** and answer using the word provided, e.g.:

Chi/nowydh.
Fatell yw an chi? Nowydh yw.

Repeat the model answers:
1. **An dra/parys.**
2. **Teylu/lowen.**
3. **Alban/teg.**
4. **An badell na/plos.**
5. **An gador-vregh/da.**
6. **An re na/bryntin.**

Oberenn 9.6

Provide the questions to which the sentences are replies, using the phrase **py par**, e.g.:

Py par lestrier yw henna? **Kembrek yw.**

Repeat the model answers:
1. **Gwin frynkek yw.**
2. **Kenderow yw.**
3. **Yeth keltek yw.**
4. **Prenn derow yw.**
5. **Rover yw.**
6. **Eglos Pow Sows yw.**

RANN 10 PERGENNIETH

Oberenn 10.1

Link each pair of words in a 'the / of the' construction, e.g.:

The son/The father. **Mab an tas.**

Repeat the model answers:
1. *The door/the hall.*
2. *The end/the road.*
3. *The head/the nail.*
4. *The story/the fisherman.*
5. *The hand/the boy.*
6. *The relative (f)/the grandmother.*
7. *The idle talk/the child.*
8. *The trees* **(gwydh)**/*the wood.*

Oberenn 10.2

Link each pair of words in a 'the / of a' construction, e.g.:

Branch/chestnut tree. **Skorrenn kestenenn.**

Repeat the model answers:
1. *The son/a fisherman.*
2. *The floor/a house.*
3. *The story/a farmer.*
4. *The tail/a dog.*
5. *The brother/a farmwife.*
6. *The end/a wood.*

Oberenn 10.3

Link each pair of words in a 'somebody's/something' construction, e.g.:

Peter's house. **Chi Peder.**

Repeat the model answers:
   1. Jori's book.   *3. Pol's nephew.*
   2. Myrna's father.   *4. Lowena's hand.*

RANN 11 SEYTH GER A VERN
Oberenn 11.1
Change each of these statements by substituting the key word for the pronoun in each case, e.g.:
Ty yw teg. *(she).* **Hi yw teg.**
Repeat the model answers:
   1. **I yw pyskadoryon.** *(We)*
   2. **My yw kloppek.** *(He)*
   3. **Hwi yw fur.** *(They)*
   4. **Ni yw warbarth lemmyn.** *(You,* pl.)

Oberenn 11.2
Put the appropriate pronoun in place of the noun in each of the sentences.e.g.:
An koes yw bras. Ev yw bras.
Repeat the model answers:
   1. **An bluvenn yw rudh.**
   2. **An diogyon yw parow.**
   3. **An vowes yw kloppek.**
   4. **An dus yw lowen.**
   5. **An fleghes yw parys.**
   6. **Karol yw teg.**

Oberenn 11.3
Put **ev** or **hi** in place of the nouns in the sentences, e.g.:
Yma leurlenn y'n hel. Yma hi y'n hel.
Repeat the model answers:
   1. **Yma lyver war an leur.**
   2. **Yma chi ryb an eglos.**
   3. **Yma eglos yn kres an dre.**
   4. **An gwin yw bretonek.**
   5. **An lovan yw berr.**
   6. **An dhavas yw gwann.**

RANN 12 DEGRE
Oberenn 12.1
Put the key word before the adjective in each of the sentences, e.g.:
An ostel yw brav. (pur)
An ostel yw pur vrav.
Repeat the model answers:
   1. **Yw an eglos ma koth? (pur)**
   2. **My yw lowen. (pur)**
   3. **An gewer yw sygh. (pur)**
   4. **Yw an voes ma poes? (re)**

5. **Ev yw moen. (re)**
6. **An hwedhel ma yw hir. (re)**

Oberenn 12.2
Complete the sentences by putting the word **lowr** in as appropriate, e.g.:
Yw an gegin bras? Yw an gegin bras lowr?
Repeat the model answers:
   1. **Eus pluvennow ena genowgh?**
   2. **Yw hemma da?**
   3. **Yw an re ma teg?**
   4. **Yns i poes?**

RANN 13 LIES TRA
Oberenn 13.1
Repeat the statements, making the singular word plural in each case, e.g.:
An chambour ma yw brav.
An chambours ma yw brav.
Repeat the model answers:
   1. **Ottomma lyver kernewek.**
   2. **Yma an genter omma**
   3. **An flogh na yw lowen..**
   4. **Kemmer an aval, mar pleg.**

Oberenn 13.2
Repeat the statements, making the plural word singular in each case, e.g.:
Eus pluvennow gesys? Eus pluvenn gesys?
Repeat the model answers:
   1. **Eus chiow ryb an pras?**
   2. **Yw an trevow bras?**
   3. **Yw an notennow berr?**
   4. **Yw an padellow ma plos?**

Oberenn 13.3
Listen to the following short passages.

1. **Margh yw mab Mr ha Mrs Toms. Tiek yw ev. Yma ev lemmyn y'n pras. Hi a wra glaw ha glyb yw Margh, pur lyb. Nyns yw lowen dell hevel.**

2. **Yma Hel an Dre yn kres an dre hag yma tus y'n drehevyans na lemmyn. Kanoryon yns, kanoryon an eglos. Kanoryon dha yns, sur.**

Now answer the following questions in Cornish. Repeat the model answers.
   1. Who is the son of Mr and Mrs Toms?
   2. What is he?

164

3. *Where is he?*
4. *What is the weather like?*
5. *How is Mark?*
6. *Where is the Town Hall?*
7. *What are the people inside the Town Hall?*

RANN 14 ONAN, DEW, TRI
Oberenn 14.1
Translate the phrases into Cornish, e.g.:
3 books   tri lyver.
Repeat the model answers:

1. 9 chairs	*5. 2 girls*	*9. 9 houses*
2. 1 person	*6. 3 boys*	*10. 2 dogs*
3. 4 women	*7. 3 chairs*	
4. 20 cars	*8. 15 plates*	

Oberenn 14.2
Put the word **an** before the phrases, e.g.:
dew dhen,   an dhew dhen.
Repeat the model answers:

1. Diw vowes.	**4. Dew hwegynn.**
2. Dew diek	**5. Dew wolow.**
3. Diw bluvenn	**6. Diw gestenenn.**

Oberenn 14.3
Increase by 2 the numbers in each case, e.g.:
peswar den,   hwegh den.
Repeat the model answers:

1. Teyr fordh	**5. Unn le**
2. Dewdhek toll	**6. Naw karrji**
3. Eth chi	**7. Pymp jynn-skrifa**
4. Etek pluvenn	**8. Unn desenn**

Oberenn14.4
Translate the sentences into Cornish, e.g.:
There is one light in the kitchen
Yma unn golow y'n gegin.
Repeat the model answers:

1. The light is bright.
2. What is this book?
3. This is a long rope.
4. What boy is that?
5. He is George's cousin.
6. This story is not true.

RANN 15 AN EUR
Oberenn 15.1
State the times given in Cornish, e.g.:
3 o'clock   **teyr eur.**
Repeat the model answers:
1. 10 minutes past 10.

2. 20 minutes to 10.
3. Half-past 7.
4. 25 minutes past 12.
5. A quarter to 8.
6. 4 o'clock exactly.
7. A quarter past eleven.
8. About 6 o'clock.
9. 20 minutes to nine.
10. Midnight exactly.

Oberenn 15.2
Increase these times by 10 minutes in each case, e.g.:
Naw eur marnas pymp mynysenn.
Pymp mynysenn wosa naw eur.
Repeat the model answers:
1. Teyr eur hanter.
2. Kwarter wosa eth eur.
3. Dewdhek eur marnas kwarter.
4. Deg mynysenn wosa deg eur.

Oberenn 15.3
State in Cornish the time given for each item, e.g.: **Dhe by eur yw hansel?** *(At 8 o'clock)*
Dhe eth eur.
Repeat the model answers:
1. Dhe by eur yw an kyttrin *(At 5-30).*
2. Dhe by eur yw an nessa tren dhe Lyskerrys? *(At 6-15).*
3. Dhe by eur yw an kerdh? *(At 2-00).*
4. Dhe by eur yw li? *(At 12-30).*
5. Dhe by eur yw an kuntelles? *(At 7-00 exactly).*

RANN 16 HWILAS TRAOW
Oberenn 16.1
Supply the questions to which the answers are given, e.g.:
Yma an amanenn y'n gegin.
Plema'n amanenn?
Repeat the model answers:
1. Yma an kuntelles yn Hel an Dre.
2. Yma an paper war an voes.
3. Yma an platys y'n lestrier.
4. Yma an arghans yn tigenn an vamm.
5. Yma an skath y'n porth.
6. Yma an spisti ryp an eglos yn kres an dre.

Oberenn 16.2
Supply short answers to the questions, e.g.:

Plema'n karr? *In the garage.*
Repeat the model answers:
  1. **Plema'n fleghes?** *(In the garden).*
  2. **Plema'n avalow?** *(In the basket).*
  3. **Plema myrgh Mr Lane?** *(With mother).*
  4. **Plema'n puskes?** *(on the plate).*

Oberenn 16.3
Make each of the statements plural by substituting **Ymons i** for **ev** or **hi**, e.g.:
Yma ev y'n hel. Ymons i y'n hel.
Repeat the model answers:
  1. **Yma hi gans an tas.**
  2. **Yma hi a-rag an chi.**
  3. **Yma ev ryb an karrji.**
  4. **Yma hi war an leur.**

Oberenn 16.4
Answer the questions by translating the phrases given, e.g.:
Plemons i?
(They are in the meadow). **Ymons i y'n pras.**
Repeat the model answers:
  1. **Plemons i?** *(They are in the cinema).*
  2. **Plemons i?** *(They are in front of the hotel).*
  3. **Plemons i?** *(They are by the road).*
  4. **Plemons i?** *(They are in Brittany).*
  5. **Plemons i?** *(They are with John's nephew).*

RANN 17 MOY A NIVEROW
Oberenn 17.1
Translate the number phrases, e.g.:
26 boats.   **Hwegh skath warn ugens.**
Repeat the model answers:
  1. 39 cups   *5. 63 farmers*
  2. 42 boys   *6. 74 pens*
  3. 58 women   *7. 84 tables.*
  4. 61 chairs   *8. 99 sheep*

Oberenn 17.2
Increase the numbers by 3, e.g.:
Onan warn ugens.   Peswar warn ugens.
Repeat the model answers:
  1. 27, 2. 39,   3. 41,   4. 89,   5. 78.   6. 97.

Oberenn 17.3
Listen to the passage and then answer the questions in Cornish.

**An gewer yw brav lemmyn, kosel ha toemm
Yma Mr Tamblyn war an woen gans an**

deves. Tiek yw ev. Yma dew gi gans Mr Tamblyn. Onan yw Duik ha onan yw Herdhyer. Yma an dhew gi ma a-dryv Mr Tamblyn. War an woen ena yma a-dro peswar ugens davas. Etek davas ha tri ugens yw gwynn ha diw dhavas yw du.

  1. **Fatell yw an gewer?**
  2. **Plema Mr Tamblyn?**
  3. **Pyth yw ev?**
  4. **Eus tri hi gans Mr Tamblyn?**
  5. **Plemons i?**
  6. **Py lies davas yw gwynn?**
  7. **Py lies davas yw du?**

RANN 18 AN LE MAY MA TRAOW
Oberenn 18.1
Link the two concepts with the Cornish preposition, e.g.:
Nyns eus paper/an voes (on).
Nyns eus paper war an voes.
Repeat the model answers:
  1. **Yma an lyver/an argh-lyvrow** *(in).*
  2. **Eus drehevyans/an eglos?** *(behind).*
  3. **A nyns eus pluvek/an gador** *(under).*
  4. **Yma an vamm-wynn/an tan** *(at).*
  5. **Nyns eus fordh/an bargen-tir** *(beside).*
  6. **Yma gwydhenn/an chi** *(beside.*
  7. **Eus fordh/an koes?** *(through).*
  8. **Yma gwin/an boes** *(with).*

Oberenn 18.2
Give the expressions the opposite meaning by changing the preposition in each case. e.g.:
Yma karrek vras a-dryv an koes.
Yma karrek vras a-rag an koes.
Repeat the model answers:
  1. **Yma paper war an leurlenn.**
  2. **Nyns eus lowarth a-rag an chi.**
  3. **Eus fordhow a-dryv an chiow na?**
  4. **Yma bolla rudh yn-dann an voes.**

Oberenn 18.3
Make the noun definite and change the verb from **eus** to **usi**, e.g.:
Eus amari ryb an daras?
Usi an amari ryb an daras?
Repeat the model answers:
  1. **Eus kanstell genes?**
  2. **Nyns eus fleghes y'n skol na.**
  3. **A nyns eus karr y'n karrji?**

4. Eus kresenn gernewek y'n dre ma?
5. Eus tarow y'n pras na?
6. Nyns eus deves ena.

Oberenn 18.4
Omit the noun subject and change the verb accordingly, e.g.:
Usi an lyvrow y'n amari?
Esons i y'n amari?
Repeat the model answers:
   1. Usi an skorr war an leur?
   2. Nyns usi an podigow y'n gegin.
   3. Usi an arghanttiow y'n stret ma?
   4. A nyns usi an puskes war an plat?

Oberenn 18.5
Make the noun indefinite and change the verb from **usi** to **eus**, e.g.:
Usi an eskisyow yn-dann an gweli?
Eus eskisyow yn-dann an gweli?
Repeat the model answers.
   1. Nyns usi an lovan y'n skath.
   2. Nyns usi an bargen-tir bras yn Kernow.
   3. Usi an chapel yn kres an dre?
   4. Usi an pronter y'n eglos?
   5. Usi an folennow gwag y'n lyver ma?
   6 Nyns usi an vyrgh tre hwath.

RANN 19 MEUR A po NEBES
Oberenn 19.1
Put the phrase **meur a** before the first noun in each sentence, e.g.:
Yma arghans y'n arghantti, sur.
Yma meur a arghans y'n arghantti, sur.
Repeat the model answers:
   1. Platow yw plos.
   2. Yma deves y'n pras.
   3. Fleghes yw re dew.
   4. Nyns eus pluvennow gesys.
   5. Kemmer bara, mar pleg!
   6. Ottena delennow yn dann an wydhenn.

Oberenn 19.2
Put the word **pals** after the plural noun in each case, e.g.: **Kanoryon yw kernewek.**
Kanoryon bals yw kernewek.
Repeat the model answers:
   1. Dornleow yw terrys.
   2. Tus yw boghosek.
   3. Yma chambours y'n ostel.
   4. Yma tiogyon y'n pow ma.

Oberenn 19.3
Put the word **lies** before the first noun in each sentence, making the plural form singular, e.g.:
Yma chiow y'n fordh ma.
Yma lies chi y'n fordh ma.
Repeat the model answers:
   1. Nyns yw fordhow salow.
   2. Hwedhlow yw re verr.
   3. Kuntellesow yw re hir.
   4. Hwegynnow yw drog.
   5. Porthow yw byghan.
   6. Delennow yw rudh.

Oberenn 19.4
Put the key word in Cornish into the sentence, making it singular to mean 'little, some' or plural to mean 'few', e.g.:
Yma nebes/y'n gegin *(wine).*
Yma nebes gwin y'n gegin.
Repeat the model answers:
   1. Nebes/yw re voen. *(person).*
   2. Nebes/yw gwynn *(flower).*
   3. Yma nebes/gesys *(beer).*
   4. Nebes/ yw re gul *(road).*
   5. Nyns/ eus nebes/lowr *(money).*
   6. Nebes/yw hweg *(drink).*
   7. Nebes/ yw du *(sheep).*
   8. Nebes yw melyn *(butter).*

RANN 20 ERGHI
Oberenn 20.1
Put the appropriate command into the statement in each sentence, using the singular form.e.g.:
An lyver ma *(take).*
Kemmer an lyver ma!
Repeat the model answers:
   1. An lyver dhe Beder *(give).*
   2. An fenester, mar pleg *(open).*
   3. An oberenn ma *(do).*
   4. Dhymm an hwedhel *(tell).*
   5. An erva *(read aloud).*
   6. Daras an chambour *(shut).*
   7. Omma dhymm *(come).*
   8. Dhe'n gegin *(go).*
   9. An bluvenn diworth Jori *(ask).*
   10. An lavar *(write).*

Oberenn 20.2
Repeat exercise 20.1, using the plural form in each case. e.g.:

An lyver ma *(take)*.
Kemmerewgh an lyver ma!
Repeat the model answers.

Oberenn 20.3
Make exercise 20.1 negative, e.g.:
An lyver ma *(do not take)*.
Na gemmer an lyver ma!
Repeat the model answers.

Oberenn 20.4
Make exercise 20.2 negative, e.g.:
An lyver ma *(do not take)*.
Na gemmerewgh an lyver ma!
Repeat the model answers.

RANN 21 MY YW...NYNS OV
Oberenn 21.1
Make the following statements negative, e.g.:
My yw parys.   Nyns ov parys.
Repeat the model answers:
1. **My yw boghosek.**
2. **My yw diek.**
3. **Ty yw flogh gokki.**
4. **Ty yw fur.**
5. **Ev yw mab Mr Pennglas.**
6. **Ev yw arghantti.**
7. **Hi yw benyn deg.**
8. **Hi yw delenn ell.**
9. **Ni yw warbarth lemmyn.**
10. **Ni yw tiogyon.**
11. **Hwi yw tus an dre.**
12. **Hwi yw parow.**
13. **I yw skorr bras.**
14. **I yw kanoryon dha.**

Oberenn 21.2
Make the negative statements into questions,
e.g.: **Nyns ov parys. Ov vy parys?**
Repeat the model answers:
1. **Nyns os Albanek.**
2. **Nyns yw koes byghan.**
3. **Nyns yw hi gerva hir.**
4. **Nyns on tew.**
5. **Nyns owgh fleghes dha.**
6. **Nyns yns plos.**

Oberenn 21.3
Change the statement putting the complement
first, e.g.:
My yw gour.   Gour ov.

Repeat the model answers:
1. **Ty yw fol.**
2. **Ev yw gyllys**
3. **Ev yw gow.**
4. **Hi yw devedhys lemmyn.**
5. **Hi yw bro vras.**
6. **Ni yw krev.**
7. **Ni yw shyndys.**
8. **Hwi yw teg.**
9. **Hwi yw gwann.**
10. **I yw lowarthow kul.**

Oberenn 21.4
Translate the statements into English.
Repeat the model answers:
1. **Lowen yns.**
2. **Nyns on pyskadoryon.**
3. **A nyns yw hi Mrs Bolitho?**
4. **I yw an re dhiek.**
5. **Ov vy salow omma? Os!**
6. **Nowydh yw an leurlenn ma? Nag yw!**
7. **Hwi yw Kembrek martesen. On!**
8. **A nyns yns i donsyow da? Yns!**

RANN 22
HEVELEPTER HA DIHEVELEPTER
Oberenn 22.1
Compare the two items in each case, using
haval orth 'similar to', e.g.:
An karr ma/karr Maria.
An karr ma yw haval orth karr Maria.
Repeat the model answers:
1. **An chi ma/ostel.**
2. **Broder Jori/mab Lynda.**
3. **An desenn/bara.**
4. **Hemm/henna.**
5. **Euryor Wella/huni Mr Pennglas.**

Oberenn 22.2
Substitute   the phrase **dihaval diworth**
'different from' for the phrase **haval orth**
'similar to' in exercise 1 above, e.g.:
An karr ma/karr Maria.
An karr ma yw dihaval diworth karr Maria.
Repeat the model answers.

Oberenn 22.3
Translate the following statements into
English. Repeat the model answers:
1. **Skrif an keth hwedhel arta!**
2. **Ymons i y'n keth chi.**

168

3. An gewer yw an keth hedhyw ha'n gewer de.
4. Kemmer an keth fordh ha'n huni gyns!
5. Yma an skathow y'n keth porth warbarth.
6. Nyns yw glas an keth liw ha gwyrdh.

Oberenn 22.4
Put the word **ken** 'other' before the noun in each case, e.g.:
Kemmer pluvenn! Kemmer ken pluvenn!
Repeat the model answers:
1. **Ro dhymm plat!**
2. **Diskwedh dhymm hanaf!**
3. **Ke dhe jambour!**
4. **Pys amanenn diworth an vamm!**
5. **Gwra tra, mar pleg!**
6. **Leverewgh hwedhel!**

RANN 23 AN TERMYN TREMENYS

Oberenn 23.1
Put the following statements into past time by replacing **yw** 'is' by **o** 'was', e.g.:
An gwydh yw marow. An gwydh o marow.
Repeat the model answers:
1. **My yw drog pes.**
2. **Lorna yw klav.**
3. **An re ma yw da lowr.**
4. **I yw pur dhiek.**
5. **Hemm yw an keth tra.**
6. **Piw yw an gwettha flogh?**

Oberenn 23.2
Make the following statements into questions by substituting an inflected form of the verb for **o** 'was' in each case, e.g.:
Ty o boghosek ena. Es jy boghosek ena?
Repeat the model answers:
1. **I o parow.**
2. **An vodrep o koth.**
3. **Hwi o kanoryon dha.**
4. **Dornla an hanaf o terrys.**
5. **My o gokki.**
6. **Ev o bargen-tir bras.**

Oberenn 23.3
Put these sentences into the present tense, e.g.:
Yth esa an re ma warbarth y'n keth hel.
Yma an re ma warbarth y'n keth hel.
Repeat the model answers:

1. **Yth esen vy omma.**
2. **Nyns eses jy ogas dhymm.**
3. **Esens i y'n ostel na?**
4. **Yth esewgh hwi yn gorsav an hynshorn**
5. **Yth esens war an treth.**
6. **Yth esa an bughes y'n pras arall.**

Oberenn 23.4
Translate into Cornish.
Repeat the model answers:
1. *We were displeased.*
2. *We were in the same car.*
3. *Dad's umbrella is broken.*
4. *The church was in the middle of the parish.*
5. *This watch is new.*
6. *They were not in the library.*
7. *They are goats, so it seems.*
8. *The clouds are grey.*
9. *Pam's sisters are lucky.*
10. *The people are not happy.*

RANN 24 PERGHENNIETH
Oberenn 24.1
Put the key word **dha** or **y** before the noun in each case, e.g.:
Ottomma kador *(your).* **Ottomma dha gador.**
Repeat the model answers:
1. **Kemmer diwes** *(your).*
2. **An traow yw parys** *(his).*
3. **Henn yw maw** *(your).*
4. **An dornleow yw terrys** *(its).*
5. **Pyth yw bro** *(your).*
6. **My yw keniterow** *(his).*
7. **Yma lyvrow genes** *(your).*
8. **Nyns eus mebyl omma hwath** *(its).*

Oberenn 24.2
Put the key word **ow**, **hy** or **aga** before the noun in each case, e.g.:
Ple'ma kota? *(my).* **Ple'ma ow hota?**
Repeat the model answers:
1. **Nyns yw plat glan** *(their).*
2. **Yth esa tarow yn mes** *(their).*
3. **Koen yw parys dhe seyth eur** *(my).*
4. **Nyns yns i plasennow** *(my).*
5. **An penn o shyndys** *(her).*
6. **I o kowethesow** *(my).*
7. **Ple'ma an fleghes?** *(their).*
8. **Gorr hansel war an voes** *(my).*
9. **Ple'ma an tas?** *(her).*
10. **Pyth yw arghantti?** *(their).*

169

Oberenn 24.3
Translate into Cornish. Note that the pronoun 'your' can be translated by **dha** or **agas**. You will be told which to use.
  1. *Do your work!* (p.)
  2. *Where are my trousers?*
  3. *Your house is old, it seems.*(s.)
  4. *Is our beach clean?*
  5. *Was their father pleased?*
  6. *Where is our umbrella?*
  7. *My male cousin is George.*
  8. *Is your sister with you?* (s.)

Oberenn 24.4
Listen to the passage. It will be read twice. Then answer the questions in Cornish.
Pan en vy yowynk yth en lowen. Yth esa agan chi yn kres tre vyghan. Pan esen ni, agan teylu, warbarth ni o unnek den, ow mamm wynn, ow vamm, hag ow thas, ow thri broder hag ow feder hwoer. Yth esa ow hi, Duik y hanow, genen ha diw gath ynwedh mes nyns ens i tus.

  1. **Fatell en vy pan en yowynk?**
  2. **Ple'th esa agan chi?**
  3. **Py lies den en ni warbarth?**
  4. **Py lies enyval esa genen y'n chi?**
  5. **Pyth o hanow ow hi?**

RANN 25 HWARVOSOW TREMENYS
Oberenn 25.1
Put the verb provided into the phrase in the third person singular of the past tense, e.g.:
Peder/lyver kernewek (prena).
Peder a brenas lyver kernewek.
Repeat the model answers:
  1. **Ty/henna (leverel).**
  2. **Hi/an hwedhel (lenna).**
  3. **Ev/y'n eglos (kana).**
  4. **My/dhis an jynn-amontya (diskwedhes)**
  5. **Maria/hy sagh ena (gorra).**
  6. **Y das/y'n mor (neuvya).**
  7. **An gath/war an gweli (esedha).**
  8. **An re na/an tiek (gweres).**

Oberenn 25.2
Put the statements of Exercise 25.1 into the Perfect tense, replacing **a** by **re**, e.g.:
Peder a brenas lyver kernewek.
Peder re brenas lyver kernewek.

Repeat the model answers:
  1. **Ty a leveris henna.**
  2. **Hi a lennas an hwedhel.**
  3. **Ev a ganas y'n eglos.**
  4. **My a dhiskwedhas dhis an jynn-amontya.**
  5. **Maria a worras hy sagh ena.**
  6. **Y das a neuvyas y'n mor.**
  7. **An gath a esedhas war an gweli.**
  8. **An re na a weresas an tiek.**

Oberenn 25.3
Translate the following sentences into Cornish. The verb **prena** 'buy' is used throughout. Repeat the model answers:
  1. *I did not buy the radio.*
  2. *Did she buy a red coat? Yes!*
  3. *We didn't buy the records.*
  4. *Didn't they buy food in town?*
  5. *Did you* (s.) *buy trousers in that new shop?*
  6. *George did not buy the beer.*
  7. *You* (p.) *didn't buy your furniture. We did!*
  8. *Didn't the children buy sweets? They didn't!*

Oberenn 25.4
Answer the following questions affirmatively and then negatively, e.g.:
A brensys jy padell nowydh?
Prenis!/Na brenis!
Repeat the model answers:
  1. **A esedhas Peder gans y gowethes?**
  2. **A lennsons i an lavarow?**
  3. **A neuvsys jy y'n avon?**
  4. **A weressowgh hwi agas mamm?**
  5. **A worras an dus aga seghyer war an voes?**
  6. **A leversys jy hemma ynwedh?**

RANN 26 HWARVOSOW Y'N EUR MA
Oberenn 26.1
Make the statements negative, e.g.:
Ni a guntell lyvrow koth.
Ny guntellyn lyvrow koth.
Repeat the model answers:
  1. **My a bren glawlenn nowydh.**
  2. **Ty a yv dowr.**
  3. **Ev a gews flows.**
  4. **Hi a guntell plasennow.**

170

5. Ni a vet orth agan koweth.
6. Hwi a vir orth an re ma.
7. I a denn an lovan warbarth.
8. Mona a yskynn an vre.
9. An byskadoryon a guntell arghans.
10. Hemma a gews kernewek da.
11. Ev a vir orth an bellwolok.
12. Hi a bren boes y'n dre.

Oberenn 26.2
Make these questions into affirmative
statements, e.g.:
A gews hi Frynkek? Hi a gews Frynkek.
Repeat the model answers:
1. **A vetyowgh hwi orth an pronter?**
2. **A yskynnons i an menydh?**
3. **A guntellav vy an kaderyow?**
4. **A viryn ni orth an folenn ma?**
5. **A bren Wella karr nowydh?**
6. **A yv an fleghes aga leth?**

Oberenn 26.3
Translate the sentences into Cornish.
Repeat the model answers:
1. I buy a new coat every year.
2. Michael **(Mighal)** *drinks tea with his
   breakfast.*
3. They don't speak Cornish.
4. These (people) collect old stamps.
5. Do you (pl.) *buy bacon in Mr Page's shop?*
6. Don't you (s.) *look at the television?.*
7. We meet your son on the way to school.
8. They always wait here.

Oberenn 26.4
Listen to the passage. It will be read twice.
Then answer in Cornish the questions which
follow.Listen to the model answers.

   Pan eth Maria dhe'n varghas y'n dre, hi
a welas ena hy howethes, Rita. "Dydh da
dhis, Rita," yn medh hi. "Fatla genes ha
fatla gans dhe deylu?"
   "Ow gour yw klav," Rita a worthybis,
mes yma an fleghes yn poynt da. Ymons i
y'n skol ha'n gour, yma ev tre yn y weli."
   "Drog yw genev," Maria a leveris.
"Martesen ev a vydh gwell kyns pell."

1. **Plema an varghas?**
2. **Fatell o gans gour Rita?**

3. **Fatell o gans an fleghes?**
4. **Ple'th esa an fleghes?**
5. **Ple'th esa an tas?**

RANN 27 VERBOW DHE LES
Oberenn 27.1
Translate the sentences into Cornish.
Repeat the model answers:
1. I will play with the children .
2. Can he help his mother with the work?
3. The river goes down to the sea.
4. John makes tables.
5. Morwenna comes to Saltash every day.

Oberenn 27.2
Translate the following sentences, putting the
action into the past as shown.
Repeat the model answers
1. I wished to play with the children.
2. Could he help his mother with the work?
3. We went down to the sea.
4. John made a table.
5. Morwenna came to Saltash this morning.

RANN 28 DHYMM ha DHIS
Oberenn 28.1
Put a preposition with a personal ending in
place of the noun in each case, e.g.:
Ro an bluvenn dhe Beder.
Ro an bluvenn dhodho.
Repeat the model answers:
1. **My a dhiskwedhas an skeusenn dhe
   Helen.**
2. **Ni a lever an hwedhel dhe'n dus.**
3. **Ev a vynn eva koffi gans aga thas.**
4. **Ty a yll esedha gans an re na.**
5. **Na worr dha arghans y'n gyst!**
6. **Yma skath vras y'n porth.**
7. **Eus bollas a gowl war an voes?**
8. **Hwi a yll gasa agas kota war an
   kaderyow.**
9. **Nyns esa le rag Tamsyn.**
10. **Ty a yll gul henna rag dha vroder.**
11. **Ny yll an dus mos heb Hykka.**
12, **Ny wonn konvedhes heb an erva.**
13. **Kemmer an lyver a Jori!**
14. **Na evewgh dowr a'n avon!**

Oberenn 28.2
Put a single suffixed pronoun after the
preposition in each case, e.g.:

Yma ow broder genev.
Yma ow broder genev vy.
Repeat the model answers:
1. Yma kath gensi.
2. Ro an bluvenn dhymm!
3. Ev a skrifas ynno.
4. Eus anwoes warnos?
5. Gwra henna hebdha!
6. Tri ahanan yw parys.
7. Kemmer an gwin ragos!
8. Meur ras dhis!
9. A vynn an flogh gwari gensi?
10. Ev eth genen.

Oberenn 28.3
Repeat exercise 2 but use doubled suffixed pronouns in place of single ones, e.g.:
Yma ow broder genev.
Yma ow broder genev evy.
Repeat the model answers:

29 HWARVOSOW OW PESYA
Oberenn 29.1
Translate the following sentences into Cornish. The verbal noun is supplied in each case, eg. (*The child is playing* (**gwari**).
Yma an flogh ow kwari.
Repeat the model answers:
1. I am waiting for my friend (**gortos**).
2. John is speaking Cornish (**kewsel**).
3. Owen is not drinking his milk (**eva**).
4. Your brother is coming now (**dos**).
5. She is not looking at the television (**mires**).
6. Father is washing the dishes (**golghi**).

Oberenn 29.2
Put the statements into the past, e.g.:
Yma an gwyns ow hwytha.
Yth esa an gwyns ow hwytha.
Repeat the model answers:
1. Nyns esov ow koslowes orto.
2. Usi an tas ow palas y'n lowarth?
3. Nyns eus karr ow tos.
4. Ymons i ow kul aga ober
5. Esos jy ow powes?
6. Yma an ki owth eva dowr.
7. Yth eson ow mos.
8. Eus tren ow nesa?

Oberenn 29.3
Replace the singular form of the verb by the

plural, e.g.:
Nyns esov owth eva gwin.
Nyns eson owth eva gwin.
Repeat the model answers:
1. Esos jy ow kweres?
2. Nyns usi ev ow kewsel dhedhi.
3. Yth esov ow tybri an boes.
4. Nyns esos ow klywes orthiv.
5. Yma hi ow kana gansa.
6. Nyns esov owth holya an wir fordh.

Oberenn 29.4
Replace the verbal phrase by the present participle construction in the following statements. The verbal noun is supplied in each case, e.g.:
Maria a gews Kernewek gans hy gour (kewsel).
Yma Maria ow kewsel Kernewek gans hy gour.
Repeat the model answers:
1. An venyn ma a veg (megi).
2. An byskadoryon a dhe'n mor (mones).
3. Aga hath a gosk war aga gweli (koska).
4. I a drig yn y ji (triga).
5. Jori a esedh orth an fenester (esedha).
6. Agan ki a neuv y'n avon (neuvya).

RANN 30 GRASSA, PANDRA, ASS!
Oberenn 30.1
Translate the following statements into Cornish. Repeat the model answers:
1. Thank you for the ice-cream.
2. Thank you for the ticket.
3. Thank you for the coffee.
4. Thank you for helping.
5. Thank you for waiting. No matter!

Oberenn 30.2
Make the statements into questions, using **pandra** 'what?' and changing the person of the verb if necessary, e.g.:
'Meur ras!' a leveris ev.
Pandr'a leveris ev?
Repeat the model answers:
1. Kath dhu y'n lowarth a welis vy.
2. Lies ger nowydh a skrifsons i.
3. Kan hweg a glywsyn ni.
4. Oberi a wra Peder pub dydh.
5. Bara ha leth a brenas an vamm y'n spisti.

172

Oberenn 30.3
Make exclamations from these statements, e.g.:

Skwith ov. Ass ov vy skwith!

Repeat the model answers:
1. Plos yw an wedrenn ma.
2. Da yw an boes omma y'n diwotti.
3. Koynt yns.
4. Krev os.
5. Drog o an gewer.
6. Klav en vy.

RANN 31 ARAYA TRAOW
Oberenn 31.1
Change the ordinal number in each sentence by the amount shown, e.g.:

An degves linenn yw hir (+ 8).

An etegves linenn yw hir.

Repeat the model answers:
1. Hedhyw yw an nawves dydh a'n mis (+ 11).
2. Hy chi o an peswera y'n stret (- 3).
3. Ni a esedhas y'n trydhegves rew (- 5).
4. Ena y kansons an trysa salm warn ugens (+ 10).
5. Dy' Gwener a vydh y bympes bloedh ha tri ugens (- 3).

RANN 32 PY DYDH YW EV?
Oberenn 32.1
Translate the following dates into Cornish, e.g.:

Tuesday 26th March.

Dy' Meurth 26es a vis Meurth.

Repeat the model answers:
1. *Wednesday 2nd October.*
2. *Saturday 15th June.*
3. *Monday 21st August.*
4. *Friday 8th February.*
5. *Sunday 31st January.*
6. *Thursday 12th September.*

Oberenn 32.2
What day will it be a week after each of the above dates (in 32.1)? e.g.:

Tuesday 26th March.

Dy' Meurth 2a a vis Ebrel.

Repeat the model answers.

RANN 33
DA YW GANS ha DROG YW GANS
Oberenn 33.1

Translate the key phrase and complete the sentence with it, e.g.: ....

donsya *(Loveday likes)*

Da yw gans Loveday donsya.

Repeat the model answers:
1. kerdhes warbarth *(We like).*
2. dos dh'agan chi *(My brother likes).*
3. dybri kig *(She doesn't like).*
4. gwari peldroes *(They prefer).*
5. kewsel yndella *(Harold is reluctant).*
6. mones dhe'n skol *(Young Tamsyn hates).*
7. dos y'ga harr ytho? *(Did they prefer).*
8. mires orth an bellwolok *(I am not keen).*
9. bos rych *(Everybody likes).*
10. omwolghi *(The boy does not like).*

Oberenn 33.2
Listen to the passage. It will be read twice. Then answer in Cornish the questions which follow.

"My a vynn daskorr dha lyver" yn medh Kolan.

Da o gans Pol klywes an nowodhow ma. "Yma hwans dhymm a redya an keth lyver ma arta," ev a leveris. Onan didhanus yw."

"Ny dhiwedhis vy an hwedhel, " Kolan a leveris. "Gwell yw genev redya hwedhlow yn kever Kernow."

1. Pandr'a leveris Kolan dhe Pol?
2. Fatell o an lyver herwydh Pol?
3. A dhiwedhas Kolan lyver Pol?
4. Py par hwedhlow yw da gans Kolan?

RANN 34 PERGHENNIETH
Oberenn 34.1
Provide questions to which the replies are given, e.g.:

Eus! Yma broder dhymm. Eus broder dhis?

Repeat the model answers:
1. Eus! Yma kath dhedhi.
2. Nag eus! Nyns eus skath dhodho.
3. Esa! Yth esa euryor dhe'n gour na.
4. Nag esa! Nyns esa hwoer dhedha.
5. Eus! Yma tokyn genes.
6. Nag eus. Nyns eus kollel-boket genev.

Oberenn 34.2
Put the statements into the past tense, e.g.:

Yma goel ledan dhe'n skath.

Yth esa goel ledan dhe'n skath.

173

Repeat the model answers:
1. **Yma lowarth bras dhe Vr Collings.**
2. **Nyns eus lyverva dhe'n dre.**
3. **Eus dewweder dhedhi?**
4. **A nyns eus meur a dir dhe'n tiek?**

Oberenn 34.3
Put each statement into the past tense, e.g.:
An mappa ma yw dhe'n dyskador.
An mappa ma o dhe'n dyskador.
Repeat the model answers:
1. **An gador ma yw dhymm.**
2. **Oll an mebyl ma yw dhe Vtrs Palmer.**
3. **An ki drog na yw dhodho.**
4. **Nyns yw an kota loes ma dhymm.**
5. **Yw an jynn-amontya nowydh dhe Beder?**
6. **A nyns yw an koffi ma dhis?**

Oberenn 34.4
Make the indefinite noun definite in each case, changing the verb and the word order where required, e.g.:
Yth esa kweth teg dhedhi.
An gweth teg o dhedhi.
Repeat the model answers:
1. **Eus pal gernewek dhis?**
2. **Yma soedhva dhe'n gesva.**
3. **Nyns esa radyo dhedha.**
4. **Nyns eus seghyer dhe'n spiser.**
5. **Yma pel dhe'n fleghes ma.**
6. **Yth esa pows dhu dhe'n vamm.**
7. **Nyns eus glawlenn dhymm.**
8. **Yma plasennow dhe'n vowes ma.**

Oberenn 34.5
Translate the sentences into Cornish using the key verb which is given together with the adjective from which it is derived, e.g.:
He lowered his voice. **(isel/iselhe)**
Ev a iselhas y lev.
Repeat the model answers:
1. *The days lengthen in summer.* **(hir/hirhe)**
2. *The fisherman shortened the rope.* **(berr/berrhe)**
3. *We didn't clean the car.* **(glan/glanhe)**
4. *The sun warms the land.* **(toemm/toemmhe)**

RANN 35 OLL, NEBES po MANN
Oberenn 35.1
Translate the key phrase and use it to complete the sentence, e.g.:

..a dheuth dhe'n kuntelles. *(All the members)*
Oll an eseli a dheuth dhe'n kuntelles.
Repeat the model answers:
1. **..o gwann, pur wann** *(All of them)*.
2. **..o terrys** *(A few jars)*.
3. **..re wrug an ober** *(Few of us)*.
4. **Ny dheuth .... dhe'n porth** *(All the ships)*.
5. **..yw teg** *(A few gardens)*.
6. **Kemmer .... y'n wedrenn** *(a little wine)*.
7. **..a vydh ena a-dhistowgh** *(You all)*.
8. **..yw leun a draow** *(All the cupboards)*.

Oberenn 35.2
Convert the sentences so that they have the opposite meaning to that given, using the key phrase given in place of **oll**, e.g.:
Oll an dus a evas koffi du.
Ny evas den vydh koffi du.
Repeat the model answers:
1. **Oll an fleghes a worthybis. (flogh vydh)**
2. **Oll an delennow o glas. (delenn vydh)**
3. **Oll an lyvrow yw dhe les. (lyver vydh)**
4. **Hi a vrojyas oll an oyow. (oy vydh)**
5. **Oll an deves a lammas dres an ke.**
   (davas vydh)

RANN 36 HA, KYNS ha WOSA
Oberenn 36.1
Link each pair of sentences together using **ha** or **hag**, e.g.:
Margh a veg. Yma ev ow liwya fos an chambour.
Margh a veg hag ev ow liwya fos an chambour.
Repeat the model answers:
1. **Mona a ganas. Yth esa hi owth omwiska.**
2. **Ny yllsyn keskewsel. Yth esov owth omwolghi.**
3. **Ass o Larri lowen. Yth esa Morwenna owth esedha rybdho.**
4. **Skwith o ow howeth. Yth esa ev ow revya a-dreus an avon.**
5. **My a vynn gorra an lestri war an voes. Yth esos jy ow pareusi an boes.**
6. **An tas a yll koska deg mynysenn. Yma an vebyon ow kwari peldroes yn-mes.**
7. **Res yw gortos a-ji. Yma hi ow kul glaw.**
8. **Fatell wrons i aga ober? Ymons i ow kewsel warbarth.**

174

Oberenn 36.2
Replace **kyns** with **wosa** in the sentences, e.g.:
An tas a veg unn sigaretenn kyns mones dh'y weli.
An tas a veg unn sigaretenn wosa mones dh'y weli.
Repeat the model answers:
1. **Yowann a welas y wreg kyns gweles y gowethes.**
2. **Maria a gewsis gans Padryk kyns y weres.**
3. **Res yw tyli kyns y brena.**
4. **Hi a jynnskrifas an oberenn kyns hy redya.**

Oberenn 36.3
Translate the following sentences into Cornish.
Repeat the model answers:
1. *I washed the wall before painting it.*
2. *The egg was bad. Mark felt ill after eating it.*
3. *Look before jumping!*
4. *They left the cups after filling them with coffee.*
5. *Read the sentences aloud after translating them into Cornish!*

RANN 37 HEVELEBI TRAOW
Oberenn 37.1
Translate the key phrase and complete the sentence with it, e.g.:
An chi ma yw....chi Mr Toms. *(as large as)*
An chi ma yw mar vras avel chi Mr Toms.
Repeat the model answers:
1. **Ev yw.... avel lew.** *(as strong)*
2. **Dy' Yow o .... avel Dy' Mergher.** *(as wet)*
3. **Ty yw .... . avello.** *(as foolish)*
4. **Ev o .... avel kolonn Pharaoh.** *(as hard)*
5. **An nos yw .... avel sagh-kroust an Jowl.** *(as black)*
6. **Yowann yw .... avella, dell dybav.** *(as bad)*

Oberenn 37.2
Translate the key phrase and complete the sentence with it, e.g.:
Tour an eglos yw .... ages to ow chi. *(higher than)*
Tour an eglos yw ughella ages to ow chi.
Repeat the model answers:
1. **Maria yw ... agesov.** *(older)*
2. **An fordh ma yw .... ages an fordh veur.**

(safer)
3. **Lannstefan yw .... ages Loundres.** *(nearer)*
4. **Piw o .... agessa?** *(more foolish)*
5. **Ty o .... agesso ytho.** *(luckier)*
6. **Mighal yw .... ages y vroder, dell hevel.** *(smaller)*

Oberenn 37.3
Translate the following phrases into Cornish, e.g.: *The nearest house.* **An nessa chi.**
Repeat the model answers:
1. *The weakest child.*
2. *The least money.*
3. *The cleanest room.*
4. *The happiest woman.*
5. *The newest book.*
6. *The sweetest cake.*

Oberenn 37.4
Listen to the passage. It will be read twice. Then answer in Cornish the questions which follow.

> Pol a drig yn Truru mes ev a ober yn Sen Ostell. Pub dydh ev a dh'y ober yn y garr. Nyns yw an karr ma an nowyttha yn Kernow na nyns yw an gwettha. Skav lowr yw, kynth yw koth. Ny yll Pol prena onan gwell hwath, onan kreffa martesen. Kepar ha lies den yw agan Pol. Ev a yv korev ha mos dhe dhonsya pub Dy' Sadorn gans y gowethes, Salli.

1. **Ple'ma chi Pol?**
2. **Ple'ma y ober?**
3. **Fatell yw karr Pol?**
4. **Pandr'a wra Pol pub Dy' Sadorn?**
5. **Pandr'a yv Pol.**
6. **Pyth yw hanow y gowethes?**

RANN 38 Y WERES
Oberenn 38.1
Replace the noun which is underlined with a possessive adjective in each case, e.g.:
Pam a vynnas gweres hy gour.
Pam a vynnas y weres.
Repeat the model answers:
1. **My a wrug gasa an karr a-rag Hel an Dre.**
2. **Y nith a vynn gorra pluvek war hy hador.**
3. **Piw a yll gorfenna an gan?**
4. **Oll anedha a wra dyski an yeth.**

5. Yowann a vynn gweres <u>an dioges</u>.
6. Py flogh a wrug skrifa <u>an notenn</u> dhymm?
7. Ny allav gweles <u>an maw</u> lemmyn.
8. Ow heniterow a allas diwedha <u>an hwedhel</u> kyns prys koen.

Oberenn 38.2
Translate the sentences into Cornish. The verbal noun is given in each case, e.g.:
Tamsyn a yll .... *(help you* [sing.] **(gweres)**.
Tamsyn a yll dha weres.
Repeat the model answers:
1. Gwra .... . *(help me)* **(gweres)**
2. A vynn'ta .... dhymm? *(bring it* [m]) **(doen)**
3. Ny vynnons i .... . *(follow them)* **(sywya)**
4. Na wra .... ! *(strike it* [f.]) **(gweskel)**
5. A wre'ta .... ? *(love him)* **(kara)**
6. A yllyn ni .... ? *(re-do it* [m.]) **(daswul)**
7. Ny wrussowgh hwi .... *(hear us)* **(klywes)**
8. Ny yllis vy .... *(see you* [sing.] **(gweles)**

Oberenn 38.3
Translate the key words and use them to complete the sentences, making any necessary mutation changes, e.g.:
Diskwedh e .... koweth! *(to my)*.
Diskwedh e dhe'm koweth!
Repeat the model answers:
1. I yw dha vamm .... tas. *(and your* [sing.])
2. Yw an lyver ma onan .... lyvrow? *(of his)*
3. Agan mamm-wynn a drig .... chi. *(in our)*
4. My a gar ow fleghes .... fleghes-wynn. *(and my)*
5. Kemmer an arghans ma .... dorn! *(in your* [sing.])
6. Morwenna a leveris, "Fatla genes?" .... broder. *(to her)*

RANN 39 AN ACHESON
Oberenn 39.1
Make the following questions negative, e.g.:
Prag y tybons i yndella?
Prag na dybons i yndella?
Repeat the model answers:
1. Prag y hwre'ta y skoedhya?
2. Prag y hworfennowgh agas ober dhe beder eur?
3. Prag y hwaytydh jy gorthyp?
4. Prag y leskons i del marow y'ga

lowarth?
5. Prag y perthyn ni kov a henna?
6. Prag y sewenas hi?
7. Prag y fynn'ta esedha omma?
8. Prag yth igoras Kolan y anow y'n kuntelles?

Oberenn 39.2
Match the answers given below (a to f) to the questions (1 to 6), using the booklet to help you.
1. Prag na worthyp ev?
2. Prag yth eth hi tre?
3. Prag yth evas Jori dew hanafas a de?
4. Prag na dheuthons i genowgh?
5. Prag yth yw an fleghes plos?
6. Prag na dhons hi?
a. Drefenn hy mamm dhe bareusi hy hoen.
b. Drefenn na vynnons i dos.
c. Drefenn bos hy throes shyndys.
d. Drefenn na yll ev klywes.
e. Drefenn bos seghes bras dhodho.
f. Drefenn i dhe wari y'n pras.

Oberenn 39.3
Listen to the following passage. It will be read twice. Then answer, in Cornish, the questions which follow.

Ass o Pedrik anfur! Nyns eth dhe'n dre gans y wreg drefenn ev dhe oberi yn y lowarth. Yth esa hwans dhodho a wortos tre.
"Gwith an baban ytho!" yn medh y wreg, Lynda.
"Prag na vynn'ta doen an baban genes tejy?" Ev a wovynnas.
"Drefenn hi dhe vos lowenna omma genes es bos genev yn gwerthjiow leun a dus." Lynda a worthybis. "Dyw genes!"
Nyns o Pedrik hegar orth y wreg mes ny sorras orti, drefenn ev dhe vos gour da.

1. Fatell o Pedrik?
2. Prag na vynnas Pedrik mos dhe'n dre?
3. Prag na vynnas Lynda doen an baban gensi?
4. Fatell o Pedrik wosa lavarow y wreg?
5. Prag na sorras Pedrik orth y wreg?

176

RANN 1 KORTESI
Oberenn 1.1
1. Gorthugher da, Padryk. Gorthugher da, Mighal. Ottomma Pol.
2. Gorthugher da, Pol. Fatla genes?
3. Da lowr, meur ras.
4. Nos dha, oll.
5. Nos dha, Margh.
6. Dyw genes, Yowann.
7. Dyw genowgh hwi oll.

RANN 2 BOSVA
Oberenn 2.1
1. Yma pluvek ena.
2. Yma eglos y'n le.
3. Yma karr a-ji an karrji.
4. Yma pluvenn ryb an lyver.

Oberenn 2.2
1. Eus aval genes?
2. Eus jynn-skrifa ena?
3. Eus moes a-ji an chi?
4. Eus lyver gesys omma

Oberenn 2.3
1. Ottomma karrji!
2. Ottomma avalow!
3. Ottomma moes!

Oberenn 2.4
1. Ottena lyver!
2. Ottena pluvek!
3. Ottena pluvennow!

RANN 3 DIBLANSNETH
Oberenn 3.1
1. An pras
2. An sinema
3. An lestrier

Oberenn 3.2
1. An leurlenn
2. An woen
3. An desenn

Oberenn 3.3
1. An arr na
2. An vowes na
3. An genter na

RANN 4 OW PESYA ANDHIBLANSNETH
Oberenn 4.1
1. Mowes
2. Pras
3. Stamp

Oberenn 4.2
1. Unn bluvenn
2. Unn desenn
3. Unn sinema

Oberenn 4.3
1. Eus neppyth gesys?
2. Eus neppyth war an voes?
3. Eus nebonan a-ji an karr?

RANN 5 HEVELEPTER
Oberenn 5.1
1. Nyns yw an dra ma prenn, dell hevel.
2. Nyns yw honna Maria.
3. Nyns yw an eglos ma bryntin.
4. Nyns yw an re ma losow.

Oberenn 5.2
1. Yw hemma kenter? Yw/Nag yw.
2. Yw an voes ma derow? Yw/Nag yw.
3 Yw an diwes ma gwin frynkek? Yw/Nag yw.
4. Yw an re ma mebyl? Yw/Nag yw

Oberenn 5.3
1. Kenter yw
2. Gweder yw
3. Eglos yw
4. Avalow yns

RANN 6 STUDH
Oberenn 6.1
1. An eglos yw koth, dell dybav.
2. An traow yw parys, sur.
3. An fleghes ma yw feusik.
4. An vowes yw lowen lemmyn.
5. An mebyl yw gwerthys, dell hevel.
6. An fordh ma yw kul.

Oberenn 6.2
1. An maw ma yw fol.
2. An losow ma yw byw.
3. An den na yw gwann.
4. An gegin yw kul.
5. An avalow ma yw hweg.
6. Henn yw da.

Oberenn 6.3
1. Nyns yw honna Fiona.
2. Nyns yw an drehevyans na Hel an Dre.
3. Nyns yw an re na gwerthys.
4. Nyns yw an gwin ma hweg.
5. Nyns yw an gweder ma dhe les.
6. Nyns yw an jynn-skrifa parys lemmyn.

Oberenn 6.4
1. Yw an gwin parys?
2. Yw an mebyl gwerthys?
3. Yw an traow dhe les?
4. Yw an den na fol?
5. Yw an drehevyans na eglos?
6. Yw an vowes lowen lemmyn?

Oberenn6. 5
1. A nyns yw an lyver ma dhe les?
2. A nyns yw Hel an Dre nowydh?
3. A nyns yw an vowes salow lemmyn?
4. A nyns yw an re ma parys?
5. A nyns yw an den ma feusik?
6. A nyns yw an gweder gwerthys?

RANN 7 DASWRIANS
Oberenn 7.1
1. Gonn. Na wonn.
2. Gonn. Na wonn.
3. Gonn. Na wonn.

Oberenn 7.2
1. Py aval yw hweg?
2. Py re yw dhe les?
3. Py pluvek yw honna?
4. Py gwin yw parys?
5. Py fleghes yw lowen?
6. Py stamp yw kembrek?

Oberenn 7.3
1. An gewer yw poeth.
2. Hi a wra glaw.
3. Hi a wra ergh.
4. An gewer yw splann.

5. Hi yw niwlek.
6. Hi yw awelek.

RANN 8 GOROW HA BENOW
Oberenn 8.1
1. An gour
2. An brithel
3. An kenderow
4. An le
5. An noy
6. An gorthugher
7. An dus
8. An diogyon
9. An byskadoryon

Oberenn 8.2
1. An nos
2. An geniterow
3. An vodrep
4. An nith
5. An genter
6. An gador
7. An gegin
8. An wreg
9. An hwoer.

Oberenn 8. 3
1. Yw an gewer teg?
2. Eus ke ryb an koes?
3. Yw an le'ti ma nowydh?
4. Eus anwoes war an den na?
5. Yw an tiek na feusik?
6. A nyns eus pluvek war an gador?

Oberenn 8.4
1. An vamm-wynn yw koth lemmyn.
2. Yma anwoes war an tas.
3. An gewer yw toemm.
4. An vamm yw Kernowes.
5. An teylu ma yw lowen.
6. Hi a wra ergh lemmyn.

RANN 9 DESKRIFA TRAOW
Oberenn 9.1
1. Ottena drehevyans nowydh.
2. Eus aval byghan ena?
3. Yowann yw maw fol, dell dybav.
4. Kernow yw pow keltek, sur.
5. Yma gweder byghan omma.
6. Nyns yw chi nowydh, dell hevel.

Oberenn 9.2
1. Eus benyn goth ena?
2. Lanstefan yw tre vras.
3. Pyth yw hemma? Kador gembrek yw.
4. Leurlenn vrav yw honna.
5. Ottena an eglos teg!
6. Yma moes vyghan omma.
7. An Tamer yw avon dhown.

Oberenn 9.3
1. An re ma yw tus kernewek.
2. An re ma yw tus vretonek.
3. Yma pyskadoryon vrav ena.
4. Pyskadoryon dha yns.
5. Ottena benynes koth.
6. Benynyes kembrek yns.
7. A nyns yw an re na fleghes vyghan?
8. Fleghes lowen yns.
9. Pluvennow byghan yns.
10. Eus chiow bras ena?

Oberenn 9.4
1. Piw yw an re na?
2. Piw yw henna?
3. Piw yw henna?
4. Piw yw honna?
5. Piw yw an re na?
6. Piw yw honna?

Oberenn 9.5
1. Fatell yw an dra? Parys yw.
2. Fatell yw an teylu? Lowen yw.
3. Fatell yw Alban? Teg yw.
4. Fatell yw an badell na? Plos yw.
5. Fatell yw an gador-vregh? Da yw.
6. Fatell yw an re na. Bryntin yns.

Oberenn 9.6
1. Py par gwin yw hemma?
2. Py par kar yw henna?
3. Py par yeth yw homma?
4. Py par prenn yw hemma?
5. Py par karr yw henna?
6. Py par eglos yw honna?

RANN 10 PERGHENNIETH
Oberenn 10.1
1. Daras an hel
2. Penn an fordh
3. Penn an genter
4. Hwedhel an pyskador

5. Dorn an maw
6. Kares an vamm-wynn
7. Flows an flogh
8. Gwydh an koes

Oberenn 10.2
1. Mab pyskador
2. Leur chi
3. Hwedhel tiek
4. Lost ki
5. Broder tioges
6. Penn koes

Oberenn 10.3
1. Lyver Jori
2. Tas Myrna
3. Noy Pol
4. Dorn Lowena

RANN 11 SEYTH GER A VERN
Oberenn 11.1
1. Ni yw pyskadoryon.
2. Ev yw kloppek.
3. I yw fur.
4. Hwi yw warbarth lemmyn.

Oberenn 11.2
1. Hi yw rudh.
2. I yw parow.
3. Hi yw kloppek.
4. I yw lowen.
5. I yw parys.
6. Hi yw teg.

Oberenn 11.3
1. Yma ev war an leur.
2. Yma ev ryb an eglos.
3. Yma hi yn kres an dre.
4. Ev yw bretonek.
5. Hi yw berr.
6. Hi yw gwann.

RANN 12 DEGRE
Oberenn 12.1
1. Yw an eglos ma pur goth?
2. My yw pur lowen.
3. An gewer yw pur sygh.
4. Yw an voes ma re boes?
5. Ev yw re voen.
6. An hwedhel ma yw re hir.

Oberenn 12.2
1. Eus pluvennow lowr ena genowgh?
2. Yw hemma da lowr?
3. Yw an re ma teg lowr?
4. Yns i poes lowr?

RANN 13 LIES TRA

Oberenn 13.1
1. Ottomma lyvrow kernewek.
2. Yma an kentrow omma.
3. An fleghes na yw lowen.
4. Kemmer an avalow, mar pleg.

Oberenn 13.2
1. Eus chi ryb an pras?
2. Yw an dre bras?
3. Yw an notenn berr?
4. Yw an badell ma plos?

Oberenn 13.3
1. Margh.
2. Tiek.
3. Y'n pras.
4. Glyb. Hi a wra glaw.
5. Glyb.
6. Yn kres an dre.
7. Kanoryon.

RANN 14 NIVEROW

Oberenn 14.1
1. Naw kador.   6. Tri maw.
2. Unn den.   7. Teyr hador.
3. Peder benyn.   8. Pymthek plat.
4. Ugens karr.   9. Naw chi.
5. Diw vowes.   10. Dew gi.

Oberenn 14.2
1. An dhiw vowes.
2. An dhew diek.
3. An dhiw bluvenn.
4. An dhew hwegynn.
5. An dhew wolow.
6. An dhiw gestenenn.

Oberenn 14.3
1. Pymp fordh.   5. Tri le.
2. Peswardhek toll.   6. Unnek karrji.
3. Deg chi.   7. Seyth jynn-skrifa
4. Ugens pluvenn.   8. Teyr thesenn.

Oberenn 14.4
1. An golow yw splann.
2. Pyth yw an lyver ma?
3. Homm yw lovan hir.
4. Py maw yw henna?
5. Ev yw kenderow Jori.
6. Nyns yw an hwedhel ma gwir.

RANN 15 AN EUR

Oberenn 15.1
1. Deg mynysenn wosa deg eur.
2. Deg eur marnas ugens mynysenn.
3. Seyth eur hanter.
4. Pymp mynysenn warn ugens wosa dewdhek eur.
5. Eth eur marnas kwarter.
6. Peder eur poran.
7. Kwarter wosa unnek eur.
8. A-dro hwegh eur.
9. Naw eur marnas ugens mynysenn.
10. Hanter nos poran.

Oberenn 15.2
1. Peder eur marnas ugens mynysenn.
2. Pymp mynysenn warn ugens wosa eth eur.
3. Dewdhek eur marnas pymp mynysenn
4. Ugens mynysen wosa deg eur.

Oberenn 15.3
1. Dhe bymp eur hanter.
2. Dhe gwarter wosa hwegh eur.
3. Dhe dhiw eur.
4. Dhe dhewdhek eur hanter.
5. Dhe seyth eur poran.

RANN16 HWILAS TRAOW

Oberenn 16.1
1. Plema'n kuntelles?
2. Plema'n paper?
3. Plema'n platow?
4. Plema'n arghans?
5. Plema'n skath?
6. Plema'n spisti?

Oberenn 16.2
1. Y'n lowarth.   3. Gans an vamm.
2. Y'n ganstell.   4. War an plat.

Oberenn 16.3
1. Ymons i gans an tas.
2. Ymons i a-rag an chi.
3. Ymons i ryb an karrji.
4. Ymons i war an leur.

Oberenn 16.4
1. Ymons i y'n sinema.
2. Ymons i a-rag an ostel.
3. Ymons i ryb an fordh.

4. Ymons i yn Breten Vyghan.
5. Ymons i gans noy Yowann.

RANN 17 MOY A NIVEROW
Oberenn 17.1
1. Nownsek hanaf warn ugens.
2. Dew vaw ha dew ugens.
3. Etek benyn ha dew ugens.
4. Unn gador ha tri ugens.
5. Tri thiek ha tri ugens.
6. Peswardhek pluvenn ha tri ugens.
7. Peder moes ha peswar ugens.
8. Nownsek davas ha peswar ugens.

Oberenn 17.2
1. Deg warn ugens.
2. Dew ha dew ugens.
3. Peswar ha dew ugens.
4. Dewdhek ha peswar ugens.
5. Onan ha peswar ugens.
6. Kans.

Oberenn 17.3
1. Brav, kosel ha toemm.
2. War an woen yma ev.
3. Tiek yw ev.
4. Nag eus. Yma dew gi gans Mr Tamblyn.
5. Ymons i a-dryv Mr Tamblyn.
6. Etek davas ha tri ugens.
7. Diw dhavas yw du.

RANN 18 AN LE MAY MA TRAOW
Oberenn 18.1
1. Yma an lyver y'n argh-lyvrow.
2. Eus drehevyans a-dryv an elgos?
3. A nyns eus pluvek yn-dann an gador?
4. Yma an vamm-wynn orth an tan.
5. Nyns eus fordh ryb an bargen-tir.
6. Yma gwydhenn ryb an chi.
7. Eus fordh der an koes?
8. Yma gwin gans an boes.

Oberenn 18.2
1. Yma paper yn-dann an leurlenn.
2. Nyns eus lowarth a-dryv an chi.
3. Eus fordhow a-rag an chiow na?
4. Yma bolla rudh war an voes.

Oberenn 18.3
1. Usi an ganstell genes?
2. Nyns usi an fleghes y'n skol na.

3. A nyns usi an karr y'n karrji?
4. Usi an gresenn gernewek y'n dre ma?
5. Usi an tarow y'n pras na?
6. Nyns usi an deves ena.

Oberenn 18.4
1. Esons i war an leur?
2. Esons i y'n gegin?
3. Esons i y'n stret ma?
4. A nyns esons i war an plat?

Oberenn 18.5
1. Nyns eus lovan y'n skath.
2. Nyns eus bargen-tir bras yn Kernow.
3. Eus chapel yn kres an dre?
4. Eus pronter y'n eglos?
5. Eus folennow gwag y'n lyver ma?
6. Nyns eus myrgh tre hwath.

RANN 19 MEUR A po NEBES
Oberenn 19.1
1. Meur a blatow yw plos.
2. Yma meur a dheves y'n pras.
3. Meur a fleghes yw re dew.
4. Nyns eus meur a bluvennow gesys.
5. Kemmer meur a vara, mar pleg!
6. Ottena meur a dhelennow yn-dann an wydhenn.

Oberenn 19.2
1. Dornleow pals yw terrys.
2. Tus pals yw boghosek.
3. Yma chambours pals y'n ostel.
4. Yma tiogyon bals y'n pow ma.

Oberenn 19.3
1. Nyns yw lies fordh salow.
2. Lies hwedhel yw re verr.
3. Lies kuntelles yw re hir.
4. Lies hwegynn yw drog.
5. Lies porth yw byghan.
6. Lies delenn yw rudh.

Oberenn 19.4
1. Nebes tus yw re voen.
2. Nebes bleujennow yw gwynn.
3. Yma nebes korev gesys.
4. Nebes fordhow yw re gul.
5. Nyns eus nebes arghans lowr.
6. Nebes diwes yw hweg.
7. Nebes deves yw du.

8. Nebes amanenn yw melyn.

RANN 20 ERGHI
Oberenn 20.1
1. Ro an lyver dhe Beder!
2. Igor an fenester, mar pleg!
3. Gwra an oberenn ma!
4. Lavar dhymm an hwedhel!
5. Lenn an erva!
6. Dege daras an chambour!
7. Deus omma dhymm!
8. Ke dhe'n gegin!
9. Pys an bluvenn diworth Jori!
10. Skrif an lavar!

Oberenn 20.2
1. Rewgh an lyver dhe Beder!
2. Igerewgh an fenester, mar pleg!
3. Gwrewgh an oberenn ma!
4. Leverewgh dhymm an hwedhel!
5. Lennewgh an erva!
6. Degeewgh daras an chambour!
7. Dewgh omma dhymm!
8. Kewgh dhe'n gegin!
9. Pysewgh an bluvenn diworth Jori!
10. Skrifewgh an lavar!

Oberenn 20.3
1. Na ro an lyver dhe Beder!
2. Na igor an fenester, mar pleg!
3. Na wra an oberenn ma!
4. Na lavar dhymm an hwedhel!
5. Na lenn an erva!
6. Na dhege darasa an chambour!
7. Na dheus omma dhymm!
8. Na ge dhe'n gegin!
9. Na bys an bluvenn diworth Jori!
10. Na skrif an lavar!

Oberenn 20.4
1. Na rewgh an lyver dhe Beder!
2. Na igerewgh an fenester, mar pleg!
3. Na wrewgh an oberenn ma!
4. Na leverewgh dhymm an hwedhel!
5. Na lennewgh an erva!
6. Na dhegeewgh an chambour!
7. Na dhewgh omma dhymm!
8. Na gewgh dhe'n gegin!
9. Na bysewgh an bluvenn diworth Jori!
10. Na skrifewgh an lavar!

RANN 21 MY YW...NYNS OV
Oberenn 21.1
1. Nyns ov boghosek.
2. Nyns ov diek.
3. Nyns os flogh gokki.
4. Nyns os fur.
5. Nyns yw ev mab Mr Pennglas.
6. Nyns yw ev arghantti.
7. Nyns yw hi benyn deg.
8. Nyns yw hi delenn ell.
9. Nyns on warbarth lemmyn.
10. Nyns on tiogyon.
11. Nyns owgh tus an dre.
12. Nyns owgh parow.
13. Nyns yns skorr bras.
14. Nyns yns kanoryon dha.

Oberenn 21.2
1. Osta Albanek?
2. Yw ev koes byghan?
3. Yw hi gerva hir?
4. On ni tew?
5. Owgh hwi fleghes dha?
6. Yns i plos?

Oberenn 21.3
1. Fol os.
2. Gyllys yw ev.
3. Gow yw ev.
4. Devedhys yw hi lemmyn.
5. Bro vras yw hi.
6. Krev on.
7. Shyndys on.
8. Teg owgh.
9. Gwann owgh.
10. Lowarthow kul yns.

Oberenn21.4
1. *We are happy.*
2. *We are not fishermen.*
3. *Isn't she Mrs Bolitho?*
4. *They are the lazy ones.*
5. *Am I safe here? You are!*
6. *Is this carpet new? No!*
7. *You are Welsh perhaps. We are!*
8. *Are they not good dances? They are!*

RANN 22 HEVELEPTER HA DIHEVELEPTER
Oberenn 22.1
1. An chi ma yw haval orth ostel.

2. Broder Jori yw haval orth mab Lynda.
3. An desenn yw haval orth bara.
4. Hemm yw haval orth henna.
5. Euryor Wella yw haval orth huni Mr Pennglas.

Oberenn 22.2
1. An chi ma yw dihaval diworth ostel.
2. Broder Jori yw dihaval diworth mab Lynda.
3. An desenn yw dihaval diworth bara.
4. Hemm yw dihaval diworth henna.
5. Euryor Wella yw dihaval diworth huni Mr Pennglas.

Oberenn 22.3
1. Write the same story again!
2. They are in the same house.
3. The weather is the same to day as the weather yesterday.
4. Take the same road as the one before!
5. The boats are in the same harbour together.
6. Green is not the same colour as green.

Oberenn 22.4
1. Ro dhymm ken plat!
2. Diskwedh dhymm ken hanaf!
3. Ke dhe gen chambour!
4. Pys ken amanenn diworth an vamm!
5. Gwra ken tra, mar pleg!
6. Leverewgh ken hwedhel!

RANN 23 AN TERMYN TREMENYS
Oberenn 23.1
1. My o drog pes.
2. Lorna o klav.
3. An re ma o da lowr.
4. I o pur dhiek.
5. Hemm o an keth tra.
6. Piw o an gwettha flogh?

Oberenn 23.2
1. Ens i parow?
2. O an vodrep koth?
3. Ewgh hwi kanoryon dha?
4. O dornla an hanaf terrys?
5. En vy gokki?
6. O ev bargen-tir bras?

Oberenn 23.3
1. Yth esov vy omma.
2. Nyns esos jy ogas dhymm.
3. Esons i y'n ostel na?
4. Yth esowgh hwi yn gorsav an hynshorn.
5. Yth esons i war an treth.
6. Yma an bughes y'n pras arall.

Oberenn 23.4
1. Ni o drog pes.
2. Yth esen y'n keth karr.
3. Glawlenn an tas yw terrys.
4. Yth esa an eglos yn kres an blu.
5. An euryor ma yw nowydh.
6. Nyns esens y'n lyverva.
7. I yw gever, dell hevel.
8. An kommol yw loes.
9. Hwerydh Pam yw feusik.
10. Nyns yw an dus lowen.

RANN 24 PERGHENNIETH
Oberenn 24.1
1. Kemmer dha dhiwes!
2. Y draow yw parys.
3. Henn yw dha vaw.
4. Y dhornleow yw terrys.
5. Pyth yw dha vro?
6. My yw y geniterow.
7. Yma dha lyvrow genes.
8. Nyns eus y vebyl omma hwath.

Oberenn 24.2
1. Nyns yw aga flat glan.
2. Yth esa aga tharow yn mes.
3. Ow hoen yw parys dhe seyth eur.
4. Nyns yns i ow flasennow.
5. Hy fenn o shyndys.
6. I o ow howethesow.
7. Ple'ma aga fleghes?
8. Gorr ow hansel war an voes!
9. Ple'ma hy thas?
10. Pyth yw aga arghantti?

Oberenn 24.3
1. Gwrewgh agas ober!
2. Plema ow lavrek?
3. Dha ji yw koth, dell hevel.
4. Yw agan treth glan?
5. O aga thas pes da?
6. Plema agan glawlenn?
7. Ow henderow yw Jori.

8. Usi dha hwoer genes?

Oberenn 24.4
1. Lowen en.   4. Tri.
2. Yn kres tre vyghan.   5. Duik.
3. Unnek den.

RANN 25 HWARVOSOW TREMENYS
Oberenn 25.1
1. Ty a leveris henna.
2. Hi a lennas an hwedhel.
3. Ev a ganas y'n eglos.
4. My a dhiskwedhas dhis an jynn-amontya.
5. Maria a worras hy sagh ena.
6. Y das a neuvyas y'n mor.
7. An gath a esedhas war an gweli.
8. An re na a weresas an tiek.

Oberenn 25.2
1. Ty re leveris henna.
2. Hi re lennas an hwedhel.
3. Ev re ganas y'n eglos.
4. My re dhiskwedhas dhis an jynn-amontya.
5. Maria re worras hy sagh ena.
6. Y das re neuvyas y'n mor.
7. An gath re esedhas war an gweli.
8. An re na re weresas an tiek.

Oberenn 25.3
1. Ny brenis an radyo.
2. A brenas hi pows rudh?
3. Ny brensyn an plasennow.
4. A ny brensons i boes y'n dre?
5. A brensys jy lavrek y'n gwerthji nowydh na?
6. Ny brenas Jori an korev.
7. Ny brensowgh agas mebyl. Prensyn!
8. A ny brenas an fleghes hwegynnow? Ny brensons!

Oberenn 25.4
1. Esedhas/Na esedhas.
2. Lennsons/Na lennsons.
3. Neuvis/Na neuvis.
4. Gweressyn/Na weressyn.
5. Gorrsons/Na worrsons.
6. Leveris/Na leveris.

RANN 26 HWARVOSOW Y'N EUR MA
Oberenn 26.1
1. Ny brenav glawlenn nowydh.
2. Ny evydh dowr.
3. Ny gews ev flows.
4. Ny guntell hi plasennow.
5. Ny vetyn orth agan koweth.
6. Ny virowgh orth an re ma.
7. Ny dennons an lovan warbarth.
8. Ny yskynn Mona an vre.
9. Ny guntell an byskadoryon arghans.
10. Ny gews hemma kernewek da.
11. Ny vir ev orth an bellwolok.
12. Ny bren hi boes y'n dre.

Oberenn 26.2
1. Hwi a vet orth an pronter.
2. I a yskynn an menydh.
3. My a guntell an kaderyow.
4. Ni a vir orth an folenn na.
5. Wella a brenn karr nowydh.
6. An fleghes a yv aga leth.

Oberenn 26.3
1. My a bren kota nowydh pub blydhen.
2. Mighal a yv te gans y hansel.
3. Ny gewssons Kernewek.
4. An re ma a guntell stampow koth.
5. A brenowgh hwi bakken yn gwerthji Mr Page?
6. A ny virydh jy orth an bellwolok?
7. Ni a vet orth dha vab war an fordh dhe'n skol.
8. I a worta omma pupprys.

Oberenn 26.4
1. Y'n dre.   4. Y'n skol yth esens.
2. Klav o.   5. Tre yn y weli.
3. Yn poynt da ymons.

RANN 27 VERBOW DHE LES
Oberenn 27.1
1. My a vynn gwari gans an fleghes.
2. A yll ev gweres y vamm gans an ober?
3. An avon a yn-nans dhe'n mor.
4. Yowann a wra moesow.
5. Morwenna a dheu dhe Essa pub dydh.

Oberenn 27.2
1. My a vynnas gwari gans an fleghes.
2. A allas ev gweres y vamm gans an ober?

3. Ni eth yn-nans dhe'n mor.
4. Yowann a wrug moes.
5. Morwenna a dheuth dhe Essa an myttin ma.

RANN 28 DHYMM HA DHIS
Oberenn 28.1
1. My a dhiskwedhas an skeusenn dhedhi.
2. Ni a lever an hwedhel dhedha.
3. Ev a vynn eva koffi ganso.
4. Ty a yll esedha gansa.
5. Na worr dha arghans ynni!
6. Yma skath vras ynno.
7. Eus bollas a gowl warnedhi?
8. Hwi a yll gasa agas kota warnedha.
9. Nyns esa le rygdhi.
10. Ty a yll gul henna ragdho.
11. Ny yll an dus mos hebdho.
12. Ny wonn konvedhes hebdhi.
13. Kemmer an lyver anodho!
14. Na evewgh dowr anedhi!

Oberenn 28.2
1. Yma kath gensi hi.
2. Ro an bluvenn dhymmo vy!
3. Ev a skrifas ynno ev.
4. Eus anwoes warnos jy?
5. Gwra henna hebdha i
6. Tri ahanan ni yw parys.
7. Kemmer an gwin ragos jy!
8. Meur ras dhiso jy!
9. A vynn a flogh gwari gensi hi?
10. Ev eth genen ni.

Oberenn 28.3
1. Yma kath gensi hyhi.
2. Ro an bluven dhymmo evy!
3. Ev a skrifas ynno eev.
4. Eus anwoes warnos tejy?
5. Gwra henna hebdha ynsi!
6. Tri ahanan nyni yw parys.
7. Kemmer an gwin ragos tejy!
8. Meur ras dhiso tejy!
9. A vynn an flogh gwari gensi hyhi?
10. Ev eth genen nyni.

RANN 29 HWARVOSOW OW PESYA
Oberenn 29.1
1. Yth esov ow kortos ow howeth.
2. Yma Yowann ow kewsel Kernewek.
3. Nyns usi Owen owth eva y leth.

4. Yma dha vroder ow tos lemmyn.
5. Nyns usi hi ow mires orth an bellwolok.
6. Yma an tas ow kolghi an lestri.

Oberenn 29.2
1. Nyns esen ow koslowes orto.
2. Esa an tas ow palas y'n lowarth?
3. Nyns esa karr ow tos.
4. Yth esens i ow kul aga ober.
5. Eses jy ow powes?
6. Yth esa an ki owth eva dowr.
7. Yth esen ow mos.
8. Esa tren ow nesa?

Oberenn 29.3
1. Esowgh hwi ow kweres?
2. Nyns esons i ow kewsel dhedhi.
3. Yth eson ow tybri an boes.
4. Nyns esowgh ow klywes orthiv.
5. Ymons i ow kana gansa.
6. Nyns eson owth holya an wir fordh.

Oberenn 29.4
1. Yma an venyn ma ow megi.
2. Yma an byskadoryon ow mones dhe'n mor.
3. Yma aga hath ow koska war aga gweli.
4. Ymons i ow triga yn y ji.
5. Yma Jori owth esedha orth an fenester.
6. Yma agan ki ow neuvya y'n avon.

RANN 30 GRASSA, PANDRA, ASS!
Oberenn 30.1
1. Meur ras dhis a'n dyenn-rew.
2. Meur ras dhis a'n tokyn.
3. Meur ras dhis a'n koffi.
4. Meur ras dhis ow kweres.
5. Meur ras dhis ow kortos. Ny vern!

Oberenn 30.2
1. Pandr'a a welsys jy y'n lowarth?
2. Pandr'a skrifsons i.
3. Pandr'a a glysowgh hwi?
4. Pandr'a wra Peder pub dydh?
5. Pandr'a brenas an vamm y'n spisti?

Oberenn 30.3
1. Ass yw ploes an wedrenn ma!
2. Ass yw da an boes omma y'n diwotti!
3. Ass yns koynt!
4. Ass os krev!

185

5. Ass o drog an gewer!
6. Ass en vy klav!

RANN 31 ARAYA TRAOW
Oberenn 31.1
1. Hedhyw yw an ugensves dydh a'n mis. .
2. Hy chi yw an kynsa y'n stret.
3. Ni a esedhas y'n ethves rew.
4. Ena y kansons an trydhegves salm warn ugens
5. Dy' Gwener a vydh y nessa bloedh ha tri ugens.

RANN 32 PY DYDH YW EV?
Oberenn 32.1
1. Dy' Mergher an nessa a vis Hedra.
2. Dy' Sadorn an pymthegves a vis Metheven.
3. Dy' Lun an kynsa warn ugens a vis Est.
4. Dy' Gwener an ethves a vis Hwevrer.
5. Dy' Sul an unnegves warn ugens a vis Genver.
6. Dy' Yow an dewdhegves a vis Gwynngala.

Oberenn 32.2
1. Dy' Mergher an nawves a vis Hedra.
2. Dy' Sadorn an nessa warn ugens a vis Metheven.
3. Dy' Lun an ethves warn ugens a vis Est.
4. Dy' Gwener an pymthegves a vis Hwevrer.
5. Dy' Sul an seythves a vis Hwevrer.
6. Dy' Yow an nownsegves a vis Gwynngala.

RANN 33
DA YW GANS ha DROG YW GANS
Oberenn 33.1
1. Da yw genen kerdhes warbarth.
2. Da yw gans ow broder dos dh'agan chi.
3. Drog yw gensi dybri kig.
4. Gwell yw gansa gwari peldroes.
5. Poes yw gans Harold kewsel yndella.
6. Kas yw gans Tamsyn yowynk mones dhe'n skol.
7. O gwell gansa dos y'ga harr ytho?
8. Nyns yw da genev mires orth an bellwolok.
9. Da yw gans puponan bos rych.
10. Drog yw gans an maw omwolghi.

Oberenn 33.2
1. My a vynn dasskorr dha lyver.
2. Onan didhanus yw.
3. Na dhiwedhas an lyver.
4. Hwedhlow yn kever Kernow.

RANN 34 PERGHENNIETH

Oberenn 34.1
1. Eus kath dhedhi?
2. Eus skath dhodho?
3. Esa euryor dhe'n gour na?
4. Esa hwoer dhedha?
5. Eus tokyn dhymm?
6. Eus kollel-boket genes?

Oberenn 34.2
1. Yth esa lowarth bras dhe Vr Collings.
2. Nyns esa lyverva dhe'n dre.
3. Esa dewweder dhedhi?
4. A nyns esa meur a dir dhe'n tiek?

Oberenn 34.3
1. An gador ma o dhymm.
2. Oll an mebyl ma o dhe Vtrs Palmer.
3. An ki drog na o dhodho.
4. Nyns o an kota loes ma dhymm.
5. O an jynn-amontya nowydh dhe Beder?
6. A nyns o an koffi ma dhis?

Oberenn 34.4
1. Yw an bal gernewek dhis?
2. An soedhva yw dhe'n gesva.
3. Nyns o an radyo dhedha.
4. Nyns yw an seghyer dhe'n spiser.
5. An bel yw dhe'n fleghes ma.
6. An bows dhu o dhe'n vamm.
7. Nyns yw an lawlenn dhymm.
8. An plasennow yw dhe'n vowes ma.

Oberenn 34.5
1. An dhydhyow a hirha y'n hav.
2. An pyskador a verrhas an lovan.
3. Ny lanhasyn an karr.
4. An howl a doemmha an tir.

RANN 35 OLL, NEBES po MANN
Oberenn 35.1
1. Oll anedha o gwann, pur wann.
2. Nebes sethow o terrys.
3. Nebes ahanan re wrug an ober.

4. Ny dheuth oll an gorholyon dhe'n porth.
5. Nebes lowarthow yw teg.
6. Kemmer nebes gwin y'n wedrenn.
7. Hwi oll a vydh ena a-dhistowgh
8. Oll an amaris yw leun a draow.

Oberenn 35.2
1. Ny worthybis flogh vydh.
2. Nyns o delenn vydh glas.
3. Nyns yw lyver vydh dhe les.
4. Ny vrojyas hi oy vydh.
5. Ny lammas davas vydh dres ke.

RANN 36 KYNS ha WOSA
Oberenn 36.1
1. Mona a ganas ha hi owth omwiska.
2. Ny yllsyn keskewsel ha my owth omwolghi.
3. Ass o Larri lowen ha Morwenna owth esedha rybdho.
4. Skwith o ow howeth hag ev ow revya a-dreus an avon.
5. My a vynn gorra an lestri war an voes ha ty ow pareusi an boes.
6. An tas a yll koska deg mynysenn ha'n vebyon ow kwari peldroes yn- mes.
7. Res yw gortos a-ji ha hi ow kul glaw.
8. Fatell wrons i aga ober hag i ow kewsel warbarth?

Oberenn 36.2
1. Yowann a welas y wreg wosa gweles y gowethes.
2. Maria a gewsis gans Padryk wosa y weres.
3. Res yw tyli wosa y brena.
4. Hi a jynnskrifas an oberenn wosa hy redya.

Oberenn 36.3
1. My a wolghas an fos kyns hy liwya.
2. An oy o drog. Margh a omglywas klav wosa y dhybri.
3. Mir kyns lamma!
4. I a asas an hanafow wosa aga lenwel a goffi.
5. Lenn an lavarow wosa aga threlya yn Kernewek!

RANN 37 HEVELEBI TRAOW
Oberenn 37.1

1. Ev yw mar grev avel lew.
2. Dy' Yow o mar lyb avel Dy' Mergher.
3. Ty yw mar fol avello.
4. Ev o mar gales avel kolonn Pharaoh.
5. An nos yw mar dhu avel sagh-kroust an Jowl.
6. Yowann yw mar dhrog avella, dell dybav.

Oberenn37. 2
1. Maria yw kottha agesov.
2. An fordh ma yw salwa ages an fordh veur.
3. Lannstefan yw nes ages Loundres.
4. Piw o folla agessa?
5. Ty o feusikka agesso ytho.
6. Mighal yw byghanna ages y vroder, dell hevel.

Oberenn37.3
1. An gwanna flogh.
2. An lyha arghans.
3. An glanna stevell.
4. An lowenna benyn.
5. An nowyttha lyver.
6. An hwekka tesenn.

Oberenn 37.4
1. Yn Truru y trig ev.
2. Yn Sen Ostell yth ober ev.
3. Skav yw kynth yw koth.
4. Mos dhe dhonsya a wra ev.
5. Korev a yv ev.
6. Salli yw hanow y gowethes.

RANN 38 Y WERES
Oberenn 38.1
1. My a wrug y asa a-rag Hel an Dre.
2. Y nith a vynn hy gorra war hy hador.
3. Piw a yll hy gorfenna?
4. Oll anedha a wra hy dyski.
5. Yowann a vynn hy gweres.
6. Py flogh a wrug hy skrifa dhymm?
7. Ny allav y weles lemmyn.
8. Ow heniterow a allas y dhiwedha kyns prys koen.

Oberenn 38.2
1. Gwra ow gweres!
2. A vynn'ta y dhoen dhymm?
3. Ny vynnons i aga sywya.
4. Na wra hy gweskel!

5. A wre'ta y gara?
6. A yllyn ni y dhaswul?
7. Ny wrussowgh hwi agan klywes.
8. Ny yllis vy dha weles.

Oberenn 38.3
1. I yw dha vamm ha'th tas.
2. Yw an lyver ma onan a'y lyvrow?
3. Agan mamm-wynn a drig y'gan chi.
4. My a gar ow fleghes ha'm fleghes-wynn.
5. Kemmer an arghans ma y'th torn!
6. Morwenna a leveris, " Fatla genes?"
   dh'y broder.

RANN 39 AN ACHESON
Oberenn 39.1
1. Prag na wre'ta y skoedhya?
2. Prag na worfennowgh agas ober dhe
   beder eur?
3. Prag na waytydh jy gorthyp?
4. Prag na leskons i del marow y'ga
   lowarth?
5. Prag na berthyn ni kov a henna?
6. Prag na sewenas hi?
7. Prag na vynn'ta esedha omma?
8. Prag na igoras Kolyn y anow y'n
   kuntelles?

Oberenn 39.2
1. Prag na worthyp ev?
d. Drefenn na yll ev klywes.
2. Prag yth eth hi tre?
a. Drefenn hy mamm dhe bareusi hy hoen.
3. Prag yth evas Jori dew hanafas a de?
e. Drefenn bos syghes bras dhodho.
4. Prag na dheuthons i genowgh?
b. Drefenn na vynnons i dos.
5. Prag yth yw an fleghes ploes?
f. Drefenn i dhe wari y'n pras.
6. Prag na dhons hi?
c. Drefenn bos hy throes shyndys.

Oberenn 39.3
1. Anfur o.
2. Drefenn bos hwans dhodho a oberi yn y
   lowarth.
3. Drefenn an baban dhe vos lowenna gans
   Pedrik es bos gans Lynda yn
   gwerthjiow leun a dus.
4. Nyns o ev hegar orth y wreg.
5. Drefenn ev dhe vos gour da.

A

a², *prep.*, of, from
a-barth (dhe), *prep.*, on behalf (of)
a-dal, *prep.*, opposite
a-dhann², *prep.* from under
a-dhelergh, *adv.*, behind, rearwards
a-dhistowgh (distowgh), *adv.*, immediately
a-dreus dhe², *prep.*, across, athwart
a-dro, *adv.*, around
a-dro dhe², *prep.*, about, concerning
a-dryv, *adv.*, behind
a-dryv dhe²(+ *noun*), *prep.*, behind
a-hys, *adv.*, along
a-hys dhe²(+ *noun*), *adv.*, along
a-ji, *adv.*, inside
a-ji dhe², *prep.*, inside
a'n par ma, of this kind
a'n par na, of that kind
a-rag, *adv.*, in front of
a-ugh, *prep.*, above
a-ves, *adv.*, outside
a-ves dhe², *prep.*, outside
a vydh, (*3s. of* **bos**) will be
a-wosa, *adv.*, afterwards
a'y anvodh, unwillingly, against his will
a'y esedh, he (is) seated
a'y sav, he (is) standing
a'y vodh, willingly, with his agreement
a'y wrowedh, he (is) lying down
acheson, -ys, *m.*, cause, reason
aga³, *poss. adj.*,their
agan, *poss. adj.*our
agas, *poss. adj.*your *(pl.)*
ages, than
Alban, *f.*, Scotland

Albanek, *adj.*, Scottish
alemma, *adv.*, from here/now
alena, *adv.*, from there/then
Almayn, *f.*, Germany
almaynek, *adj.*, German
als, -yow, *f.*, cliff
amanenn, *m.*, butter
amari, -s *f.*, cupboard
ammeth, *f.*, agriculture
anfur, *adj.*, unwise
anfurra, *adj.*, more unwise
ankor, -s, *m.*, anchor
anwoes, *m.*, cold (ailment)
   yma anwoes war
   Beder, Peter has a cold
appos-ya, (-yas) *vb.*, examine
apposyans, -ow, *m.*, examination
arall, erell, *adj.*, other
argh-lyvrow,
   arghow-l, *f.*, bookcase
arghans, *m.*, silver, money
arghantti, -ow, *m.*, bank
arvor, -yow, *m.*, shore, coast
askloes, *pl*, chips
aswonn (-is), *vb.*, acknowledge, know, realise
aval, -ow, *m.*, apple
avel, *adv.*,as
avon, -yow, *f.*, river
awel, -ow, *f.*, wind, gale
awelek, *adj.*, very windy

B

baban, -es, *m.*, baby
bakken, *m.*, bacon
bal, -yow, *m.*, mine
baner, -yow, *m.*, flag
bara, *m.*, bread
bardhonieth, *m.*, poetry
bargen-tir, -yow-t., *m.*, farm
bedh, -ow, *m.*, grave
benow, *f./adj.*, female
benyn, -es, *f.*, woman
berr, *adj.*, short
berra, *adj.*, shorter
berrheans, -ow, *m.*, abbreviation, abridgement
bewin, *m.*, beef
bleujenn, -ow, *f.*, flower

blew, *coll.*, hair
blewenn, -ow, *f.*, a hair
bloedh, *m.*, year of age
boes, *m.*, food
boesti, -ow, *m.*, café
boghosek, *adj.*, poor
boghosekka, *adj.*, poorer
bolla, bollow, *m.*, bowl
bowji, -ow, *m.*, cowshed
bownder, -yow, *f.*, lane
bras, *adj.*, big
brassa, *adj.*, bigger
brav, *adj.*, fine, excellent
braffa, *adj.*, finer
bre, -ow, *f.*, hill
bregh, -ow, *f.*, arm
bresel, -yow, *f.*, war
Breten, *f.*, Britain
Breten Veur, *f.*, Great Britain
Breten Vyghan, *f.*, Brittany
Breton, *m.*, Breton (person)
breus, -ow, *f.*, judgement
brithel, brithyli, *m.*, mackerel
bro, -yow, *f.*, country
broder, breder, *m.*, brother
bronn, -ow, *f.*, hill
bryjyon, bros (brojyas), *vb.*, boil
bryjys, *adj.*, boiled
bryntin, *adj.*, noble, fine
bryntinna, *adj.*, nobler
bugh, -es, *f.*, cow
byghan, *adj.*, small
byghanna, *adj.*, smaller
bys (yn, dhe), *prep.*, up to, until
bys, -yes, *m.*, finger
   bys vykken, for ever
bysi, *adj.*, busy, important
bythkweyth, *adv.*, ever, never *(with neg.)*
byttegyns, *adv.*, nevertheless
byw, *adj.*, alive
byw-a (-as), *vb.*, live
bywnans, -ow, *m.*, life

Ch

chambour, -s, *m.*, bedroom
chapel, -yow, *m.*, chapel
chi, -ow, *m.*, house
chymbla, -blow, *m.*, chimney

D

da, *adj.*, good
daffar, *m.*, kit, gear
dalleth, *m.*, beginning
dalleth (dallathas), *vb.*, begin
dannvon (-as), *vb.*, send
dans, dens, *m.*, tooth
daras, -ow, *m.*, door
dargan, -ow, *f.*, forecast
dargan-a (-as), *vb.*, forecast
daskorr (-as), *vb.*, restore
dassergh-i (-as), *vb.*, revive
dasserghyans, *m.*, revival
davas, deves, *f.*, sheep
de, *adv.*, yesterday
deg, *num.*, ten
dege-a (-as), *m.*, shut
dehwel-es (-is), *vb.*, return
del, *coll.*, leaves, foliage
delenn, -ow, *f.*, leaf
dell, *conj.*, as, so
   dell dybav, so I think
   dell glywav, I hear
   dell hevel, so it seems
   dell lavarav, as I say
   dell leverir, as is said, one says
   dell vydh usys, as is usual
den, tus, *m.*, person
den bal, tus bal, *m.*, miner
der, *prep*, see **dre**
derow, *adj.*, oak
derow, *coll.*, oak trees
derwenn, -ow, *f.*, oak tree
desedhys, *adj.*, situated
desk, -ow, *m.*, desk
devedhys, *adj.*, come, arrived
dew², *num.*, two *(m.)*
dewweder, *pl.*, spectacles
dha², *poss. adj.*, your
   dha weles!, see you!
dhe², *prep.*, to
   dhe les, useful
   meur dhe les, very useful
   dhe-ves, *adv.*, away
didhanus, *adj.*, amusing
diek, *adj.*, lazy
diekka, *adj.*, lazier
dien, *adj.*, complete

difun, *adj.*, awake
dihaval, *adj.*, different
dihwans, *adj.*, eagerly
diskwedh-es (-as), *vb.*, show
distowgh, *adj.*, immediately
diwedh, *m.*, end, finish
diwedh (-as), *vb.*, end, finish
diwedhes, *adj.*, late
diw², *num.*, two *(f.)*
   diwleuv, *dual.*, (two) hands
diwes, -osow, *m.*, drink
diwisk-a (-as), *vb.*, take off clothing
diworth, *prep.*, from
diwotti, -ow, *m.*, inn, pub
diwros, -ow, *f.*, bicycle
doen deg (dug), *vb.*, carry
dohajydh, *m.*, afternoon
dons, -yow, *m.*, dance
dons-ya (-yas), *vb.*, dance
dorn, -ow, *m.*, hand
dornla, -leow, *m.*, handle
dos, deu (deuth), *vb.*, come
down, *adj.*, deep
dowr, -ow, *m.*, water
dre², *prep.*, through (**der** *before vowels*)
drefenn, *conj.*, because
drehedh-es (-as), *vb.*, reach
drehev-el (-is), *vb*, raise
drehevyans, -ow, *m.*, building
dres, *prep.*, through, beyond
dri, dre (dros), *vb.*, bring
drog, *adj.*, bad
drog pes, *adj.*, displeased
drog yw genev, I'm sorry
du, *adj.*, black
Dy', *abbreviation of* **dydh**
   Dy' Sul, Sunday
   Dy' Lun, Monday
   Dy' Meurth, Tuesday
   Dy' Mergher, Wednesday
   Dy' Yow, Thursday
   Dy' Gwener, Friday
   Dy' Sadorn, Saturday
dybr-i, deber (-is), *vb.*, eat
dydh, -yow, *m.*, day
   (an jydh)
dydhlyver, -vrow, *m.*, diary
dyenn, *m.*, cream

dyenn-rew, *m.*, ice-cream
dyskador, -yon, *m.*, teacher
dyskadores, -ow, *f.*, teacher
dyskans, *m.*, lesson
dysk-i (-as), *vb.*, learn, teach
Dyw, *m.*, God
Dyw genes!, *(s)* goodbye!
Dyw genowgh!, *(pl)* goodbye!

E

e, = **ev**, *pron.*, him, it
ebrenn, *f.*, sky
edhen, ydhyn, *f.*, bird
efan, *adj.*, wide, spacious
eglos, -yow, *f.*, church
ena, *adv.*, there, then
ensampel, -plow, *m.*, example
enyval, -es, *m.*, animal
erell, *pl.adj.*, other, others
ergh, *m.*, snow
   ergh a wra, it's snowing
es, *adj.*, easy, comfortable
es, *conj.*, than
esya, *adj.*, easier, more comfortable
esedh-a (-as), *vb.*, sit
esedhva, -ow, *f.*, sitting-room
esel, -i, *m.*, member, limb
eskis, -yow, *f.*, shoe
estyllenn, -ow, *f.*, shelf
eth, *num.*, eight
euryor, -yow, *m.*, (wrist)watch
euth, *m.*, terror, dread
euthek, *adj.*, frightful
ev, *pron.*, he *or* it
ev-a yv (-as), *vb.*, drink
ewn, *adj.*, correct, straight
ewna, *adj.*, straighter
ewnter, -tres, *m.*, uncle
eythin, *coll.*, gorse
eythinenn, -ow, *f.*, gorse bush

F

fals, *adj.*, false
fatell², *conj.*, how
fenester, -tri, *f.*, window
fenten, -tynyow, *f.*, spring (water)
fest, *adv.*, very
fest da, very good

190

fest yn ta, very well
feusik, *adj.,* lucky
feusikka, *adj.,* luckier
fisten-a (-as), *vb.,* hurry
flogh, fleghes, *m.,* child
flows, *m.,* idle talk
fol, *adj.,* foolish
folla, *adj.,* more foolish
folenn, -ow, *f.,* page
fordh, -ow, *f.,* road
fordh-a-dro, fordhow-a-d, *f.,* roundabout (road)
forn, -ow, *f.,* stove, oven
fos, -ow, *f.,* wall
fur, *adj.,* wise
furra, *adj.,* wiser
furv, -ow, *f.,* form, shape
fylm, -ow, *m.,* film
fyrv, *adj.,* firm
fyrffa, *adj.,* firmer

G

gall-oes gyll (as), *vb.,* to be able, 'can'
ganow, -ow, *m.,* mouth
gans, *prep.,* with
garm-a (-as), *vb.,* shout
garth, -ow, *m.,* ya
garr, -ow, *f.,* leg
garth-gwari, garthow-g., *m.,* playground
gas-a (-as), *vb.,* leave
gaver, gever, *f.,* goat
gell, *adj.,* brown
genes, with you *(s.)*
genowgh, with you *(pl.)*
genys, *adj.,* born
ger, -yow, *m.,* word
gerlyver, -vrow, *m.,* dictionary
gerva, -ow, *f.,* word list
gesys, *adj.,* left, remaining
glan, *adj.,* clean
glanna, *adj.,* cleaner
glanh-e (-as), *vb.,* clean
glas, *adj.,* blue *(and green of plants)*
glaw, *m.,* rain
glaw a wra, it's raining
glawlenn, -ow, *f.,* umbrella
glesin, -yow, *m.,* lawn

glow, *m.,* coal
glyb, *adj.,* wet
glyppa, *adj.,* wetter
goedh, -ow, *f.,* goose
goel, -yow, *m.,* sail
goel-ya (-yas), *vb.,* sail
goen, -yow, *f.,* down
goes, *m.,* blood
gokki, *adj.,* silly
golgh-i (-as), *vb.,* wash
golow, -ys, *m.,* light
gols, *coll.,* hair of the head
gorfenn-a (-as), *vb.,* finish
gorhel, -holyon, *m.,* ship
gorher, -yow, *m.,* cover, lid
gorow, *m/adj.,* male
gorr-a (-as), *vb.,* put
gorsav, -ow, *m.,* station
　gorsav an hyns-horn, *m.,* railway station.
　gorsav an kyttrin, *m.,* bus station.
gorthugher, *m.,* evening
gorthyb-i (-is), *vb.,* answer, reply
gorthyp, -ybow, *m.,* answer, reply
gort-os, gorta (-as), *vb.,* wait for
goslow-es (-as), *vb.,* listen (**orth** to)
gour, gwer, *m.,* man, husband
gover, -ow, *m.,* brook
govynn, -ow, *m.,* question
govynn (-as), *vb.,* ask
gow, -yow, *m.,* lie
gradh, -ow, *m.,* step, grade
gras, -ow, *m.,* thanks
gul, gwra (gwrug), *vb.,* do, make
gwann, *adj.,* weak
gwanna, *adj.,* weaker
gwari, -ow, *m.,* game, play
gwari (-as), *vb.,* play
gwas, gwesyon, *m.,* fellow
gwayt-ya (-yas), *vb.,* want, expect, hope
gweder, -drow, *m.,* glass, mirror
gwedrenn, -ow, *f.,* glass,

tumbler
gwedrennas, -ow, *f.,* glassful
gwel, -yow, *m.,* open field
gwel-es (-as), *vb.,* see
gweli, -ow, *m.,* bed
gwell, *adj.,* better
　(an) gwella, *adj.,* (the) best
gweres, *m.,* help
gweres (-as), *vb.,* help
gwerth-a (-as), *vb.,* sell
gwerther -oryon, *m.,* seller, salesman
gwerthji, -ow, *m.,* shop
gwerthys, *adj.,* sold
gwesk-el (-is), *vb.,* strike
gweth, *adj.,* worse
　(an) gwettha, *adj.,*(the) worst
gweythva -ow, *f.,* factory
gwin, *m.,* wine
gwir, *adj.,* true
gwisk-a (-as), *vb.,* wear, dress
gwith-a (-as), *vb.,* guard
gwithyas, gwithysi, *m.,* guardian
gwithyas kres, gwithysi kres, *m.,* policeman
gwiver, -ow, *coll.,* wire (material)
gwivrenn, -ow, *f.,* wire
gwlas, -ow, *f.,* country, land
gwreg, gwragedh, *f.,* wife
gwrys, *adj.,* made, done
gwydh, *coll.,* trees
gwydhenn, -ow, *f.,* tree
gwynn, *adj.,* white, fair
gwynnrudh, *adj.,* pink
gwyns, -ow, *m.,* wind
gwynsek, *adj.,* windy
gwyrdh, *adj.,* green *(not plants)*
gyllys, *adj.,* gone, departed

H

ha, *conj.,* and (**hag** *before vowels*)
hager, *adj.,* ugly
hakkra, *adj.,* more ugly
hal, -ow, *f.,* moor, marsh
hanaf, -ow, *m.,* cup
hanafas, -ow, *m.,* cupful

haneth, *adv.*, this evening
hanow, henwyn, *m.*, name
hansel, -yow, *m.*, breakfast
harth -a (-as), *vb.*, bark
heb, *prep.*, without
    heb dout, without doubt
    heb mar, certainly
hedhyw, *adv.*, today
hegar, *adj.*, well disposed (**orth to**)
hegarra, *adj.*, better disposed
hel, -yow, *f.*, hall
hel an dre, *f.*, the town hall
hepken, *adv.*, only
herdh -ya (-yas), *vb.*, chase, push
herwydh, *prep.*, according to
herwydh usadow, as usual
heskenn, -ow, *f.*, saw
heyl, -yow, *m.*, estuary
hi, *pron.*, she *or* it
hir, *adj.*, long, tall
hirra, *adj.*, longer, taller
hoelan, *m.*, salt
hogh, -es, *m.*, pig
horner, -oryon, *m.*, ironmonger
hos, heyji, *m.*, duck
howl, *m.*, sun
howldrevel, *m.*, sunrise, the east
howlsedhes, *m.*, sunset, the west
howlsplann, *m.*, sunshine
(an) huni, *pron.*, (the) one
hwans, -ow, *m.*, desire, want
    yma hwans dhymm a², I want *(+ verb)*
hware, *adv.*, immediately
hwarvos hwer (hwarva), *vb.*, happen
hwath, *adv.*, yet, still
hwedhel, -dhlow, *m.*, story
hweg, *adj.*, sweet
hweger, *f.*, mother-in-law
hwegh, *num.*, six
hwegron, *m.*, father-in-law
hwegynn, -ow, *m.*, sweet
hwekka, *adj.*, sweeter
hwel, -yow, *m.*, work
hwerth-in (hwarthas), laugh

hwi, *pron.*, you *(pl.)*
hwoer, hwerydh, *f.*, sister
hwil-as hwilas (-as), *vb.*, look for, try
hwyth-a (-as), *vb.*, blow
hy³, *poss. adj.* her
hyns, -yow, *m.*, path

I

i, *pron.*, they
iger-i (igoras), *vb.*, open
igor, *adj.*, open
igorra, *adj.*, more open
isel, *adj.*, low
isella, *adj.*, lower
Iwerdhon, *f.*, Ireland
iwerdhonek, *adj.*, Irish

J

jynn, -ow, *m.*, engine, machine
jynn-amontya, *m.*, computer
jynn-ebrenn, *m.*, aeroplane
jynn-skrifa, *m.*, typewriter
jynnskrif-a (-as), *vb.*, type

K

kador, -yow, *f.*, chair
kador-vregh, -yow-bregh, *f.*, armchair
kales, *adj.*, hard
kalessa, *adj.*, harder
kalter, -yow, *f.*, kettle
kamera, -s, *m.*, camera
kamm, *adj.*, wrong, bent
kamma, *adj.*, more wrong, more bent
kampoell-a (-as), *vb.*, mention
kan, -ow, *f.*, song
kan-a (-as), *vb.*, sing
kaner, -oryon, *m.*, singer
kansblydhen, -ynyow, *f.*, century
kanstell, -ow, *f.*, basket
kar, kerens, *m.*, relative
kar-a (-as), *vb.*, love
kares, -ow, *f.*, relative
karr, kerri, *m.*, car
karrek, kerrek, *f.*, rock
karrji, -ow, *m.*, garage
kas, *m.*, hate

kath, -es, *f.*, cat
kav-oes, kyv (-as), *vb.*, have, get, obtain
kay, -ow, *m.*, platform, quay
ke, -ow, *m.*, hedge
ke!, go! *(s.) (from mos)*
kewgh!, go! *(pl.)(from mos)*
kegin, -ow, *f.*, kitchen
kell-i (kollas), *vb.*, lose
kelorn, kelern, *f.*, bucket
Kelt, -yon, *m.*, Celt
keltek, *adj.*, Celtic
Kembra, *f.*, Wales
Kembrek, *adj.*, Welsh
Kembro, -yon, *m.*, Welshman
Kembroes, -ow, *f.*, Welshwoman
kemmer-es (as), *vb.*, take
kemmyn, *adj.*, common
kemmynna, *adj.*, more common
ken, *adj.*, other
kenderow, *m.*, cousin
keniterow, *f.*, cousin
kenter, -trow, *f.*, nail
kepar ha, like, just as *(with noun or pron.)*
kepar dell², just as *(with vb.)*
ker, *adj.*, dear *(both senses)*
kerra, *adj.*, dearer
kerdh, -ow, *m.*, walk
kerdh-es (-as), *vb.*, walk
Kerneweger, -goryon, *m.*, Cornish speaker
kernewek, *adj*, Cornish,
Kernewek, *m.*, the Cornish language
Kernow, *f.*, Cornwall
Kernow, -yon, *m.*, Cornishman
Kernowes, -ow, *f.*, Cornishwoman
kert, -ow, *m.*, lorry
keskews-el (-is), *vb.*, converse
keskows, -ow, *m.*, conversation
kesten, *coll.*, chestnut trees
kestenenn, -ow, *f.*, chestnut tree
kesva, -ow, *f.*, board, organisation
keth, *adj.*, same

an keth, the same
an keth tra, the same thing
an keth tra ma/na, this/that very (same) thing
kettermyn ha, the same time
kettoth ha, as soon as
keur, -yow, *m.*, choir
kevoethek, *adj.*, rich powerful
kevoethekka, *adj.*, richer, more powerful
kewer, *f.*, weather
kews-el (-is), *vb.*, speak
kewsys, *adj.*, spoken
ki, keun, *m.*, dog
kibell, -ow, *f.*, bath, tub
kig, *m.*, meat
kiger, -oryon, *m.*, butcher
kikti, -ow, *m.*, butcher's shop
kinyow, -yewow, *m.*, dinner
klapp-ya (-yas), *vb.*, talk, chatter
klav, *adj.*, ill
klaffa, *adj.*, more ill
kleudh, -yow, *m.*, ditch
kloes, -yow, *f.*, rack
klokk, -ow, *m.*, clock
kloppek, *adj.*, lame
klyw-es (-as), *vb.*, hear, sense, perceive
koen, -yow, *f.*, dinner, cooked supper
koes, *m.*, wood *(natural feature)*
koffi, *m.*, coffee
kok, -ow, *m.*, fishing boat
kollell, kellylli, *f.*, knife
koloven, -yow, *f.*, column
kommol, *coll.*, clouds
kommolek, *adj.*, cloudy
kommolekka, *adj.*, more cloudy
kommolenn, -ow, *f.*, cloud
kons, -yow, *m.*, pavement
korev, -ow, *m.*, beer
kornell, -ow, *f.*, corner
kosel, *adj.*, calm
kosella *adj.*, calmer
kosk-a (-as), *vb.*, sleep
kost, -yow , *m.*, cost
kota, -ow, *m.*, coat
koth, *adj.*, old

kottha, *adj.*, older
koweth, -a, *m.*, friend (*m.*)
kowethas, -ow, *m.*, fellowship
kowethes, -ow, *f.*, friend (*f.*)
kowl, *m.*, soup
kowrvargh, -vergh, *m.*, camel
koynt, *adj.*, strange
koynta, *adj.*, stranger
kreg-i (krogas), *vb.*, hang
kres, *m.*, middle
kresenn, -ow, *f.*, centre
krev, *adj.*, strong
kreffa, *adj.*, stronger
kroust, *m.*, picnic meal, crib
krow, -yow, *m.*, hut
krys, -yow, *m.*, shirtt
kudh-a, (-as), *vb.*, hide
kul, *adj.*, narrow
kulla, *adj.*, narrower
kuntell (-as), *vb.*, collect
kuntelles, -ow, *m.*, meeting
kweth, -ow, *f.*, cloth, garment
kyn⁵, *conj.*, though
kyns, *adj.*, former
kyns, *adv.*, before
kynsa, *adj.*, first, former
kyrgh-es (-as), *vb.*, fetch
kyttrin, -yow, *m.*, bus

L

lamm-a (-as), *vb.*, jump
lavar, -ow, *m.*, expression, saying, sentence
lavrek, -vregow, *m.*, trousers
le, *adj.*, less
le, -ow, *m.*, place
ledan, *adj.*, wide
ledanna, *adj.*, wider
lemmyn, *adv.*, now
lenn-a (-as), *vb.*, read aloud, recite
lent, *adj.*, slow
lenta, *adj.*, slower
lenw-el (-is), *vb.*, fill (a² with)
les, *m.*, use, advantage
dhe les, useful
lesk-i (loskas), *vb.*, burn
lester, -tri, *m.*, vessel (*dish or boat*)
lestrier, -yow, *m.*, kitchen

dresser
leth, *m.*, milk
le'ti, -ow, *m.*, dairy
leun (a²), *adj.*, full (of)
leur, -yow, *m.*, floor
leurlenn, -ow , *f.*, carpet
lever-el (-is), *vb.*, say
lew, -es, *m.*, lion
lewes, -ow, *f.*, lioness
li, livyow, *f.*, lunch
lies, *adj.*, many
lin, -yow, *m.*, line
lin, *coll.*, linen, flax
linenn, -ow, *f.*, line, thread
linenn, -ow, *f.*, piece of linen, flax plant
liw, -yow, *m.*, colour
liw-ya (-yas), *vb.*, colour
lo, -yow, *f.*, spoon
loas, -ow, *f.*, spoonful
loer, -yow, *f.*, moon
loes, *adj.*, grey
losow, *coll.*, plants
losow-kegin, *coll.*, vegetables
losowenn, -ow, *f.*, plant
losowenn-gegin, *f.*, vegetable
losowennow-kegin, *pl.*, vegetables
lost, -ow, *m.*, tail, queue
lovan, -ow, *f.*, rope
lowarth, -yow, *m.*, garden
lowen, *adj.*, happy
lowena, *f.*, joy
lowenna, *adj.*, happier
lowr, *adj.*, enough
lows, *adj.*, loose
lowsa, *adj.*, looser
lugarn, lugern, *m.*, lamp
lyha, *adj.*, least
an lyha, *adj.*, the least
dhe'n lyha, at least
lynn, -ow, *m.*, lake
lyther, -ow, *m.*, letter (*post*)
lytherenn, -ow, *f.*, letter (*of alphabet*)
lytherennek, *m.*, alphabet
lytherva, -ow, *f.*, post-office
lyver, -vrow, *m.*, book
lyverji, -ow, *m.*, bookshop
lyverva, -ow, *f.*, library

lyw-ya (-yas), *vb.,* drive
lywyer, -yoryon, *m.,* driver, pilot

M

mab, mebyon, *m.,* son
mag-a (-as), *vb.,* rear, nourish
mamm, -ow, *f.,* mother
mamm-wynn, mammow-gwynn, *f.,* grandmother
mammik, -igow, *f.,* mummy
managh, menegh, *m.,* monk
managhti, -ow, *m.,* monastery
Manow, *f.,* Isle of Man
mappa, -ow, *m.,* map
mar², *f.,* so
mar⁴, *f.,* if
    mar pleg, *f.,* please, if it pleases
marghas, -ow, *f.,* market
marow, *adj.,* dead
martesen, *adv.,* perhaps
maw, mebyon, *m.,* boy
mebyl, *coll.,* furniture
medhyk, -ygyon, *m.,* doctor
medhel, *adj.,* soft
metthla, *adj.,* softer
meg-i (mogas), *vb.,* smoke
melin, -yow, *f.,* mill
melyn, *adj.,* yellow
menydh, -yow, *m.,* mountain
mernans, -ow, *m.,* death
merw-el (-is), *vb.,* die
mes, *conj.,* but
met-ya (-yas), *vb.,* meet **(orth** with)
:neur, *m./adj.,* much, many
meur a², *(with plural noun)* many
mil², -yow, *num.,* thousand
mildir, -yow, *m.,* mile
milvil, *m./num.,* million
minhwerth-in (minhwarthas), *vb.,* smile
mir-es (-as), *vb.,* look **(orth** at)
mis, -yow, *m.,* month
    mis Genver, January
    mis Hwevrer, February
    mis Meurth, March
    mis Ebryl, April

    mis Me, May
    mis Metheven, June
    mis Gortheren, July
    mis Est, August
    mis Gwynngala, September
    mis Hedra, October
    mis Du, November
    mis Kevardhu, December
modrep, modrebedh, *f.,* aunt
moen, *adj.,* slender
moenna, *adj.,* more slender
moes, -ow, *f.,* table
mogh, *pl.,* pigs
mor, -yow, *m.,* sea
morthol, -ow, *m.,* hammer
mos/mones, a (eth), *vb.,* go *(no **a** article preceeding vowel forms)*
mowes, -i, *f.,* girl
moy, *adj.,* more
moyha, *adj.,* most
    an moyha, the most
    dhe'n moyha, for the most
my, *pron.,* I
mynn-es (-as), *vb.,* want to, wish, mean, intend
mynys, *coll.,* minutes
mynysenn, -ow, *f.,* minute *(time)*
myrgh, -es, *f.,* daughter
myttin, *m.,* morning

N

na *conj.,* nor *(**nag** before all vowels)*
na fors!, *interj.,* it doesn't matter
namoy, *adv.,* any more
nans, -ow, *m.,* valley
nebes, *m./adj.,* few, little
nebes, *adv.,* somewhat, a little
nebonan, *pron.,* someone
nebonan arall, someone else
nes, *adj.,* nearer
nes-a (-as), *vb.,* approach
nessa, *adj.,* next, second
neuv-ya (-as), *vb.,* swim
nevra, *adv.,* ever *(with neg.* never)
ni, *pron.,* we
nij-a (-as), *vb.,* fly

nith, -ow, *f.,* niece
niver, -ow, *m.,* number
niverenn, -ow, *f.,* numeral
niwl, -ow, *m.,* mist
niwlek, *adj.,* misty
nos, -ow, *f.,* night
notenn, -ow, *f.,* note
nown, *m.,* hunger
nowodhow, *pl.,* news
nowydh, *adj.,* new
nowyttha, *adj.,* newer
noy, -ens, *m.,* nephew
ny², *adv.,* not *(**nyns** before vowels in **bos** and **mos**)*
ny vern, it doesn't matter
nyhewer, *m./adv,* last night, yesterday evening

O

ober, -ow, *m.,* work, job
ober-i (-as), *vb.,* work
oer, *adj.,* very cold
oerra, *adj.,* very much colder
ogas (dhe²), *adj.,* near (to)
olifans, -es, *m.,* elephant
oll, *adj.,* all
omglyw-es (-as), *vb.,* feel, be aware
omguntell (-as), *vb.,* gather, meet together
omma , *adv,* here
omwisk-a (-as), *vb.,* dress oneself
omwolgh-i (-as), *vb.,* wash oneself
onan, *num.,* one
ors, -es, *m.,* bear *(animal)*
orses, -ow, *f.,* she bear
orth, *prep.,* at
ostel, -yow, *m.,* hotel
ottena, *interj.,* look! see there!
ottomma, *interj,* look! see here!
our, -yow, *m.,* hour *(duration)*
ow³, *poss. adj..,* my
oy, -ow, *m.,* egg
oyl, *m.,* oil

P

padell, -ow, *f.,* saucepan

pal, -yow, *f.,* spade
pal-as (-as), *vb.,* dig
pals, *adj.,* many
pan², *adv.,* when
pandra, *pron.,* what (thing)
paper, -yow, *m.,* paper
par, -ow, *m./adj,* equal
  a'n par ma, of this kind
  a'n par na, of that kind
pareus-i (pareusas), *vb.,*
  prepare
park, -ow, *m.,* field
park kerri, *m.,* car park
parys, *adj.,* ready
pasti, -ow, *m.,* pasty
peder, *num. f.,* four
pel, -yow, *f.,* ball
peldroes, *m.,* football game
pell, *adj.,* far
pella, *adj.,* further (time and
  distance)
pellgews-el (-is), *vb.,* telephone
pellgowser, -ow, *m.,* telephone
pellwolok, *f.,* television
penn, -ow, *m.,* head, end
penn-bloedh, *m.,* birthday
pennseythun, -yow, *f.,*
  weekend
perghenn, -ow, *m.,* owner
perth-i (porthas), *vb.,* bear
perthi kov a², *vb.,* remember
pes da, *adj.,* pleased
peswar, *num. m.,* four
pes-ya (-yas), *vb.,* continue
peub, *pron.,* each, every
plasenn, -ow, *f.,* disc, record
plat, -ow, *m.,* plate
pleg-ya (-yas), *vb.,* fold, bend,
  be pleasing to
plos, *adj.,* dirty
plu, -yow, *f.,* parish
pluvek, -ogow, *f.,* cushion,
  pillow
pluvenn, -ow, *f.,* pen
po, *conj.,* or
poder, *adj.,* rotten
podik, -igow, *m.,* jug
poen-ya (-yas), *vb.,* run hard
poes, *adj.,* heavy
poessa, *adj.,* heavier

poeth, *adj.,* very hot
poettha *adj.,* even hotter
poll, -ow, *m.,* pool, pit
pons, -yow, *m.,* bridge
porth, -ow, *m.,* port, harbour
pott, -ow, *m.,* pot
pow, -yow, *m.,* country
Pow Frynk, *m.,* France
Pow Sows, *m.,* England
powes (-as), *vb.,* rest
pows, -yow, *f.,* gown, frock
prag, -ow, *adv.,* why
pras, -ow, *m.,* meadow
pren-a (-as), *vb.,* buy
prenn, *m.* wood (material)
prev-i (provas), *vb.,* prove, test
pronter, -yon, *m.,* preacher
prys, -yow, *m.,* time, occasion
prysk, *coll.,* bushes
pryskenn, -ow, *f.,* a bush
pub, *adj.,* each, every
puber, *m.,* pepper
pubonan, *pron.,* everyone
pupprys, *adv.,* always
puptra, *pron.,* everything
py, *int.adv.,* what, how many
py lies, how many
pymp, *num.,* five
pys-i (-is), *vb.,* ask, pray
pysk, puskes, *m.,* fish
pyth, *int.pron,* what

R

radyo, *m.,* radio
rag, *prep.,* for
ranndir, -yow, *m.,* region
re², *adv.,* too
re, *pron.,* some
  re erell, other ones
red-ya (-as), *vb.,* read
redyans, *m.,* reading
res yw, it is necessary
resek, (-as) *vb.,* run
rev, -ow, *f.,* oar
rev-ya (-yas), *vb.,* row
rewer, -oryon, *m.,* freezer
rewl, -ow, *f.,* rule
rewler, -oryon, *m.,* manager
ri, re (ros), *vb.,* give
ros, -ow, *f.,* wheel

rudh, *adj.,* red
ruttha, *adj.,* redder
rudhvelyn, *adj.,* orange
ryb, *prep.,* beside
rych, *adj.,* rich
ryccha, *adj.,* richer

S

sagh, seghyer, *m.,* sack, bag
salow, *adj.,* safe
salwa, *adj.,* safer
sans, sens, *m.,* saint
sebon, *m.,* soap
selsik, *coll.,* sausages
selsigenn, -ow, *f.,* sausage
sen-i (sonas), *vb.,* ring, sound
serr-i (sorras), *vb.,* make/be
  angry
  serri orth, *vb.,* be angry with
serrys (orth), *adj.,* angry (with)
seth, -ow, *m.,* jar, vase
seulabrys, *adv.,* formerly
sev-el (sevis), *vb.,* stand
sewen, *adj.,* successful
sewenna, *adj.,* more successful
sewen-i (-as), *vb.,* succeed
seyth, *num.,* seven
seythun, -yow, *f.,* week
shyndys, *adj.,* hurt, damaged
sim, -es, *m.,* monkey
sinema, *m.,* cinema
skath, -ow, *f.,* small boat
skav, *adj.,* light, nimble
skaffa, *adj.,* lighter, nimbler
skentel, *adj.,* clever
skentella, *adj.,* cleverer
skeul, -yow, *f.,* ladder
skiber, -yow, *f.,* barn
skoedh-ya (-yas), *vb.,* support
skol, -yow, *f.,* school
skon, *adv.,* quickly
skonna, *adv.,* more quickly
skorr, *coll.,* branches
skorrenn, -ow, *f.,* a branch
skrif-a (-as), *vb.,* write
skub-a (-as), *vb.,* sweep
skubell, -ow, *f.,* brush
skwith, *adj.,* tired
skwittha, *adj.,* more tired
soedh, -ow, *f.,* work, office

195

soedhva, -ow, *f.*, office (place)
souder, -oryon, *m.*, soldier
soweth, *excl.*, unfortunately
sowsnek, *adj.*, English
Sowsnek, *m.*, English language
spas, -ow, *m.*, space,
  opportunity
spisti, -ow, *m.*, grocery shop
splann, *adj.*, bright
splanna, *adj.*, brighter
splann-a (-as), *vb.*, shine
stamp, -ow, *m.*, postage stamp
stevell, -ow, *f.*, room
strel, -yow, *m.*, mat, rug
stret, -ow, *m.*, street
sugra, *m.*, sugar
sur, *adv.*, surely, certainly
sygh, *adj.*, dry
syggha, *adj.*, drier
syghes, *m.*, thirst
Syllan, *f.*, Isles of Scilly
syns-i (-is), *vb.*, hold, seize
synsys, *adj.*, held, beholden
syw-ya (-yas), *vb.*, follow

T

taklow, *pl.*, things, gear
taksi, -ow, *m.*, taxi
tamm, temmyn, *m.*, piece, bit
  tamm ha tamm, bit by bit
tan, -yow, *m.*, fire
tanow, *adj.*, thin, scarce
tanwa, *adj.*, thinner, scarcer
tansys, -yow, *m.*, bonfire
tarow, terewi, *m.*, bull
tas ow, *m.*, father (*note* an
  tasow *not* an *dasow)
tas-gwynn, tasow-wynn, *m.*,
  grandfather
tasik, *m.*, daddy
tassans, tassens, *m.*, patron
  saint
tavern, -yow, *m.*, inn
taves, -vosow, *m.*, tongue,
  language
teg, *adj.*, fine, beautiful
tekka, *adj.*, finer, more
  beautiful
tenn-a (-as), *vb.*, pull
terr-i (torras), *vb.*, break, pick

terrys, *adj.*, broken
tesenn, -ow, *f.*, cake
tew, *adj.*, fat
tewa, *adj.*, fatter
tewl, *adj.*, dark
teylu -yow, *m.*, family
teyr[3], *num. f.*, three
tiek, tiogyon, *m.*, farmer
tigenn, -ow, *f.*, wallet, handbag
tioges, -ow, *f.*, farmwife
tir, -yow, *m.*, land
to, -how, *m.*, roof
toell-a (-as), *vb.*, deceive
toemm, *adj.*, warm
toemma, *adj.*, warmer
tokyn, -yow, *m.*, ticket
toll, tell, *m.*, hole
tour, -yow, *m.*, tower
towlenn, -ow, *f.*, programme,
  plan
tra, -ow, *m./f.*, thing, object
travydh, *pronf.*, anything, (with
  neg. verb) nothing
tre, -vow, *f.*, town, farm, home
tredan, *m.*, electricity
tregh-i (troghas), *vb.*, cut
trey-ya (-as), *vb.*, turn, translate
  (yn to, into)
tren, -ow, *m.*, train
treth, -ow, *m.*, beach
treweythyow, *adv.*, sometimes
tri[3], *num. m.*, three
trig-a (-as), *vb.*, live, dwell
trigva, -ow, *f.*, address
trigys, *adj.*, settled, dwelling
trist, *adj.*, sad
trista, *adj.*, sadder
tros, -yow *m.*, noise
tu, -yow, *m.*, side, direction
tus, *pl.*, people
ty, *pron.*, you (*one person*)
tyb-i (-is), *vb.*, think, have an
  opinion
tyl-i, tal, tylis, *vb.*, pay, owe
tynn, *adj.*, tight, intense
tynna, *adj.*, tighter

U

ughel *adj.*, high
ughella, *adj.*, higher

unn, *num.*, one, a
unnver, *adj.*, in agreement
usadow, *m.*, use, usage
uskis, *adj.*, quick, immediate
uvel, *adj.*, humble
uvella, *adj.*, more humble

V

vydh, *adj.*, any

W

war[2], *prep.*, on
warbarth, *adv.*, together

Y

y[2], *poss. adj.*, his, its *(m.)*
yagh, *adj.*, healthy
yaggha , *adj.*, healthier
yet, -tow, *f.*, gate
yeth, -ow, *f.*, language
yeyn, *adj.*, cold
yeynna, *adj.*, colder
yeynell, -ow, *f.*, refrigerator
yma, *vb.*, there is/are
  yma anwoes warnav, I
have a   cold
yn, *prep.*, in
  y'n (= yn an), , in the
  yn-bann, *adv.*, upwards
  yn-dann, *prep.*, under
  yn hwir, *adv.*, really
  y'n eur ma, *adv.*, now
  y'n eur na, *adv.*, then
  yn kever, *prep.*, about,
  concerning
  yn le, *prep.*, in place (of)
  yn-mes (a[2]), *prep.*, out (of)
  yn mysk, *prep.*, amidst
  yn-nans, *adv.*, downwards
  yn ta, *adv.*, well
yndella, *adv.*, thus, so
ynter, *prep.*, between (*before
  vowels*)
yntra , *prep.*, between
ynwedh, *adv.*, as well, also
ynys, -ow, *f.*, island
yowynk, *adj.*, young
yowynka, *adj.*, younger
yskynn-a (-as), *vb.*, ascend
ystynn-a (-as), *vb.*, extend

ystynnans, -ow , *m.*, extension
ytho, *conj.*, so, then

A

able (to be), galloes, *vb.*
abbreviation, berrheans, *m.*
about, concerning, a-dro, yn
  kever *prep.*
above, a-ugh, *prep.*
according to, herwydh, *prep.*
acknowledge, aswonn (-is), *vb.*
across, a-dreus, *prep.*
address, trygva, -ow, *f.*
advantage, les, *m.*
aeroplane, jynn-ebrenn, *m.*
affair, tra, -ow, *m./f.*
afternoon, dohajydh, *m.*
afterwards, a-wosa, *adv.*
agriculture, ammeth, *f.*
alive, byw, *adj.*
all, oll
along, a-hys, *adv.*
also, ynwedh, *adv.*
always, pup-prys, *adv.*
amidst, yn mysk, *prep.*
amongst, yn mysk, *prep.*
amusing, didhanus, *adj.*
anchor, ankor, -s, *m.*
and, ha, *conj.* (hag *before*
  vowels)
angry (with), serrys (orth), *adj.*
animal, enyval, -es, *m.*
answer, gorthyb-i (-is), *vb.*
answer, gorthyp, -ybow, *m.*
any, vydh, *adj.*
any more, namoy, *adj.*
apple, aval, -ow, *m.*
approach, nes-a (-as), *vb.*
April, mis Ebryl
arm, bregh, -ow, *f.*
armchair, kador-vregh, *f.*
as, avel *adv.*
as, dell, *adv.*
  as I hear, dell glywav

as I say, dell lavarav
as is said, dell leverir
as is usual, dell vydh usys
as one says, dell leverir
as soon as, kettoth ha
as usual, herwydh usadow, *adv.*
as well, (also) ynwedh, *adv.*
ascend, yskynn-a (-as), *vb.*
ask, govynn (-as), *vb.*
ask, pys-i (-is), *vb.*
at, orth, *prep.*
athwart, a-dreus, *prep.*
August, mis Est
aunt, modrep, modrebedh, *f.*
awake, difun, *adj.*
away, dhe-ves, *adv.*

B

baby, baban, -es, *m.*
bacon, bakken, *m.*
bad, drog, *adj.*
bag, sagh, seghyer, *m.*
ball, pel, -yow, *f.*
bank, arghantti, -ow , *m.*
barn, skiber, -yow, *f.*
basket, kanstell, -ow, *f.*
bath, kibell, -ow, *f.*
be, bos, *vb.*
be angry with, serri orth, *vb.*
bear, perth-i (porthas), *vb.*
bear *(animal)* ors, -es, *m.*
because, drefenn, *conj.*
bed, gweli, -ow, *m.*
bedroom, chambour, -s, *m.*
beef, bewin, *m.*
beer, korev, -ow, *m.*
before, kyns, *adv.*
begin, dalleth (dallathas), *vb.*
beginning, dalleth, *m.*
behind, a-dhelergh, *adv.*
behind, a-dryv , *prep.*
beholden, synsys, *adj.*
bend, pleg-ya (-yas), *vb.*
bent, kamm, *adj.*
beside, ryb, *prep.*
best (the), (an) gwella, *adj.*
better, gwell, *adj.*
better disposed to, hegarra
  orth, *adj.*
between , yntra, *prep.*(*before*

vowels) ynter
beyond, dres, *prep.*
bicycle, diwros, -ow, *f.*
big, bras, *adj.*
bigger, brassa, *adj.*
bird, edhen, ydhyn, *f.*
birthday, penn-bloedh, *m.*
bit, tamm, temmyn, *m.*
  bit by bit, tamm ha tamm
black, du, *adj.*
blood, goes, *m.*
blue *(and* **green** *of plants)*
  glas, *adj.*
board *(organisation)* kesva,
  -ow, *f.*
boil, bryjyon, bros (brojas), *vb.*
boiled, bryjys, *adj.*
bonfire, tansys, -yow, *m.*
book, lyver, -vrow, *m.*
bookcase, argh-lyvrow,
  arghow-l, *f.*
bookshop, lyverji, -ow, *m.*
born, genys, *adj.*
bowl, bolla, bollow, *m.*
boy, maw, mebyon, *m.*
branch, skorrenn, -ow, *f.*
branches, skorr, *coll.*
bread, bara, *m.*
break, pick, terr-i (torras), *vb.*
breakfast, hansel, -yow, *m.*
Breton *(person)* Breton, *m*
bridge, pons, -yow, *m.*
bright, splann, *adj.*
brighter, splanna, *adj.*
bring, dri, dre (dros), *vb.*
Britain, Breten, *f.*
Brittany, Breten Vyghan, *f.*
broken, terrys, *adj.*
brook, gover, -ow, *m.*
brother, broder, breder, *m.*
brown, gell, *adj.*
brush, skubell, -ow, *f.*
bucket, kelorn, kelern , *f.*
build, drehev-el (-is) *vb.*
building, drehevyans, -ow, *m.*
bull, tarow, terewi, *m.*
burn, lesk-i (-as) *vb.*
building, drehevyans, -ow, *m.*
bus, kyttrin, -yow, *m.*
bus station, gorsav an kyttrin, *m.*

bush, pryskenn, -ow, *f.*
bushes, prysk, *coll.*
busy, bysi, *adj.*
but, mes, *conj.*
butcher, kiger, -oryon, *m.*
butcher's shop, kikti, -ow, *m.*
butter, amanenn, *m.*
buy, pren-a (-as), *vb.*

C

café, boesti, -ow, *m.*
calm, kosel, *adj.*
calmer, kosella, *adj.*
camel, kowrvargh,
　　-vergh, *m.*
camera, kamera, -s, *m.*
car, karr, kerri, *m.*
car park, park kerri, *m.*
carpet, leurlenn, -ow , *f.*
carry, doen, deg (dug), *vb.*
cat, kath, -es, *f.*
cause, reason, acheson, -ys, *m.*
Celt, Kelt, -yon, *m.*
Celtic, keltek, *adj.*
centre *(middle)* kres, *m.*
centre, kresenn, -ow, *f.*
century, kansblydhen, -ynyow,
　　f.
certainly, heb mar, *adv.* sur
chair, kador, -yow, *f.*
chapel, chapel, -yow, *m.*
chatter, klapp-ya (-yas), *vb.*
chestnut tree, kestenenn,
　　-ow, *f.*
chestnut trees, kesten, *coll.*
child, flogh, fleghes, *m.*
chimney, chymbla, -blow, *m.*
chips, askloes, *pl.*
choir, keur, -yow, *m.*
church, eglos, -yow, *f.*
cinema, sinema, *m.*
clean, glan, *adj.*
clean, glanh-e (-as), *vb.*
cleaner, glanna, *adj.*
clever, skentel, *adj.*
cleverer, skentella, *adj.*
cliff, als, -yow, *f.*
clock, klokk, -ow, *m.*
cloth, kweth, -ow, *f.*
cloud, kommolenn, -ow, *f.*

clouds, kommol, *coll.*
cloudy, kommolek, *adj.*
coal, glow, *m.*
coast, arvor, -yow, *m.*
coat, kota, -ow, *m.*
coffee, koffi, *m.*
cold, *(ailment)* anwoes, *m.*
　　I have a cold, yma anwoes
　　　warnav,
cold, yeyn, *adj.*
colder, yeynna, *adj.*
collect, kuntell (-as), *vb.*
colour, liw, -yow, *m.*
colour, liw-ya (-yas), *vb.*
column, koloven, -yow, *f.*
come, arrived, devedhys, *adj.*
come, dos, deu (deuth), *vb.*
comfortable, es, *adj.,*
　　(more comfortable, esya)
common, kemmyn, *adj.*
computer, jynn-amontya, *m.*
continue, pes-ya (-yas), *vb.*
conversation, keskows,
　　-ow, *m.*
converse, keskews-el (-is), *vb.*
corner, kornell, -ow, *f.*
Cornish, kernewek, *adj.*
Cornish language, Kernewek,
Cornish speaker, kerneweger,
　　-goryon, *m.*
Cornishman, Kernow,
　　-yon, *m.*
Cornishwoman, Kernowes, -
　　ow *f.*
Cornwall, Kernow, *f.*
correct, ewn, *adj.*
cost, kost, -yow , *m.*
country, *(district)* bro, -yow, *f.*
country, *(land)* gwlas, -ow, *f.*
countryside, pow, -yow, *m.*
cousin, kenderow, *m.*
cousin, keniterow, *f.*
cover, *(lid)* gorher, -yow, *m.*
cow, bugh, -es, *f.*
cowshed, bowji, -ow, *m.*
cream, dyenn, *m.*
cup, hanaf, -ow, *m.*
cupboard, amari, -s, *f.*
cupful, hanafas, -ow, *m.*
cushion, pluvek, -ogow, *f.*

cut, tregh-i (troghas), *vb.*

D

daddy, tasik, *m.*
dairy, le'ti, -ow, *m.*
damaged, shyndys, *adj*
dance, dons, -yow, *m.*
dance, dons-ya (-yas), *vb.*
dark, tewl, *adj.*
daughter, myrgh, -es, *f.*
day, dydh, -yow, *m.*
　　abbreviation used with
　　days of the week, dy'
dead, marow, *adj.*
dear, *(both senses)* ker, *adj.*
dearer, kerra, *adj.*
death, mernans, *m.*
December, mis Kevardhu,
deep, down, *adj.*
departed, gyllys, *adj.*
desire, hwans, -ow, *m.*
desk, desk, ow, *m.*
diary, dydhlyver, -vrow, *m.*
dictionary, gerlyver, -vrow, *m.*
die, merw-el, merow (-is), *vb.*
dig, pal-as (-as), *vb.*
dinner, kinyow, -yewow, *m.*
dinner, koen, -yow, *f.*
direction, tu, -yow, *mj.*
dirty, plos, *adj.*
disc, *(record)* plasenn, -ow , *f.*
displeased, drog pes, *adj.*
distinct, diblans, *adj.*
ditch, kleudh, -yow, *m.*
do, gul, gwra (gwrug), *vb.*
doctor, medhyk, -ygyon, *m.*
dog, ki, keun, *m.*
done, gwrys, *adj.*
door, daras, -ow, *m.*
down, goen, -yow, *f.*
downwards, yn-nans, *adv.*
dress, gwisk-a (-as), *vb.*
dress oneself, omwisk-a
　　(-as), *vb.*
drier, syggha, *adj.*
drink, diwes, -osow, *m.*
drink, ev-a. yv (-as), *vb.*
driver, lywyer, -yoryon, *m.*
dry, sygh, *adj.*
duck, hos, heyji, *m.*

198

dwell, tryg-a (-as), *vb.*

E

each, peub, *pron.*
each, every, pub, *adj.*
easier, esya, *adj.*
easy, es, *adj.*
eat, dybr-i, deber (-is), *vb.*
egg, oy, -ow, *m.*
electricity, tredan, *m.*
elephant, olifans, -es , *m.*
end, penn, -ow, *m.*
engine, jynn, -ow, *m.*
England, Pow Sows, *m.*
English, sowsnek, *adj.*
enough, lowr, *adj.*
equal, par, -ow, *m./adj.*
estuary, heyl, -yow, *m.*
evening, gorthugher, *m.*
    this evening, haneth, *adv.*
ever, bythkweyth, *adv.*
every, pub, *adj.*
everyone, pubonan, *pron.*
everything, puptra, *pron.*
examination, apposyans, -ow, *m.*
examine, appos-ya (-yas), *vb.*
example, ensampel, -plow, *m.*
extend, ystynn-a (-as), *vb.*
extension, ystynnans, -ow, *m.*

F

factory, gweythva -ow, *f.*
fair, gwynn, *adj.*
false, fals, *adj.*
family, teylu, -yow, *m.*
far, pell, *adj.*
farm, bargen-tir, -yow-t. , *m.* tre, -vow, *f.*
farmer, tiek, tiogyon, *m.*
farmwife, tioges, -ow, *f.*
fat, tew, *adj.*
father, tas, -ow, *m.(note* an tasow *not* an *dasow)
father-in-law, hwegron, *m.*
fatter, tewa, *adj.*
February, mis Hwevrer
feel, *(be aware)* omglyw-es (-as), *vb.*
fellow, gwas, gwesyon, *m.*

female, benow, *adj.*
fetch, kyrgh-es (-as), *vb.*
few, nebes, *m.*
field, park, -ow, *m.*
fill (with), lenw-el (-is) (a²), *vb.*
film, fylm, -ow, *m.*
fine *(excellent)*, brav, *adj.*
fine *(beautiful)*, teg , *adj.*
finer, braffa , *adj,* tekka, *adj.*
finger, bys, -yes, *m.*
finish, diwedh, *vb.*
fire, tan -yow, *m.*
firm, fyrv, *adj.*
firmer, fyrffa, *adj.*
first, former, kynsa, *adj.*
fish, pysk, puskes, *m.*
fishing boat, kok, -ow, *m.*
flag, baner, -yow , *m.*
flax plant, linenn, -ow, *f.*
flax, lin, *coll.*
floor, leur, -yow , *m.*
flower, bleujenn, -ow, *f.*
fly, nij-a (-as), *vb.*
fold, pleg-ya (-yas), *vb.*
foliage, del, *coll.*
follow, syw-ya (-yas)
food, boes, *m.*
foolish, fol, *adj.*
football game, peldroes, *m.*
for, rag, *prep.*
    for ever, bys vykken
forecast, dargan, -ow, *f.*
forecast, dargan-a (-as), *vb.*
form, shape, furv, -ow, *f.*
former, kyns, *adj.*
formerly, seulabrys , *adv.*
fountain, fenten, -ynyow, *f.*
France, Pow Frynk, *m.*
French, frynkek, *adj.*
freezer, rewer, -oryon, *m.*
Friday, Dy' Gwener
friend *(f.)*, kowethes, -ow, *f.*
friend *(m.)*, koweth, -a, *m.*
frightful, euthek, *adj.*
frock, pows, -yow, *f.*
from, diworth, a² *prep.*
    from here, alemma, *adv.*
    from now, alemma, *adv.*
    from /then, alena, *adv.*
    from there, alena, *adv.*

from under, a-dhann *adv.*
full (of), leun (a²), *adj.*
furniture, mebyl, *coll.*
further, pella, *adj.*

G

game, play, gwari, -ow, *m.*
garage, karrji, -ow, *m.*
garden, lowarth, -yow, *m.*
gate, yet, -tow, *f.*
gear, taklow, *pl.,* daffar *m.*
German, almaynek, *adj.*
Germany, Almayn, *f.*
get, kav-oes, kyv (-as), *vb.*
give, ri, re (ros), *vb.*
glass *(mirror)*, gweder, *m.*
glass, *(tumbler)*, gwedrenn, -ow, *f.*
glassful, gwedrennas, -ow, *f.*
go, mos/mones, a (eth), *vb.*
go! *(from* mos) ke!/kewgh!,
goat, gaver, gever, *f.*
God, Dyw, *m.*
gone, departed, gyllys, *adj.*
good, da, *adj.*
goodbye! Dyw genes! *(s.),* Dyw genowgh! *(pl.)*
goose, goedh, -ow, *f.*
gorse eythin, *coll.*
gorse bush, eythinenn, -ow, *f.*
gown, pows, -yow, *f.*
grade, gradh, -ow, *m.*
grand, bryntin, *adj.*
grandfather, tas-gwynn, tasow-wynn, *m.*
grandmother, mamm-wynn, *f.*
grave, bedh, -ow , *m.*
Great Britain, Breten Veur, *f.*
green *(not plants)* gwyrdh, *adj.*
green *(plants)* glas *adj.*
grey, loes, *adj.*
grocery shop, spisti, -ow, *m.*
guard, gwith-a (-as), *vb.*
guardian, gwithyas, gwithysi, *m.*

H

hair, blewynn, -ow, *m.*
hair, blew, *coll.*
hall, hel, -yow, *f.*

hammer, morthol, -ow, *m.*
hand, dorn, -ow, *m.*
handbag, tigenn, -ow, *f.*
handle, dornla, -leow, *m.*
happen, hwarvos, hwer (hwarva), *vb.*
happier, lowenna, *adj.*
happy, lowen, *adj.*
hard, kales, *adj.*
    hard working, diwysek *adj.*
harder, kalessa, *adj.*
hate, kas, *m.*
    I hate, kas yw genev
have *(get, obtain)* kav-oes, kyv (-as), *vb.*
he *or* **it,** ev, *pron.*
    (he is) lying down, a'y wrowedh
    (he is) seated, a'y esedh
    (he is) standing, a'y sav
head, penn, -ow, *m.*
healthier, yaggha, *adj.*
healthy, yagh, *adj.*
hear, klyw-es (-as), *vb.*
heavier, poessa, *adj.*
heavy, poes, *adj.*
hedge, ke, -ow, *m.*
held, synsys, *adj.*
help, gweres, *m.*
help, gweres (-as), *vb.*
here, omma, *adv.*
high, ughel, *adj.*
higher, ughella, *adj.*
hill, bre, ow, *f.*, bronn, ow, *f.*
hold, syns-i (-is), *vb.*
hole, toll, tell, *m.*
home, tre, -vow, *f.*
hot, toemm, *adj.*
hotel, ostel, -yow, *m.*
hotter, toemma, *adj.*
hour *(duration)* our, -yow, *m.*
house, chi, -ow, *m.*
how, fatell, *conj.*
how many, py lies,
humble, uvel, *adj.*
humbler, uvella, *adj.*
hunger, nown , *m.*
hurry, fisten-a (-as), *vb.*
hurt *(damaged)* shyndys, *adj.*
husband, gour, gwer, *m.*

hut, krow, -yow, *m.*

I

I, my, *pron.*
    I want, yma hwans dhymm a[2]
    I'm sorry, drog yw genev
ice-cream, dyenn-rew, *m.*
idle talk, flows, *m.*
ill, klav, *adj.*
iller, klaffa, *adj.*
immediately, a-dhistowgh (distowgh), *adv.*
important, bysi, a vern *adj.*
in, yn, *prep.*
    in the, y'n (= yn an)
    in agreement, unnver, *adj.*
    in front of, a-rag *adv.*
    in place (of), yn le, *prep.*
inn, tavern -yow, *m.*
inside, a-ji, *adv.*
inside, a-ji dhe[2], *prep.*
intense, tynn,
Ireland, Iwerdhon, *f.*
Irish, iwerdhonek, *adj.*
ironmonger, horner, -oryon, *m.*
island, ynys, -ow, *f.*
Isle of Man, Manow , *f.*
Isles of Scilly, Syllan , *f.*
it, ev *pron. (m.)*, hi *pron. (f.)*
    it is necessary, res yw,

J

January, mis Genver
jar, vase, seth, -ow, *m.*
job, soedh, -ow, *m.*
joy, lowena, *f.*
judgement, breus, -ow, *f.*
jug, podik, -igow, *m.*
July, mis Gortheren
jump, lamm-a (-as), *vb.*
June, mis Metheven
just as *(with vb.)* kepar dell[2]

K

kettle, kalter, -yow, *f.*
kit *(gear)* daffar, *m.*
kitchen, kegin, -ow, *f.*
kitchen dresser, lestrier, -yow, *m.*
knife, kollell, kellylli, *f.*

know *(a person, place)* aswonn, *vb. (a fact)* godhvos, *vb.*

L

ladder, skeul, -yow, *f.*
lake, lynn, -ow, *m.*
lame, kloppek, *adj.*
lamp, lugarn, lugern, *m.*
land, tir, -yow, *m.*
lane, bownder, -yow, *f.*
language, yeth, -ow, *f.*, taves, -vosow, *m.*
last night, nyhewer, *adv.*
late, diwedhes, *adj.*
later, diwettha, *adj.*
laugh, hwerth-in (hwarthas), *vb.*
lawn, glesin, -yow, *m.*
lazier, diekka, *adj.*
lazy, diek, *adj.*
leaf, delenn, -ow, *f.*
learn, teach, dysk-i (-as), *vb.*
least, lyha, *adj.*
    the least, an lyha, *adj.*
leave, gas-a (-as), *vb.*
leaves, del, *coll.*
left *(remaining)* gesys, *adj.*
less, le, *adj.*
letter *(post)* lyther, -ow, *m.*
letter *(of alphabet)* lytherenn, -ow, *f.*
library, lyverva, -ow, *f.*
lie, gow, -yow, *m.*
life, bywnans, *m.*
light, golow, -ys, *m.*
light *(weight)* skav, *adj.*
lighter, skaffa, *adj.*
like *(with n. or adj.),* kepar ha,
limb, esel, -i, *m.*
line, lin, -yow, *m.*
line *(thread)* linenn, -ow, *f.*
linen, lin, *coll.*
lion, lew, -es, *m.*
lioness, lewes, -ow, *f.*
listen (to), goslow-es (-as), (orth) *vb.*
little, byghan *adj.*
    a little, nebes, *m.*
live *(exist)* byw-a (-as), *vb.*

live *(reside)* tryg-a (-as), *vb.*
long, hir, *adj.*
longer, hirra, *adj.*
look! *(see here!)* ottomma, *interj*
look! *(see there!)* ottena, *interj.*
look (at), mir-es (-as), (orth), *vb.*
look for, hwil-as (-as), *vb.*
lorry, kert, -ow, *m.*
lose, kell-i, (kollas), *vb.*
love, kar-a (-as), *vb.*
low, isel, *adj.*
lower, isella, *adj.*
luckier, feusikka, *adj.*
lucky, feusik, *adj.*
lunch, li, livyow, *f.*

M

machine, jynn, -ow, *m.*
mackerel, brithel, brithyli, *m.*
made *(or done)* gwrys, *adj.*
make, gul, gwra (gwrug), *vb.*
make/be angry, serr-i (sorras), *vb.*
male, gorow, *m./adj.*
man, gour, gwer, *m.*
manager, rewler, -oryon, *m.*
many, lies, *adj.*, meur a² (with plural noun)
many, pals, *adj.*
map, mappa, -ow, *m.*
March, mis Meurth
market, marghas, -ow, *f.*
mat, rug, strel, -yow, *m.*
matter
    it doesn't matter, na fors!, ny vern, *interj.*
May, mis Me
meadow, pras, -ow, *m.*
meat, kig, *m.*
meet (with), met-ya (-yas), (orth) *vb.*
meeting, kuntelles, -ow, *m.*
member, esel, -i , *m.*
mention, kampoell-a (-as), *vb.*
mile, mildir, -yow, *m.*
milk, leth, *m.*
mill, melin, -yow, *f.*
million, milvil, *m.*
mine, bal, -yow, *m.*

miner, den bal, tus bal, *m.*
minute, mynysenn, -ow, *f.*
minutes, mynys, *coll.*
mirror, gweder, -drow, *m.*
mist, niwl, -ow, *m.*
misty, niwlek , *adj.*
monastery, managhti, -ow, *m.*
Monday, Dy' Lun
money, arghans, *m*
monk, managh, menegh, *m.*
monkey, sim, -es, *m.*
month, mis, -yow, *m.*
moon, loer, -yow, *f.*
moor, marsh, hal, -ow, *f.*
more, moy, *adj.*
morning, myttin, *m.*
most, moyha, *adj.*
    the most, an moyha, *adj.*
mother, mamm, -ow, *f.*
mother-in-law, hweger, *f.*
mountain, menydh, -yow, *m.*
mouth, ganow, -ow, *m.*
much, meur, *m. adj.*
mummy, mammik, -igow, *f.*

N

nail, kenter, -trow, *f.*
name, hanow, henwyn, *m.*
narrow, kul, *adj.*
narrower, kulla, *adj.*
near (to), ogas (dhe), *adj.*
nearer, nes, *adj.*
necessary, res *adj.*
    it is necessary, res yw
nephew, noy, -ens, *m.*
never *(with neg. verb)* bythkweyth, *adv. (past)* nevra, *adj. (present/future)*
nevertheless, byttegyns, *adv.*
new, nowydh, *adj.*
newer, nowyttha, *adj.*
news, nowodhow, *pl.*
next, nessa, *adj.*
niece, nith, -ow, *f.*
night, nos, -ow, *f.*
nimble, skav, *adj.*
nimbler, skaffa, *adj.*
noble, bryntin, *adj.*
nobler, bryntinna, *adj.*
noise, tros, -yow, *m.*

note, notenn, -ow, *f.*
nourish, mag-a (-as), *vb.*
November, mis Du
now, lemmyn, *adv.*
now, y'n eur ma, *adv.*
numeral, niverenn, -ow, *f.*
number, niver, -ow, *m.*

O

oak, derow, *adj.*
oak tree, derwenn, -ow, *f.*
oak trees, derow, *coll.*
oar, rev, -ow, *f.*
object, tra, -ow, *m./f.*
obtain, kav-oes, kyv (-as) *vb.*
occasion, prys, -yow, *m.*
October, mis Hedra
of, a², *prep.*
    of that kind, a'n par na
    of this kind, a'n par ma
office *(place)* soedhva, -ow, *f.*
oil, oyl, *m.*
old, koth, *adj.*
older, kottha, *adj.*
on, war², *prep.*
on behalf (of), a-barth (dhe²), *prep.*
one, unn, *adj.*, onan, *num.*
    (the one), an huni
only, hepken, *adv.*
open, iger-i (igoras), *vb.*
open, igor, *adj.*
open field, gwel, -yow, *m.*
opportunity, spas, -ow, *m.*
opposite, a-dal, *prep.*
or, po, *conj.*
orange, rudhvelyn , *adj.*
other, arall *(s.)*, erell *(pl.)*, *adj.*
other, ken, *adj*
    other ones, re erell
out (of), yn-mes (a²), *prep.*
outside, a-ves, *adv.*
oven, forn, -ow, *f.*
owe, tyl-i,. tal (tylis), *vb.*
owner, perghenn, -ow, *m.*

P

page, folenn, -ow, *f.*
paper, paper, -yow, *m.*
parish, plu, -yow, *f.*

pasty, pasti, -ow, *m.*
path, hyns, -yow, *m.*
patron saint, tassans, tassens, *m.*
pavement, kons, -yow, *m.*
pay, tyl-i,. tal (tylis), *vb.*
pen, pluvenn, -ow, *f.*
people, tus, *pl.*
pepper, puber, *m.*
perceive, klyw-es (-as), *vb.*
perhaps, martesen, *adv.*
person, den, tus, *m.*
picnic meal, kroust, *m.*
piece, bit, tamm, temmyn, *m.*
pig, hogh, -es, *m.*
pigs, mogh, *pl.*
pillow, pluvek, -ogow, *f.*
pink, gwynnrudh, *adj.*
pit, poll, -ow, *m.*
place, le, -ow, *m.*
plan, towl, -ow, *m.*
plant, losowenn, -ow, *f.*
plants, losow, *coll.*
plate, plat, -ow, *m.*
platform, quay, kay, -ow, *m.*
play, gwari (-as), *vb.*
playground, garth-gwari,
    garthow-g., *m.*
please, mar pleg
pleased, pes da, *adj.*
    (to be) pleasing to pleg-ya
    (-yas), *vb.*
poetry, bardhonieth, *m.*
policeman, gwithyas kres,
    gwithysi kres, *m.*
pool, poll, -ow, *m.*
poor, boghosek, *adj.*
poorer, boghosekka, *adj.*
port *(harbour)* porth, -ow, *m.*
post-office, lytherva, -ow, *f.*
postage stamp, stamp, -ow, *m.*
pot, pott, -ow, *m.*
powerful, kevoethek, *adj.*
pray, pys-i (-is), *vb.*
preacher, pronter, -yon, *m.*
prepare, pareus-i (-as), *vb.*
programme, towlenn, -ow, *f.*
prove, prev-i (provas), *vb.*
pub, diwotti, -ow, *m.*
pull, tenn-a (-as), *vb.*
put, gorr-a (-as), *vb.*

Q
quay, kay -ow, *m.*
question, govynn, -ow, *m.*
queue, lost, -ow, *m.*
quick, uskis, *adj.*
quickly, skon, *adv.*

R
race, resek, *vb.*
rack, kloes, -yow, *f.*
railway station, gorsav an
    hyns-horn, *m.*
rain, glaw, *m.*
    it's raining, glaw a wra
raise, drehev-el (-is), *vb.*
reach, drehedh-es (-as), *vb.*
read, red-ya (-yas), *vb.*
    read aloud, lenn-a (-as), *vb.*
reading, redyans , *m.*
ready, parys, *adj.*
really, yn hwir, *adv.*
rear, nourish, mag-a (-as), *vb.*
rearwards, a-dhelergh, *adv.*
reason, acheson, *m.*
record, plasenn, -ow, *f.*
red, rudh, *adj.*
redder, ruttha, *adj.*
refrigerator, yeynell, -ow, *f.*
region, ranndir, -yow, *m.*
relative, kar, kerens, *m.*
relative, kares, -ow, *f.*
remember, perthi kov a², *vb.*
reply, gorthyb-i (-is), *vb.*
reply, gorthyp, -ybow, *m.*
restore, daskorr (-as), *vb.*
return, dehwel-es (-is), *vb.*
revival, dasserghyans, *m.*
revive, dassergh-i (-as), *vb.*
rich, rych, kevoethek *adj.*
richer, ryccha, *adj.*
ring, sen-i (sonas), *vb.*
river, avon, -yow, *f.*
road, fordh, -ow, *f.*
rock, karrek, kerrek, *f.*
roof, to, -how, *m.*
room, stevell, -ow, *f.*
rope, lovan, -ow, *f.*
rotten, poder, *adj.*
roundabout *(road)*, fordh-a-

dro, fordhow a-dro, *f.*
row, rev-ya (-yas), *vb.*
rule, rewl, -ow, *f.*
run, poen-ya (-yas), *vb.*,
    res-ek (-as) *(run a race)*

S
sack, sagh, seghyer, *m.*
sad, trist, *adj.*
sadder, trista, *adj.*
safe, salow, *adj.*
safer, salwa, *adj.*
sail, goel, -yow, *m.*
sail, goel-ya (-yas), *vb.*
saint, sans, sens, *m.*
salt, hoelan, *m.*
same, keth, *adj.*
    the same time, kettermyn ha
Saturday, Dy' Sadorn
saucepan, padell, -ow, *f.*
sausage, selsigenn, *f.*
sausages, selsik, *coll.*
saw, heskenn, -ow, *f.*
say, lever-el (-is), *vb.*
saying, lavar, -ow, *m.*
scarce, tanow, *adj.*
scarcer, tanwa, *adj.*
school, skol, -yow, *f.*
Scotland, Alban, *f.*
Scottish, albanek, *adj.*
see, gwel-es (-as), *vb.*
    see you! dha weles!
sell, gwerth-a (-as), *vb.*
seller *(salesman)*, gwerther
    -oryon, *m.*
send, dannvon (-as), *vb.*
sense, klyw-es (-as), *vb.*
September, mis Gwynngala
settled *(dwelling)* trygys, *adj.*
she *(or it)* hi, *pron.*
sheep, davas, deves, *f.*
sheet, folenn, -ow, *f.*
shelf, estyllenn, -ow, *f.*
shine, splann-a (-as), *vb.*
ship, gorhel, -holyon, *m.*
shoe, eskis, -yow, *f.*
shop, gwerthji, -ow, *m.*
shore *(coast)* arvor, -yow, *m.*
short, berr, *adj.*
shorter, berra, *adj.*

202

shout, garm-a (-as), *vb.*
show, diskwedh-es (-as), *vb.*
shut, dege-a (-as), *m.*
side *(direction)* tu, -yow, *m.*
silly, gokki, *adj.*
silver, arghans, *m.*
sing, kan-a (-as), *vb.*
singer, kaner, -oryon, *m.*
sister, hwoer, hwerydh, *f.*
sit, esedh-a (-as), *vb.*
sitting-room, esedhva, -ow, *f.*
situated, desedhys, *adj.*
sky, ebrenn, *f.*
sleep, kosk-a (-as), *vb.*
slender, moen, *adj.*
slow, lent, *adj.*
slower, lenta, *adj.*
small, byghan, *adj.*
   small boat, skath, -ow, *f.*
smaller, byghanna, *adj.*
smile, minhwerth-in
   (minhwarthas), *vb.*
smoke, meg-i (mogas), *vb.*
snow, ergh, *m.*
   it's snowing, ergh a wra
so *(as)* dell[2]
   so I think, dell dybav
   so it seems, dell hevel
so *(then)*, ytho, *adv.*
so *(thus)*, yndella, *adv.*
soap, sebon, *m.*
soft, medhel, *adj.*
softer, metthla, *adj.*
sold, gwerthys, *adj.*
soldier, souder, -oryon, *m.*
some, re, *pron.*
someone, nebonan, *pron.*
someone else, nebonan arall
sometimes, treweythyow, *adv.*
son, mab, mebyon, *m.*
song, kan, -ow, *f.*
sound, sen-i (sonas), *vb.*
soup, kowl, *m.*
space, spas, -ow, *m.*
spade, pal, -yow, *f.*
speak, kews-el (-is), *vb.*
spectacles, dewweder, *pl.*
splendid, bryntin, *adj.*
spoken, kewsys, *adj.*
spoon, lo, -yow, *f.*

spoonful, loas, -ow, *f.*
spring *(water)* fenten,
   -tynyow, *f.*
stand, sev-el (sevis), *vb.*
station, gorsav, -ow, *m.*
step, gradh, -ow, *m.*
still *(yet)* hwath, *adv.*
story, hwedhel, hwedhlow, *m.*
stove, forn, -ow, *f.*
straight, ewn, *adj.*
straighter, ewna, *adj.*
strange, koynt, *adj.*
stranger, koynta, *adj.*
street, stret, -ow, *m.*
strike, gwesk-el (-is), *vb.*
strong, krev, *adj.*
stronger, kreffa, *adj.*
succeed, sewen-i (-as), *vb.*
successful, sewen, *adj.*
suddenly, distowgh, *adv.*
sugar, sugra, *m.*
sun, howl, *m.*
Sunday, Dy' Sul
sunrise, howldrevel, *m.*
   (also the east*)*
sunset, howlsedhes, *m.*
   (also the west*)*
sunshine, howlsplann, *m.*
support, skoedh-ya (-yas), *vb.*
supper *(cooked)* koen, -yow, *f.*
surely, sur, *adv.*
sweep, skub-a (-as), *vb.*
sweet, hweg, *adj.*
sweet, hwegynn, -ow, *m.*
sweeter, hwekka, *adj.*
swim, neuv-ya (-yas), *vb.*

T

table, moes, -ow, *f.*
tail, lost, -ow, *m.*
take, kemmer-es (as), *vb.*
talk, klapp-ya (-yas), *vb.*
tall, hir, *adj.*
taxi, taksi -ow, *m.*
teach, dysk-i (-as), *vb.*
teacher, dyskador, -yon, *m.*
teacher, dyskadores, -ow, *f.*
telephone, pellgews-el (-is), *vb.*
telephone, pellgowser, -ow, *m.*
television, pellwolok, *f.*

tell, lever-el (-is) dhe[2], *vb.*
terror, euth, *m.*
test, prev-i (provas), *vb.*
than, ages, es, *conj.*
thanks, gras,-ow, *m.*
the, an
then, y'n eur na, *adv., ena, adv.*
there, ena, *adv.*
there is/are, yma, *vb.*
they, i, *pron.*
thin, tanow, *adj.*
thinner, tanwa, *adj.*
thing, tra, -ow, *m./f.*
things, gear, taklow, *pl.*
think *(have an opinion)* tyb-i
   (-is), *vb.*
thirst, syghes, *m.*
though, kyn[5], *conj.*
thousand, mil[2], -yow, *num..*
through, beyond, dres, *prep.*
through, dre[2], *prep.*(der
   before vowels)
Thursday, Dy' Yow
thus, yndella, *adv.*
ticket, tokyn, -yow, *m.*
tight, tynn, *adj.*
tighter, tynna, *adj.*
time, prys, -yow, *m.*
tired, skwith , *adj.*
to, dhe[2], *prep.*
today, hedhyw, *adv.*
together, warbarth, *adv.*
tongue, taves, -vosow, *m.*
tooth, dans, dens, *m.*
tower, tour, -yow, *m.*
town, tre, -vow, *f.*
   town hall, hel an dre, *f.*
train, tren, -ow, *m.*
translate (into), trelya (yn) *vb.*
tree, gwydhenn, -ow, *f.*
trees, gwydh, *coll.*
trousers, lavrek, -vrogow, *m.*
true, gwir, *adj.*
try, hwil-as, hwila (-as), *vb.*
Tuesday, Dy' Meurth
turn, trelya (yn) *vb.*
two *(m.)* dew[2], *num.*
two *(f.)* diw[2], *num.*
tub, kibell, -ow, *f.*
tumbler gwedrenn, -ow *f.*

tub, kibell, -ow, *f.*
type, jynnskrif-a (-as), *vb.*
typewriter, jynn-skrifa, *m.*

U

uglier, hakkra, *adj.*
ugly, hager, *adj.*
umbrella, glawlenn, -ow, *f.*
uncle, ewnter, -tres, *m.*
under, yn-dann², *prep.*
undress, omdhiwisk-a (-as), *vb.*
unfortunately, soweth, *interj.*
until, bys yn/dhe², *prep.*
unwillingly, a'y anvodh
unwise, anfur, *adj.*
up to, bys yn/dhe², *prep.*
upwards, yn-bann, *adv.*
usage, usadow, *m.*
use, les, *m.*
use, usadow, *m.*
useful, dhe les

V

valley, nans, -ow, *m.*
vegetable, losowenn-gegin, *f.*
vegetables, losow-kegin, *coll.*
vegetables, losowennow-kegin, *pl.*
very, fest, *adv.* pur²
  very cold, oer, *adj.*
  very good, fest da
  very hot, poeth, *adj.*
  very useful, meur dhe les
  very well, fest yn ta
  very windy, awelek, *adj.*
vessel *(dish or boat)* lester, lestri, *m.*

W

wait for, gort-os, gorta (-as), *vb.*
Wales, Kembra, *f.*
walk, kerdh, -ow, *m.*
walk, kerdh-es (-as), *vb.*
wall, fos, -ow, *f.*
wallet, tigenn, -ow, *f.*
want, hwans, -ow, *m.*
  I want, yma hwans dhymm a²
war, bresel, -yow, *f.*
warm, toemm, *adj.*

warmer, toemma, *adj.*
wash, golgh-i (-as), *vb.*
wash oneself, omwolgh-i (-as), *vb.*
watch *(timepiece)* euryor, -yow, *m.*
water, dowr, -ow, *m.*
we, ni, *pron.*
weak, gwann, *adj.*
weaker, gwanna, *adj.*
wear, gwisk-a (-as), *vb.*
weather, kewer, *f.*
Wednesday, Dy' Mergher
week, seythun, -yow, *f.*
weekend, pennseythun, -yow, *f.*
well disposed (to), hegar (orth) *adj.*
Welsh, kembrek, *adj.*
Welshman, Kembro, -yon, *m.*
Welshwoman, Kembroes, -ow, *f.*
wet, glyb, *adj.*
wetter, glyppa, *adj.*
what, pandra, pyth, *int.pron.*
what, how many, py, *int.adv.*
wheel, ros, -ow, *f.*
when, pan², *adv.*
white, gwynn, *adj.*
wide, efan, *adj.*
wide, ledan, *adj.*
wider, ledanna, *adj.*
wife, gwreg, gwragedh, *f.*
willingly, a'y vodh,
wind *(gale)* awel, -ow, *f.*
wind, gwyns, -ow, *m.*
window, fenester, -tri, *f.*
windy, gwynsek, *adj.*
wine, gwin, *m.*
wire, gwivrenn, -ow, *f.*
wise, fur, *adj.*
wiser, furra, *adj.*
with, gans, *prep.*
  with you *(pl.)* genowgh,
  with you *(s.)* genes,
without, heb, *prep.*
woman, benyn, -es , *f.*
wood *(material)* prenn, *adj.*
wood *(natural feature)* koes, *m.*
word, ger, -yow, *m.*

word list, gerva, -ow, *f.*
work, hwel, -yow,
work, *(job)* ober, -ow, *m.*
work, ober-i (-as), *vb.*
work *(office)* soedh, -ow, *f.*
worse, gweth, *adj.*
worst, gwettha, *adj.*
write, skrif-a (-as), *vb.*
wrong, kamm, *adj.*

Y

yard *(court)* garth, -ow, *m.*
year, blydhen, *f.*
  year of age, bloedh, *m.*
yellow, melyn, *adj.*
yesterday, de, *adv.*
yet, still, hwath, *adv.*
you *(more than one person)* hwi, *pron.*
you *(one person),* ty, *pron.*
young, yowynk, *adj.*
younger, yowynka, *adj.*

key to abbreviations

adj.	adjective
adv.	adverb
coll.	collective (noun)
conj.	conjunction
excl.	exclamation
f.	feminine (noun)
int.	interrogative
interj.	interjection
m.	masculine (noun)
num.	numeral
pl.	plural
poss.	possessive
prep.	preposition
pron.	pronoun
s.	singular
vb.	verb/verbal noun

Further information on the Cornish language, classes, publications and activities can be obtained by contacting

The Cornish Language Board
(Kesva an Taves Kernewek)
at 65 Churchtown, Gwinear,
near Hayle, Cornwall G.B.
☎ and fax 01736 850878

or, The Cornish Language Fellowship
(Kowethas an Yeth Kernewek)
1 Gyllynvase Road, Falmouth,
Cornwall TR11 4DH

Notes

Notes

Notes

Notes

Notes

Notes

Notes